IMAGES
of America

GUNTERSVILLE

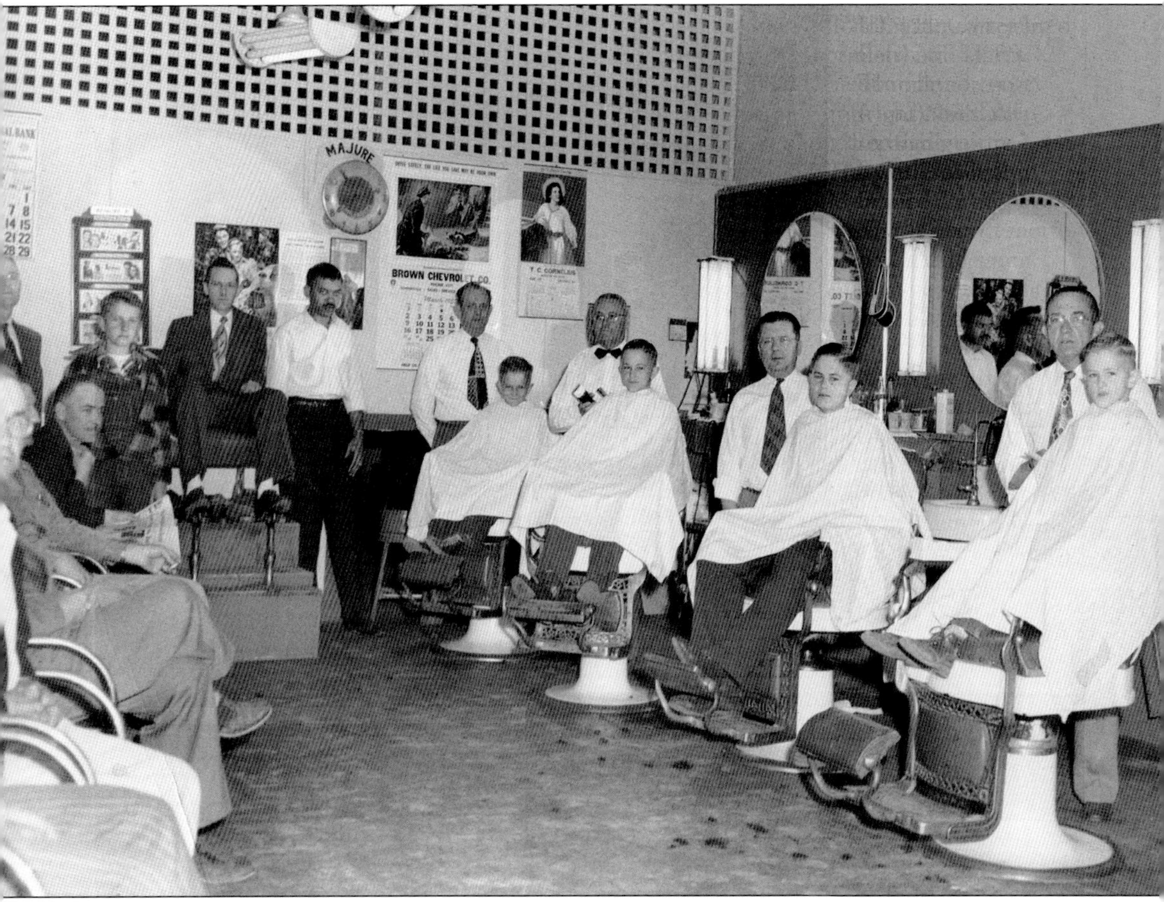

ON THE COVER: Ed Douglas operated a popular barbershop on north Gunter Avenue. Patrons enjoyed local news and sports while waiting for a turn in the chair. The barbers pictured in this 1952 photograph are, from left to right, Gordon Berry, Coy Hudson, Gordon Baird, and Fred Scott. The children in the barbers' chairs are the sons of Clifton Smith; they are, from left to right, Jerry, Robert, Leon, and Neal. Standing beside the shoeshine chair are Gilbert Smith (left) and Jim Poe, shoeshine attendant. (Marshall County Archives.)

IMAGES
of America

GUNTERSVILLE

Whitney A. Snow and Barbara J. Snow

ARCADIA
PUBLISHING

ISBN 978-1-4671-0564-4

Published by Arcadia Publishing
Charleston, South Carolina

Printed in the United States of America

Library of Congress Control Number: 2020935748

For all general information, please contact Arcadia Publishing:
Telephone 843-853-2070
Fax 843-853-0044
E-mail sales@arcadiapublishing.com
For customer service and orders:
Toll-Free 1-888-313-2665

Visit us on the Internet at www.arcadiapublishing.com

For cousin Ronald Nabors, a fellow history lover who has long provided friendship, wisdom, and laughter

Contents

ACKNOWLEDGMENTS

The authors greatly appreciate the vast litany of people who made this project a reality. Many photographs are from the Guntersville Museum and Cultural Center (Julie Patton, director), the *Advertiser-Gleam* (Anthony Campbell, editor), and the Marshall County Archives (Betty Taylor, director). We extend special thanks to Meredith McDonough at the Alabama Department of Archives and History for doing research in closed stacks. Both John Moseley (curator, Alabama Music Hall of Fame) and Bryan Jones (still image librarian and editor, Country Music Hall of Fame and Museum) proved extremely helpful in securing pictures of some of the celebrities. At the Lister Hill Library, Timothy L. Pennycuff (university archivist, University of Alabama at Birmingham) suggested the Rosser Papers, which offered a treasure trove of images. At the M. Louis Salmon Library, Reagan Grimsley (head of Special Collections and Archives, University of Alabama in Hunstville) helped locate photographs of old Marshall County. At the US Space & Rocket Center, Audrey Glasgow (collections manager and registrar) and Carolyn Lawson (archives and exhibits) sent us images of various Operation Paperclip scientists. Shalis Worthy (archivist, Huntsville–Madison County Public Library) provided assistance with looking through files on Lillie Moore and scientist Wernher von Braun. Heather McCann (park operations assistant, Lake Guntersville State Park) invited us to review photographs of the park. Tony Vellano (founder, Professional Wrestling Hall of Fame) offered his expertise regarding the wrestlers who performed in Guntersville. Simon Elliott (public services/licensing, UCLA Library Special Collections) aided us in securing a photograph of Louise Fletcher. Professional photographers Stacie Joy, Karen Ducey, and Bryan Leazenby generously provided shots of actor Gary Burghoff, author Jonathan Raban, and the award-winning boat *Au Revoir*, respectively. Additional assistance came from the City of Guntersville and the Tennessee Valley Authority (TVA).

At the Marshall County Archives, suggestions were provided by the following volunteers: Billy Alexander, Tyrus Dorman, Keith R. Finley, Neal Johnson, William E. "Sonny" Lewis, Danny Maltbie, John "Chip" Manning, John Ross, Larry Smith, Dale Strange, and Lynn Tipton. Photographs were provided by the following people: Hodge Alves III, George Barnett, Kathryn Baucom, Jonnie Ray Baxter, Jennifer Bearden, Johnny Brewer, Jacob Bright, Miles Burghoff, Sandra Campbell, Nancy Gilbreath Graham, Mary Ben Heflin, Nall Hollis, Carmen Hurff, Gail Smith Ingrum, Betty McGowin Jones, David Jones, Mike Jones, George Kappler, David Kennamer, Milla Kennamer, Richard Kennamer, Seaborn Kennamer, Jane Kohl, Gail Sams Lanning, Dennis Mitchell, Max Snow, Buddy Taylor, and Morri Yancy. The authors also want to thank those who provided leads, unused photographs, image identifications, or ideas: Louella Alves, Nancy Barker, Zachary Clemons, Carol Drake, Tyler Hawkins, Nancy Hill, Jimmy Hindman, Nancy Hindman, David Huff (David and the Giants), Lisa Jones, Nancy Larson, Sheila Mahathey, Judy Manning, Karen Noblitt, Lynn Upton, and Charles Whisenant. Last but not least, Dr. Julian "Pete" Sparks and Macey Taylor deserve merit for proofreading the draft.

In the process of collecting materials for *Guntersville*, the authors accumulated three or four times the photographs they needed. Evaluating and choosing a select few required prioritizing quality, historical significance, and—if possible—rarity. To that end, the authors are indebted to Caitrin Cunningham, senior title manager at Arcadia Publishing.

Introduction

The Tennessee River has made Guntersville an attractive place for generations. In 1785, John Gunter arrived at the "great bend" in the river in what is now north Alabama. Gunter started a trading post while negotiating an agreement with Chief Bushyhead to sell salt to the tribe. To seal the pact, Catherine, one of the chief's daughters, married Gunter, bringing him into the family. Around 1818, Gunter's son Edward established a ferry, which led to the community being called Gunter's Landing. The residents of the village, which prospered with a bustling economy, shipped agricultural products and imported manufactured goods. In 1819, Alabama became a state, and in 1836, the state legislature formed Marshall County from portions of Blount and Jackson Counties. The Indian Removal Act resulted in the displacement of Native Americans and a subsequent flurry of settlers arriving in the area. When John Gunter died in August 1835, a fight erupted over his will. In fact, actual shoot-outs—with loss of life—ensued. Even so, the area's population continued to grow.

Through an act of the state legislature, Gunter's Landing officially became Guntersville in 1847. Three communities—Claysville, Warrenton, and Guntersville—vied for the position of county seat. The vote was delayed until military units returned from the Mexican-American War, and Guntersville emerged victorious. The city constructed a brick courthouse on land donated by Judge Louis Wyeth. Though this structure succumbed to flames during the Civil War, locals erected a new building in 1870 at the current location. Needless to say, the courthouse has undergone numerous transitions, renovations, and technological alterations over the years.

In the 1850s, transportation moved to center stage as steamboats and railroads enhanced Guntersville's access to the outside world. Ease of travel permitted locals, such as mercantile owner Albert G. Henry, to move easily to places like Chattanooga and even New York City. Construction began on the Tennessee & Coosa Railroad, with Hugh Carlisle and Samuel King Rayburn lending momentum. After the Civil War interrupted the laying of track, it took decades before Guntersville got a depot. In the meantime, a complex system of rail and ferry transfer boats moved train cars from Ditto's Landing to Guntersville.

In 1861, at the onset of the Civil War, Marshall County's delegates to the Secession Convention were Arthur Campbell Beard and James Lawrence Sheffield, both cooperationists who voted "nay" in line with the northern, mountainous region of Alabama. When the "yeas" outweighed the "nays," many locals supported the Confederate government. In May 1861, the Marshall Boys and the Irish Railroad Guard departed to join the 9th Alabama Infantry and left for Virginia. Beard acquiesced to serve as a major in the 4th Alabama Infantry. Sheffield donated $50,000 to raise a company for the 48th Alabama Infantry and was promoted to colonel; the regiment saw action in Virginia, Pennsylvania, and Tennessee.

During the Civil War, Guntersville held value as a port city and was targeted by both Union and Confederate forces. The harbor had the capacity to berth boats and ship supplies. At that time, Guntersville lay closer to the water, so Union troops put cannons on the hills north of the river. In July 1862, Union forces began shelling the area, resulting in the deaths of Evergreen Findley Rayburn, the wife of Alabama militia general Samuel King Rayburn, and Henry Clay McNairy, a native of Nashville. In subsequent years, gunboats also had occasion to fire on Guntersville. In January 1865, men from the gunboats USS *General Sherman* and USS *General Thomas* torched the town.

After having been shelled and almost completely burned, Guntersville emerged from the Civil War a very different community than it had been. In 1864 and 1865, a devastating drought wrought havoc upon any agriculture. At the end of the war, Confederate veterans did not arrive home in time for spring planting. Moreover, the lack of seeds and equipment meant little harvesting until 1867. During these years, famine affected the region. In an effort to attract aid, the aforementioned Judge Wyeth traveled to northern cities, gave speeches, and distributed promotional materials. He organized generous, philanthropic donations and convinced the railroads to transport goods to Decatur for free. Wyeth also dispensed food, clothing, medicine, seeds, and miscellaneous goods/supplies from centrally located sites. His efforts saved many families from starving. Guntersville slowly recovered and relied on cotton as its primary crop.

By the late 19th century, Guntersville, while still largely agricultural, had become more focused on industry. Wyeth City, adjacent to Guntersville, boasted the Woodenware Company, Standard Basket Factory, and Nedofik Surgical Sofa Company. Of the three, Nedofik attracted the most publicity because it produced surgical sofas that sold around the world. Prominent New York City surgeon Dr. John Allan Wyeth, son of Judge Wyeth, proposed and funded industrialization to improve local employment opportunities. Though neighbors, Guntersville and Wyeth City plunged into friction over which city had dominance. The depot, built in 1891, was within the limits of Wyeth City. However, train tickets to the depot often read "Guntersville," likely due to the fact that it remained the county seat. Ultimately, in 1909, Wyeth City merged into Guntersville.

Three businesses key to Guntersville's industrial history are the cotton mill, feed mill, and Kappler, Inc. By the early 1930s, Guntersville had the Saratoga Victory Mills, a textile mill on Gunter Avenue. It became Julia Cade Mills in 1949 and changed its name to Lakeside Mills the following year. After textile production ceased, the building was used by tech company Comptronix in the mid- to late 1980s and early 1990s. In 1998, entrepreneur Mike Jones purchased the building and later opened Mike's Merchandise. The Ralston Purina Feed Mill at Eastlake opened in 1957 and is currently Wayne Farms Feedmill. Founded by George Kappler in 1976, Kappler, Inc., is headquartered in Guntersville and manufactures hazard suits. Kappler products are shipped and sold internationally.

While these businesses did much for Guntersville's economy, the most significant event that impacted the city began with the actions of the Tennessee Valley Authority. In 1939, the TVA completed the Guntersville Dam, and the resulting 69,000-acre lake utterly transformed Guntersville. Guntersville may not have changed its name, but it was nevertheless referred to as Lake Guntersville by many tourists who flocked to the water to swim, fish, or sail. As a vacation mecca, Guntersville greets guests each year with water sports, art shows, bass fishing, eagle watching, and hydroplane racing. The city also benefits from the presence of Lake Guntersville State Park, a scenic area famous for bald eagles and breathtaking lake vistas. *Southern Living* called Lake Guntersville the "best lake in Alabama." Likewise, *Living on the Water* extolled Lake Guntersville as "best lake in the South." In 2020, *Bassmaster Magazine* named Lake Guntersville the second-best lake for bass fishing in the country. Given these accolades, Guntersville has secured a position in the annals of southern tourism.

One

Settlers, Developers, and Workers

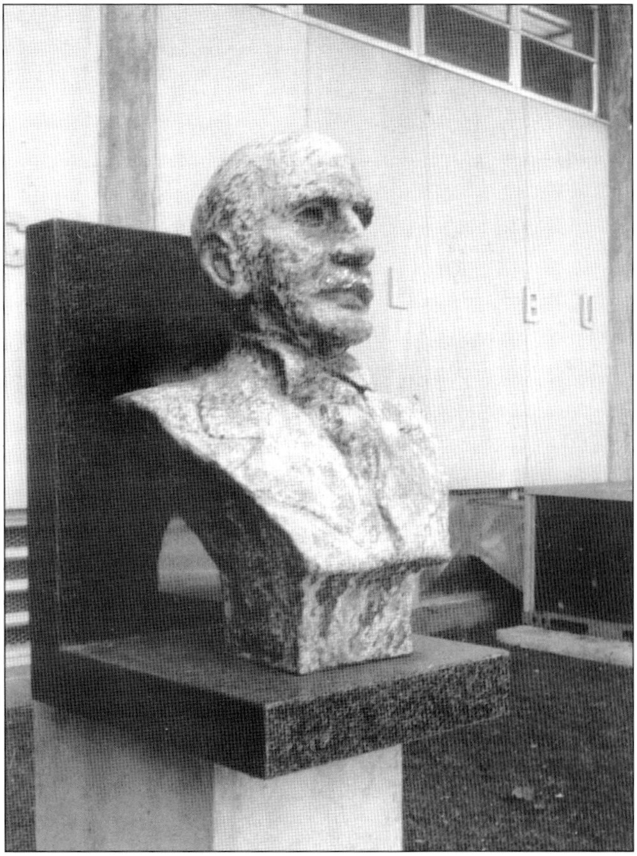

This bust of Dr. John Allan Wyeth sits outside the Guntersville Municipal Building. Born in 1845 to Louis and Euphemia Wyeth, Wyeth attended LaGrange Military Academy and later served in the Confederacy's 4th Alabama Cavalry. After earning a medical degree at the University of Louisville, he moved to New York City; years later, in 1881, he opened the New York Polyclinic Graduate Medical School and Hospital, the country's first postgraduate medical school. His brainchild, Wyeth City, Alabama, was annexed into Guntersville in 1909 and boasted several factories. A prolific author, Wyeth wrote medical articles as well as books, poems, and newspaper columns. In 1902, he became president of the American Medical Association. Wyeth visited Guntersville often until his death in 1922. (*Advertiser-Gleam*.)

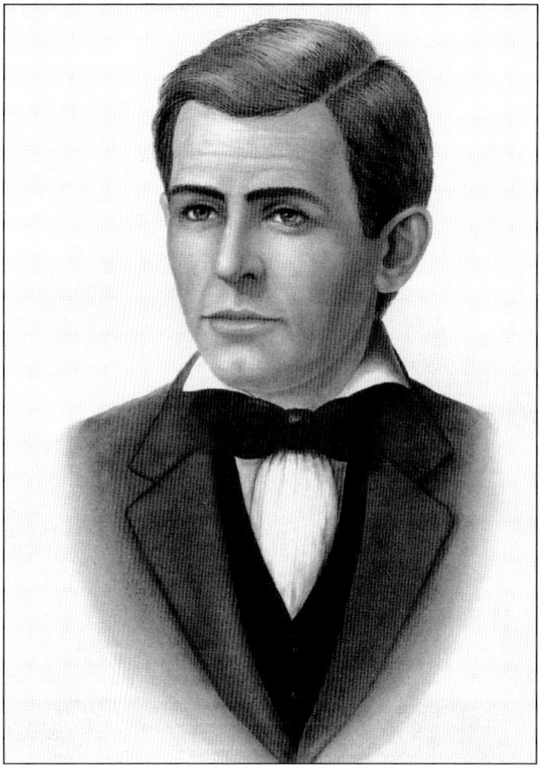

John Gunter, shown here in an artist's rendering, came to the area in 1785 and opened a trading post; the Gunter family later established a ferry landing. Some historians theorize that Gunter, a Loyalist during the Revolutionary War, migrated to the frontier to establish a new life and escape ostracism from Patriots. He married the daughter of a Cherokee chief. His 1835 death resulted in great consternation over his will. (*Advertiser-Gleam.*)

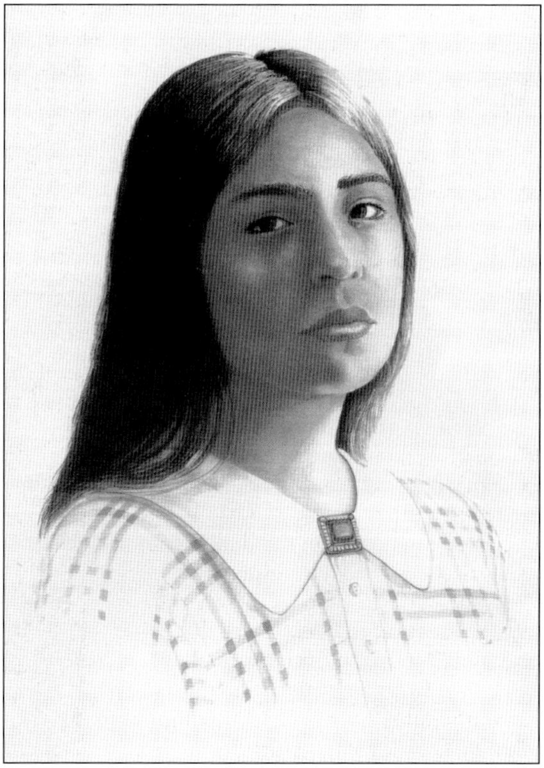

Chief Bushyhead's daughter, shown here in an artist's rendering, married John Gunter as part of an agreement for her father's purchase of salt. Ghi-Go-Ne-Li, pronounced "Jeejonahly," was given the Christian name Catherine. Their children inherited prosperous business enterprises but were forced to move to Oklahoma as a result of the Indian Removal Act. (*Advertiser-Gleam.*)

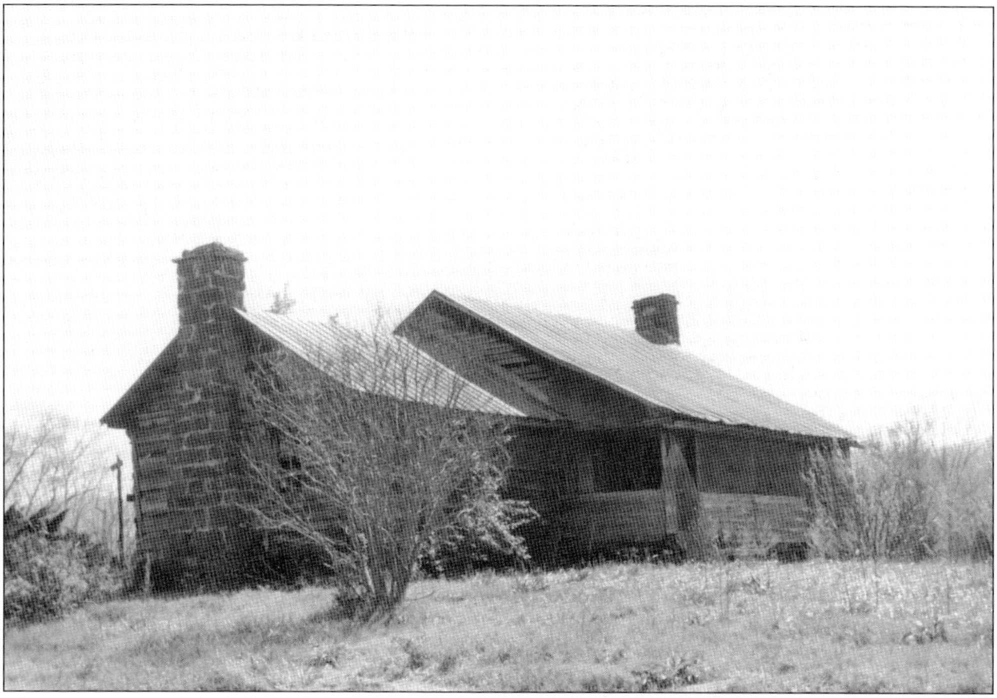

This is an image labeled "Gunter's Village." After John Gunter established a trading post, a village emerged to accommodate merchants, teamsters, and farmers. The harbor's bustling activity soon led to the opening of boardinghouses and hotels. In 1847, Gunter's Landing became Guntersville. (Salmon Library, University of Alabama in Huntsville.)

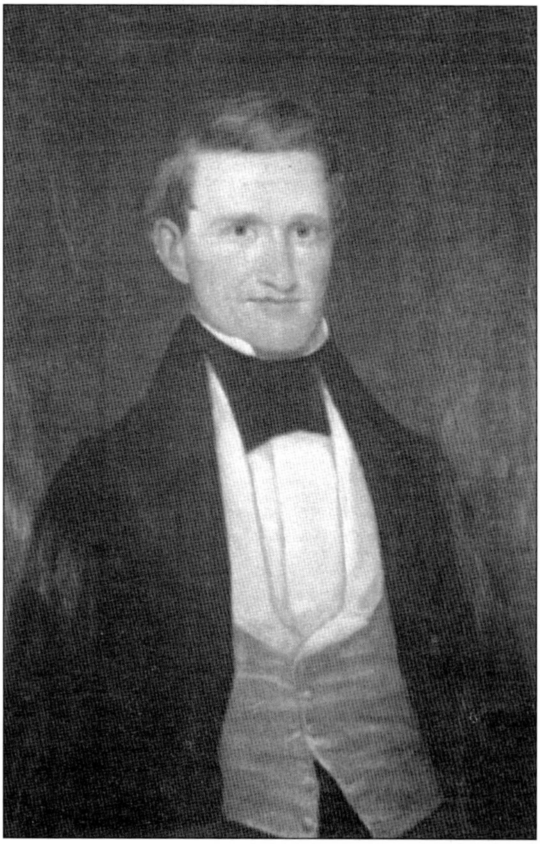

In the mid-1830s, Dr. James W. Fennell (shown) and his wife, Matilda Allison, settled five miles from Guntersville at Deposit Ferry. A planter and physician, Fennell also served as a minister in the Methodist Episcopal Church and opposed secession. He fathered 10 children. A portion of the Fennell estate is now under water. The rest is currently home to the YMCA Camp Cha-La-Kee. (Carmen Hurff.)

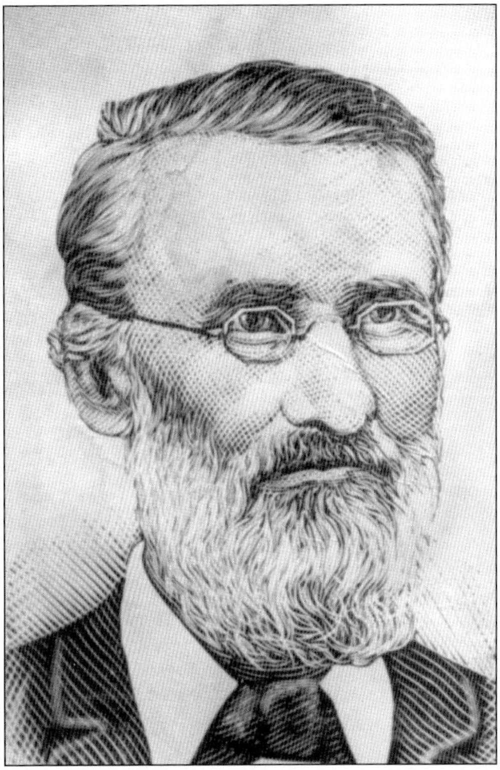

Born on June 20, 1812, in Harrisburg, Pennsylvania, Louis Wyeth (shown) moved to Guntersville at the age of 24. He became a county court judge in 1837 and a state legislator 10 years later. Judge Wyeth donated land for the courthouse, cemetery, school, and various churches. He and his wife, Euphemia Allan, had three children: John Allan (married to Florence Sims), Louisa (married to W.H. Todd), and Mary (married to Hugh Carlisle). (Marshall County Archives.)

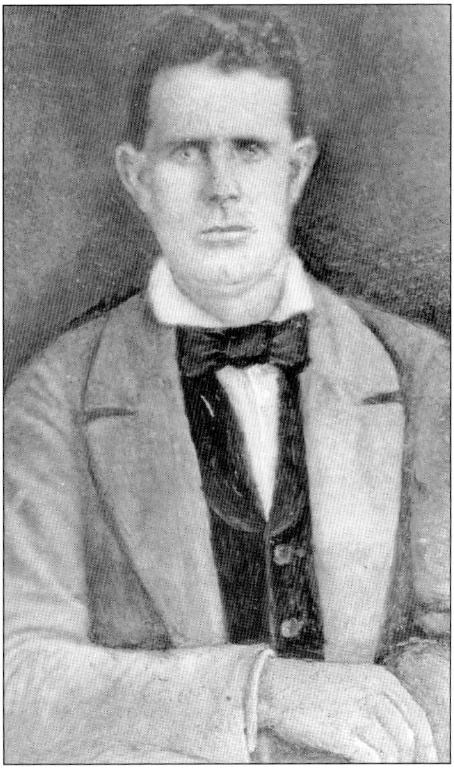

After moving to Gunter's Landing in 1834, Samuel King Rayburn (shown) opened a mercantile and later served as militia general, captain in the Confederate army, state senator, president of Tennessee & Coosa Railroad Company, and chancery judge. A dominant figure, he is also remembered as the husband of Evergreen Findley Rayburn, one of the casualties of the 1862 shelling of Guntersville. (Alabama Department of Archives and History.)

This is Nannie Nix, who arrived in Guntersville to teach school in 1862. A native of Lawrence County, Nix had been educated in common schools, a female academy, and Mary Sharpe College. Asked about teaching, she claimed to be "stamping character for eternity." She married twice-widowed Samuel King Rayburn in December 1862, and the couple's children were Bessie, Samuel Jr., William, John, and Jenny. (Alabama Department of Archives and History.)

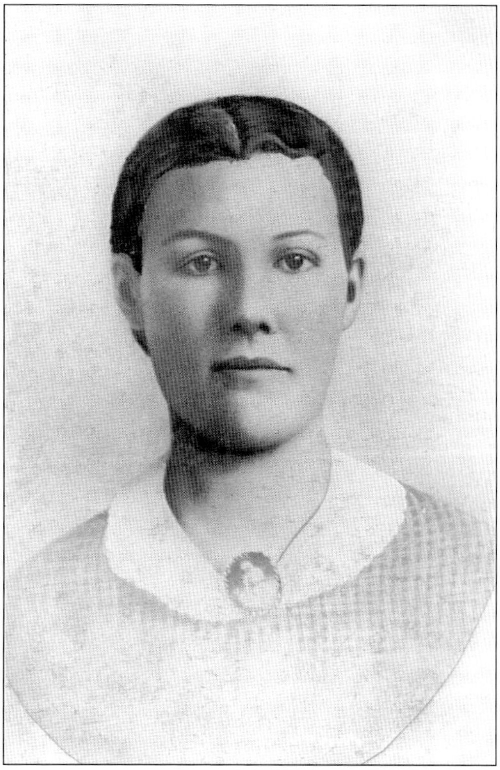

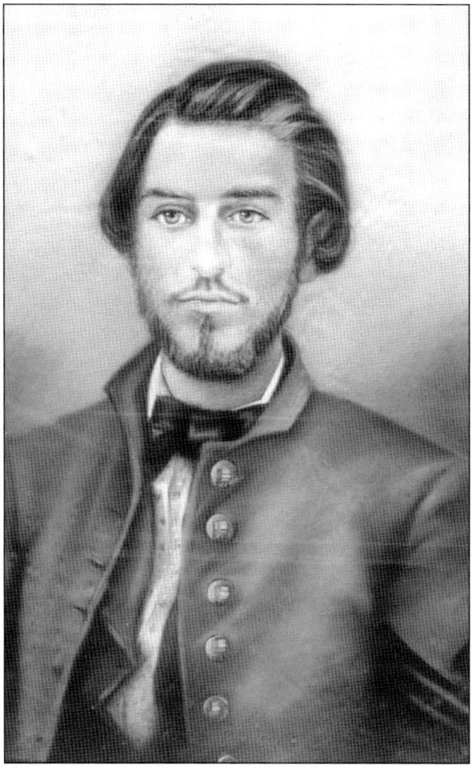

Shown is John Rayburn, the only child of Samuel King Rayburn and his first wife, Sarah Davenport. John received an education at Tennessee's Cumberland College. He enlisted in the Confederate army as a sergeant and departed Guntersville with the Marshall Boys to join the 9th Alabama Infantry. He achieved the rank of captain and died during the Battle of Antietam in 1862. (Alabama Department of Archives and History.)

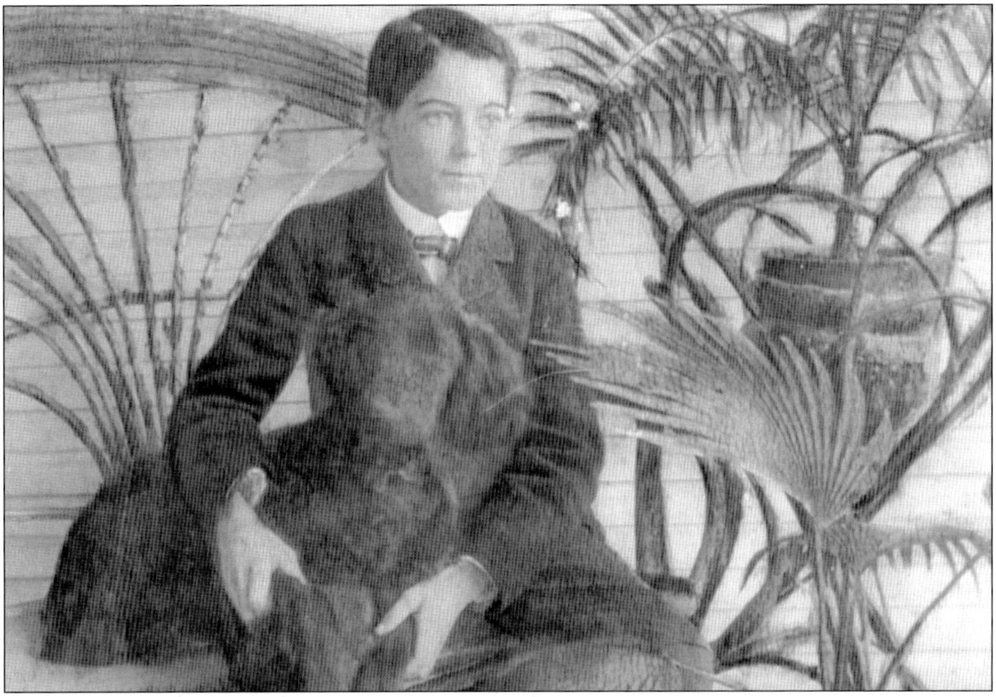

Samuel King Rayburn Jr. (shown) was born in 1890 to William and Lazinka Rayburn. He suffered from illness, perhaps asthma, and died in 1904. Named for his paternal uncle Samuel King Rayburn Jr., young Sam was buried at City Cemetery beside his grandfather, Gen. Samuel King Rayburn. (Alabama Department of Archives and History.)

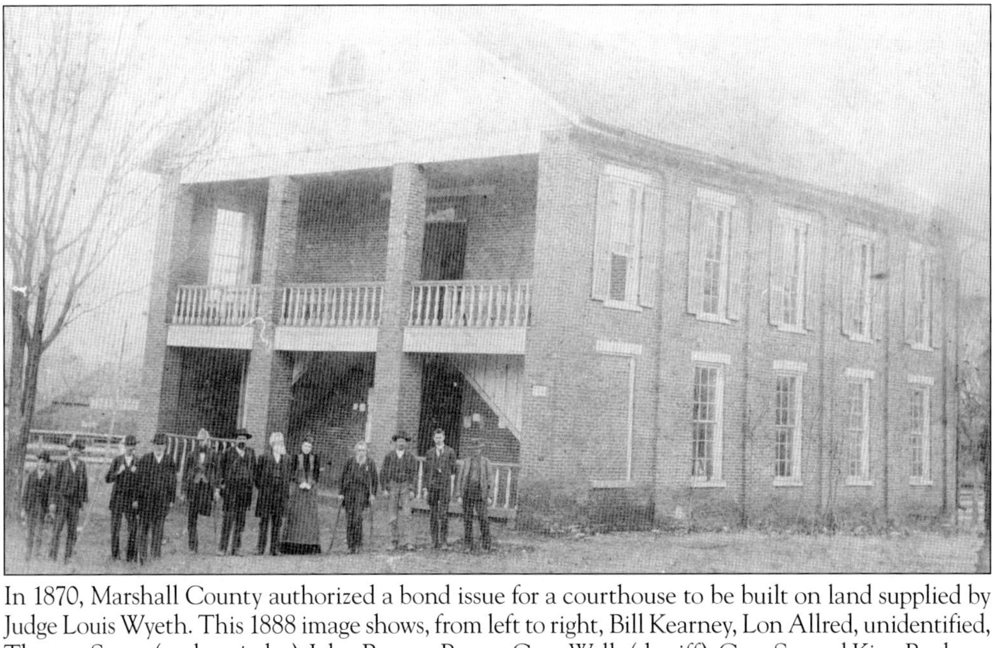

In 1870, Marshall County authorized a bond issue for a courthouse to be built on land supplied by Judge Louis Wyeth. This 1888 image shows, from left to right, Bill Kearney, Lon Allred, unidentified, Thomas Street (probate judge), John Burgett Pettus, Gum Wells (sheriff), Gen. Samuel King Rayburn (judge of chancery), Bessie Rayburn Samuel, Willis Curry (circuit clerk), unidentified, William C. Rayburn (probate clerk), and John Greenwood. (Marshall County Archives.)

Pictured is Illinois native John Dispennett, who served in the western theater during the Civil War. He reenlisted with the 7th Cavalry under the command of Gen. George Armstrong Custer. In 1876, at the Battle of the Little Big Horn, Dispennett was trapped for two days on Reno's Hill. After marrying Martha Skinner, he moved to Warrenton, Alabama, where he farmed and worked at a sawmill. (Sandra Campbell.)

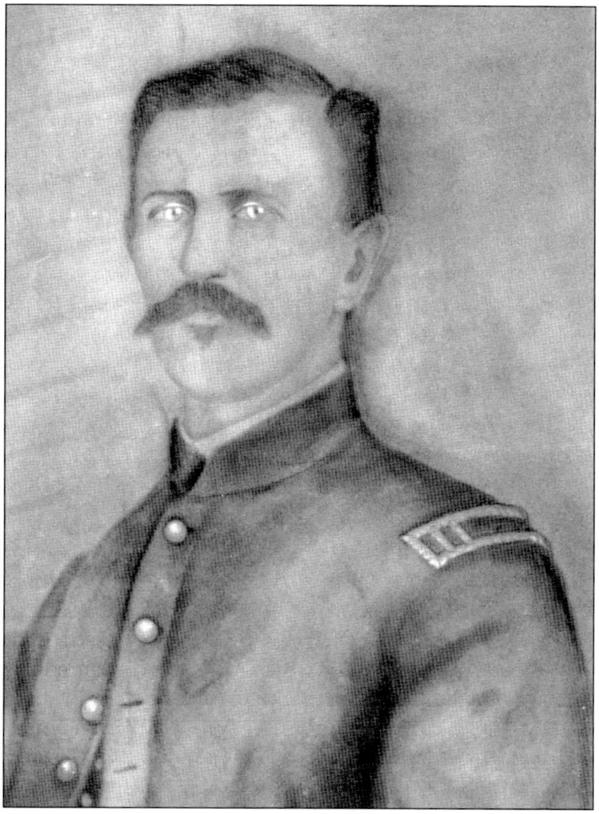

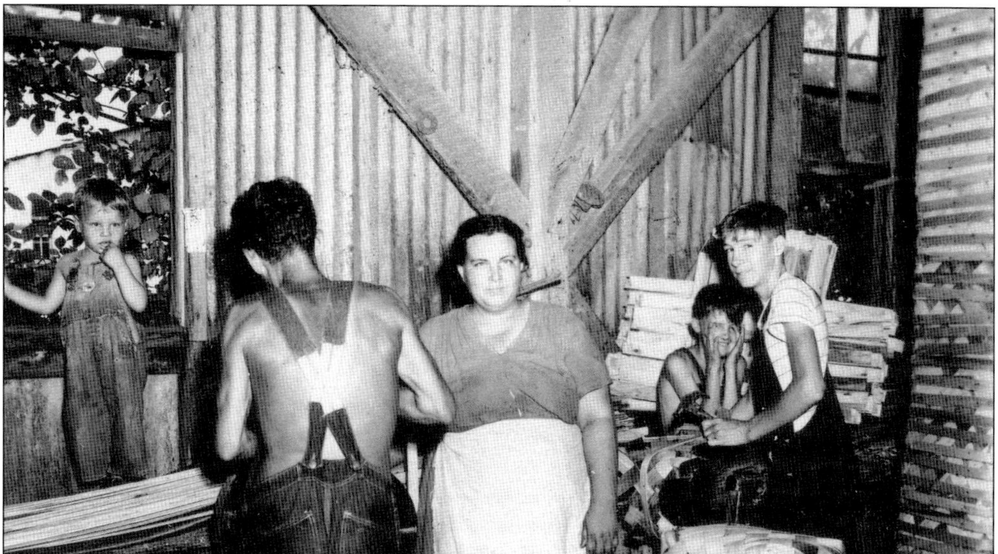

This 1949 photograph of Standard Basket Factory workers shows, from left to right, Frank Rainwater, James Swords, Venie Swords, Jim Barnes, and Bobby Swords. The young boys are making tomato baskets. After attending school for half a day, children joined their parents at the factory. Some employees produced as many as 50 baskets per day. When deadlines for contracts were imminent, families worked well into the night. (Marshall County Archives.)

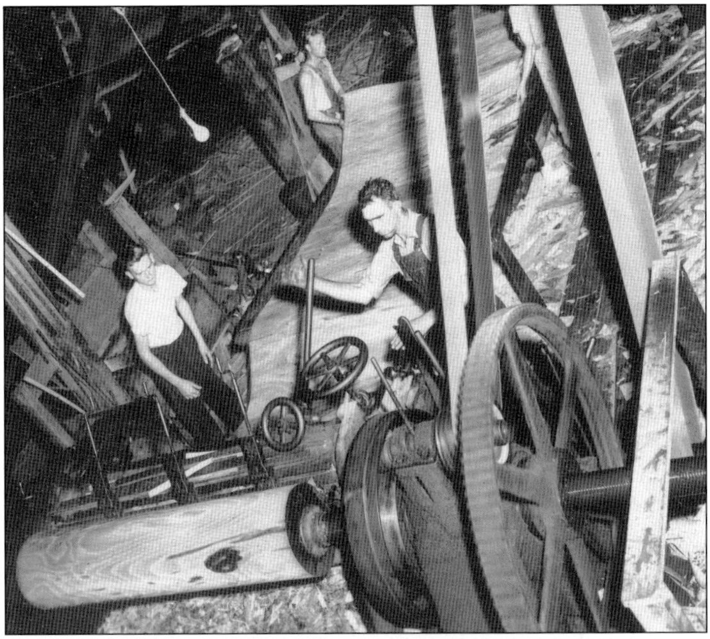

The veneering machine at the Standard Basket Factory functioned like a lathe. Pictured are J.D. Walden (holding the lever) with operator Ray Elliott on his right. Paul Holcomb and a partially visible W.L. Payne are shown holding the sheets, which were ultimately cut into strips. The factory required massive supplies of wood to manufacture 3,000 baskets per day. Multiple generations worked at the Standard Basket Factory. (Marshall County Archives.)

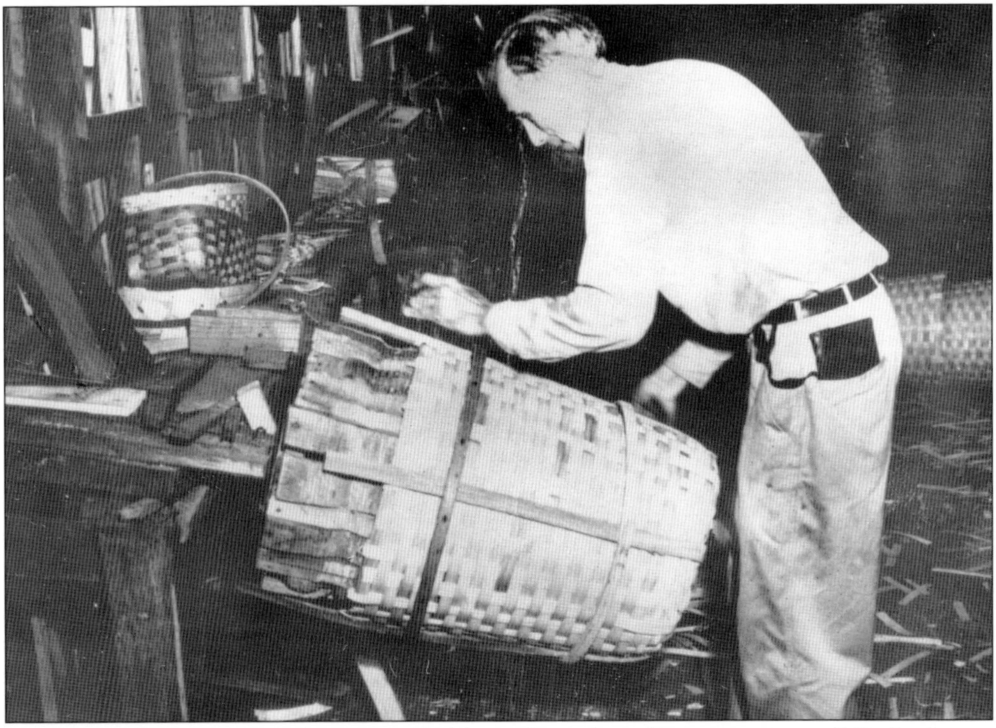

Standard Basket Factory employee Dave Walden is shown here. Upon opening in 1891, the factory used hardwoods and employed between 50 and 100 workers, and the payroll reached $1,500 to $2,000 per month. Early employees included Quintus Bailey (carpenter), John Bowers (boiler room), Albert Cookson (sawmill department), Charlie Reynolds, Joe Spurgeon (shipping clerk), and John Wright. Ownership changes and devastating fires caused the company to close in 1950. (Marshall County Archives.)

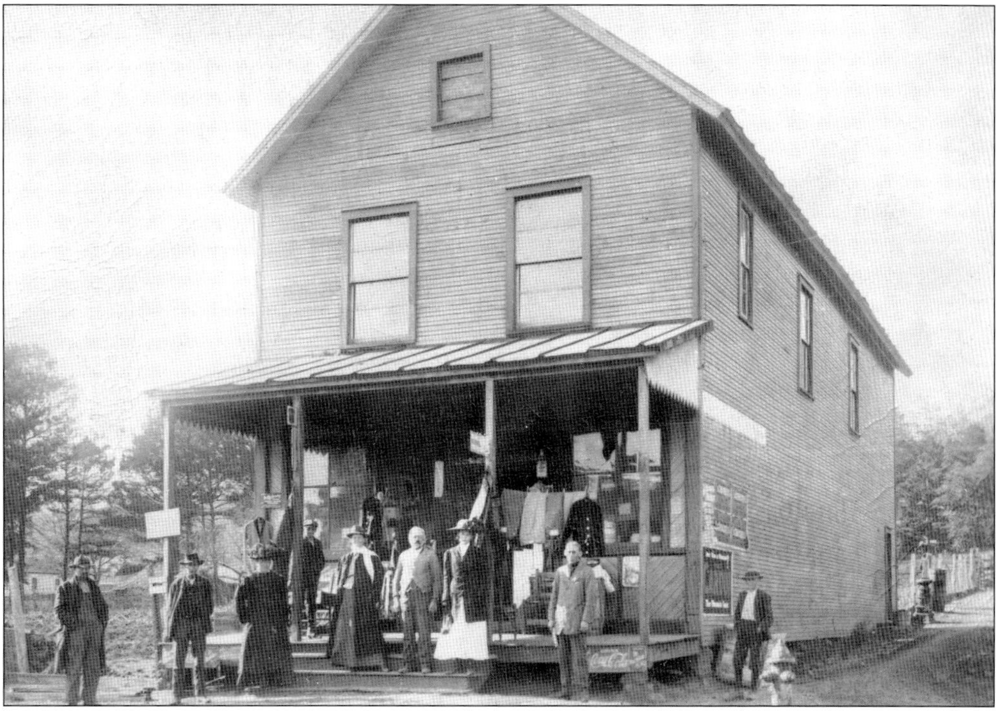

Charles Fricke (1851–1922), born in Bremen, Germany, immigrated to the United States around 1865. He and his wife, Alwina, operated a general merchandise store at the corner of Dunlap and Gilbreath Streets in Wyeth City. The building had been constructed by John Seibold. Pictured in 1918 are, from left to right, two unidentified, Alwina Fricke, Roland Fricke, unidentified, Charlie Fricke (on steps), Emma Fricke, John Fricke, and unidentified. (Marshall County Archives.)

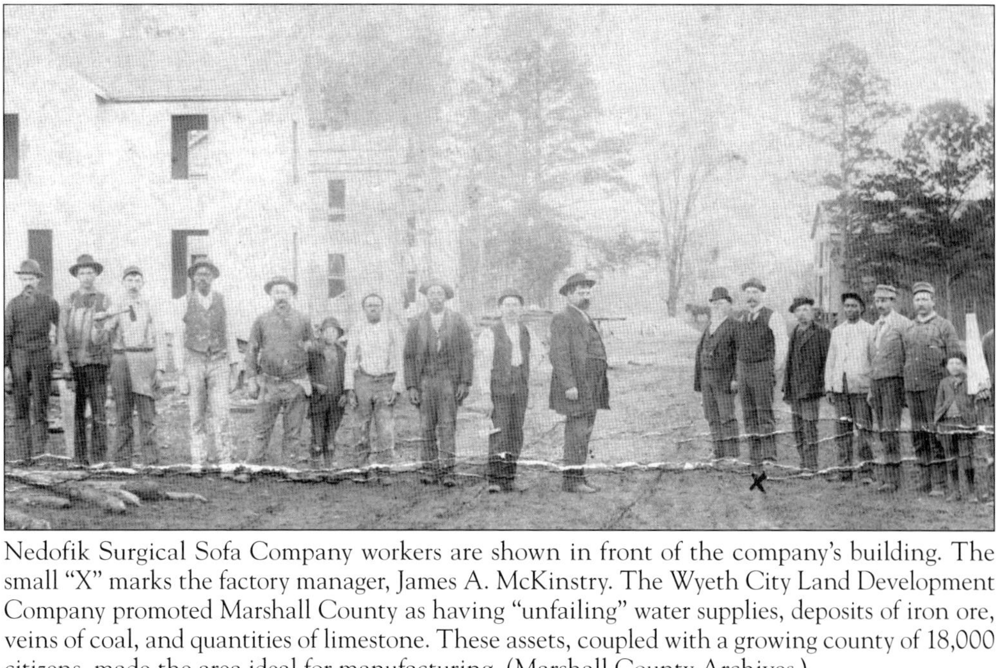

Nedofik Surgical Sofa Company workers are shown in front of the company's building. The small "X" marks the factory manager, James A. McKinstry. The Wyeth City Land Development Company promoted Marshall County as having "unfailing" water supplies, deposits of iron ore, veins of coal, and quantities of limestone. These assets, coupled with a growing county of 18,000 citizens, made the area ideal for manufacturing. (Marshall County Archives.)

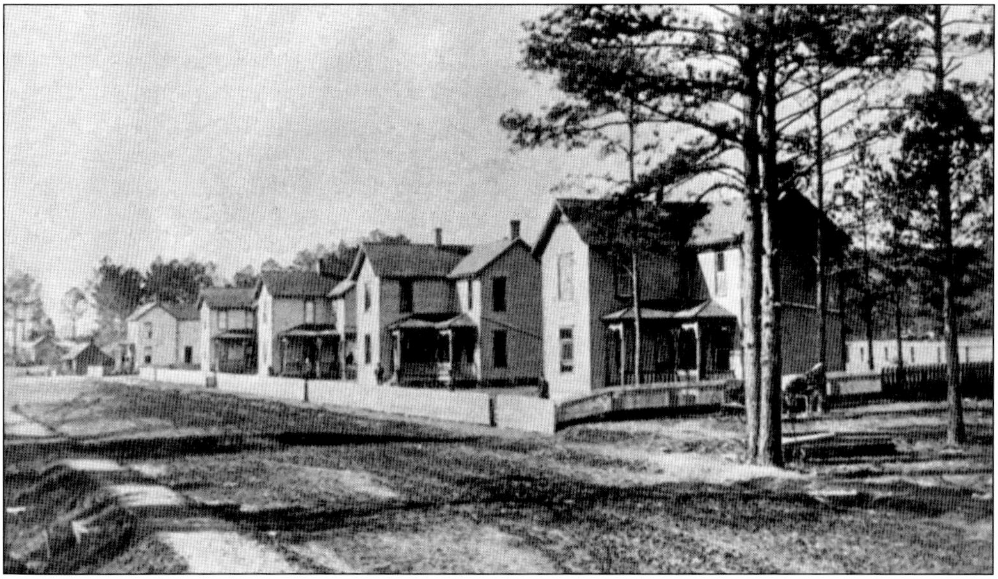

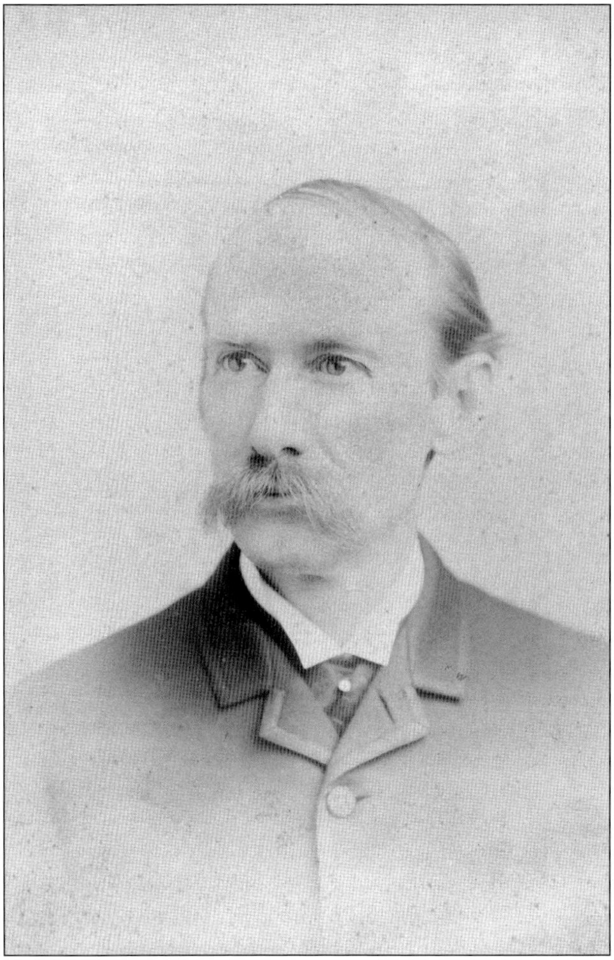

In 1891, Dr. John Allan Wyeth built the Nedofik Surgical Sofa Company in Wyeth City. Opened in 1892, the company shipped wooden, padded, adjustable sofas throughout the world. At Wyeth City, developers sold lots and encouraged modern homes like the ones shown on Nedofik Row. These attractive homes had different paint schemes and made the community quite colorful. (Marshall County Archives.)

Dr. John Allan Wyeth (shown) had many titles—soldier, surgeon, inventor, developer, and author. A devotee to the written word, Wyeth wrote *With Sabre and Scalpel: The Autobiography of a Soldier and Surgeon*; *That Devil Forrest: Life of General Nathan Bedford Forrest*; and *History of La Grange Military Academy*. In addition to Guntersville's bust, Montgomery erected a statue in honor of Wyeth. (Huntsville–Madison County Public Library.)

Florence Nightingale Sims (shown), the daughter of Dr. Marion Sims, a noted physician, married Dr. John Allan Wyeth in 1886. The couple had three children—Florence Sims Wyeth, Marion Sims Wyeth, and John Allan Wyeth Jr. After Florence died in 1915, Dr. Wyeth married Marguerite Chalifoux, a dietitian at his polyclinic. Headlines reported the couple's 50-year age difference. (Marshall County Archives.)

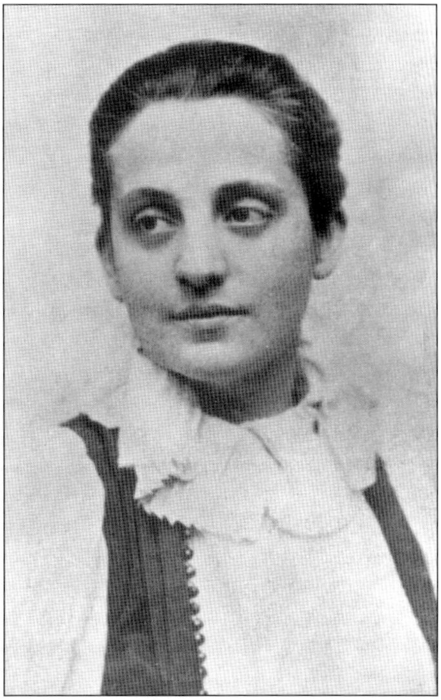

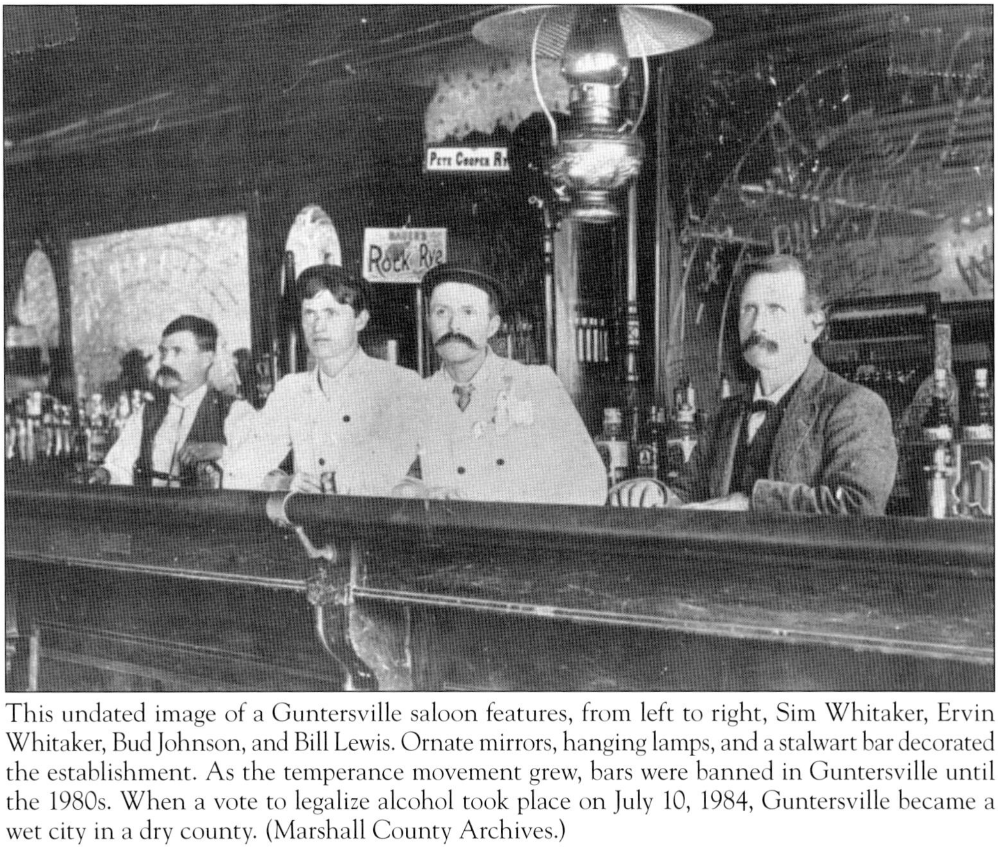

This undated image of a Guntersville saloon features, from left to right, Sim Whitaker, Ervin Whitaker, Bud Johnson, and Bill Lewis. Ornate mirrors, hanging lamps, and a stalwart bar decorated the establishment. As the temperance movement grew, bars were banned in Guntersville until the 1980s. When a vote to legalize alcohol took place on July 10, 1984, Guntersville became a wet city in a dry county. (Marshall County Archives.)

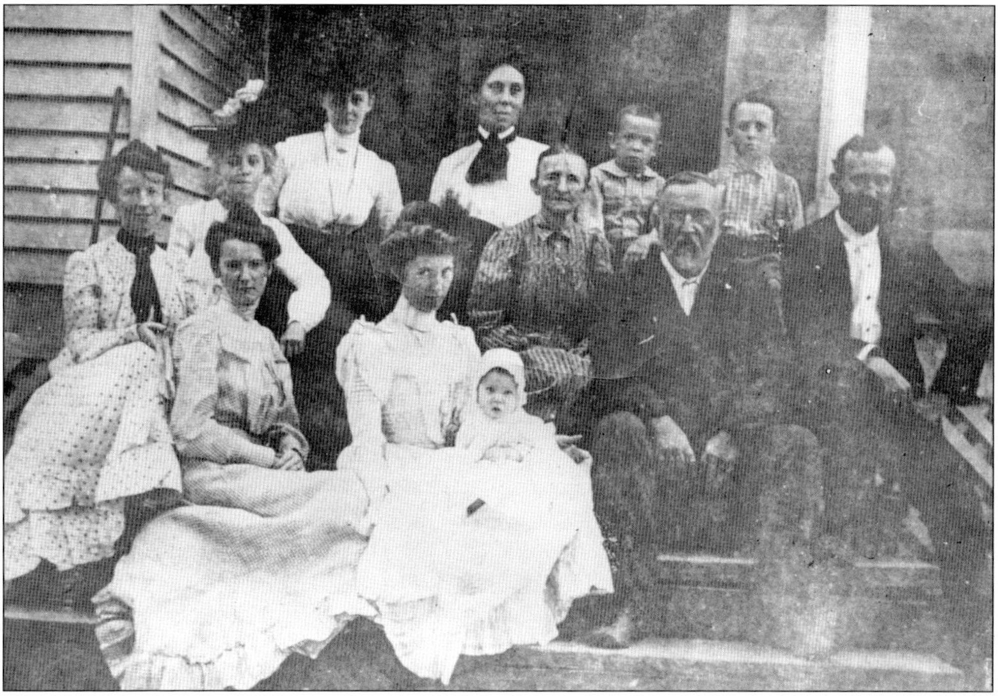

Pictured are, from left to right: (first row) Mary Tate Street, Maymie Lusk Street, Oliver Street Jr., Judge Thomas Street, and Oliver Street; (second row) Julia Street Snead, Annie Jordan Henry, Emma Hunter, Margaret Lusk Farrow, Julia Beard Street, Guy Whitman, and Edward Whitman. The Street family lived at Beard's Bluff (now Street's Bluff) on property originally settled by Arthur Beard. (Marshall County Archives.)

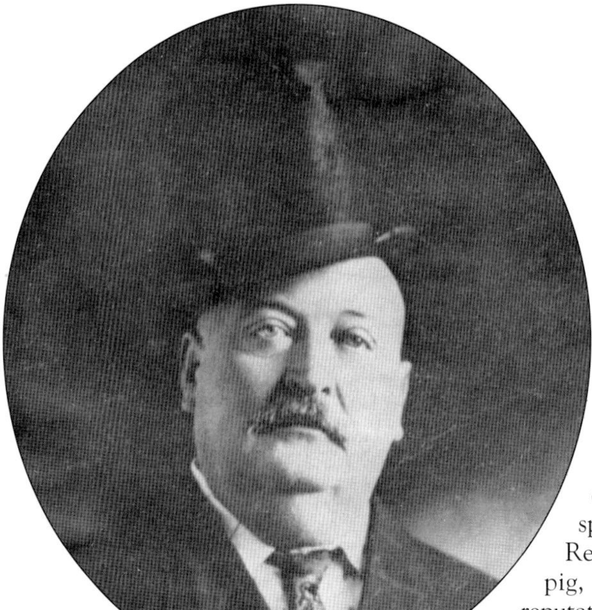

Pictured is riverboat captain William Simpson McKee (1859–1917), who had a cavalier attitude about federal regulations. When he lost his license, Captain "Simp" defied the law and continued with his entrepreneurial spirit, running bars and even brothels. Remembered for drinking with his pet pig, McKee loved advancing his "blue" reputation. He was quoted as saying, "Hell is not big enough for the devil and 'Simp' McKee." (Marshall County Archives.)

Stonecutter Hugh Carlisle built bridges, tunnels, and roadbeds for railroads. During the construction of the Tennessee & Coosa Railroad, he received 150,000 acres of land, which made him one of the most significant property owners in Alabama history. In later lawsuits filed by homesteaders, Carlisle received a favorable judgment but agreed to sell at $2.50 per acre. He married Mary Wyeth, Judge Louis Wyeth's daughter. (Marshall County Archives.)

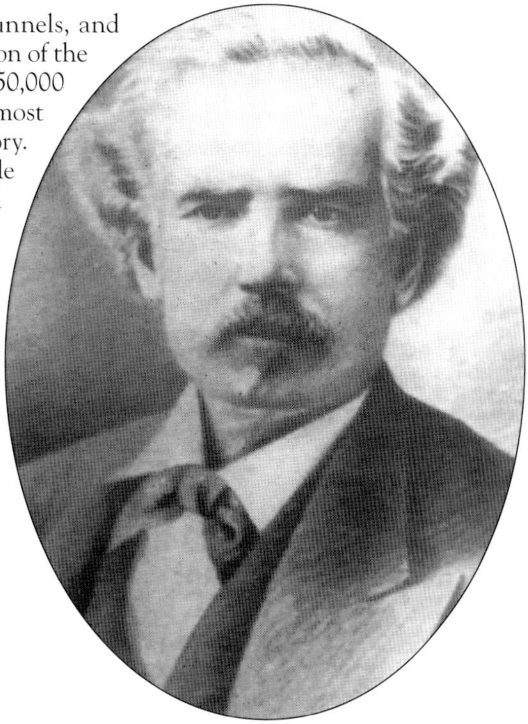

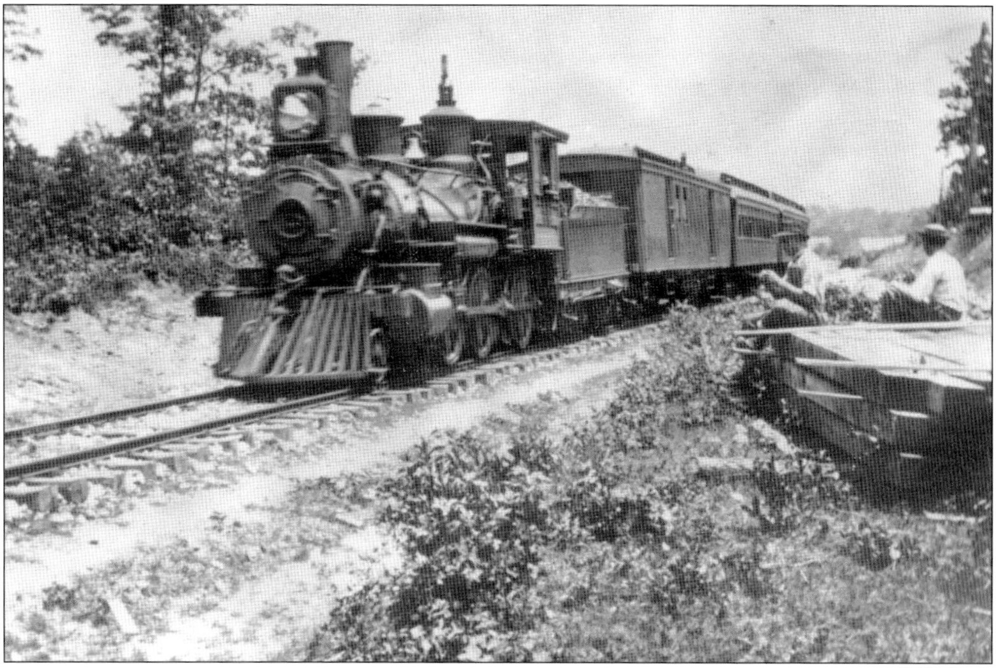

Initially discussed in the 1850s, the railroad from Guntersville to Gadsden was finally completed in 1891. The connection to Huntsville was approximately 20 miles long and required transfer boats from Hobbs' Island to Guntersville, where the trains were loaded and unloaded. Steamers and stern-wheelers like *Huntsville*, *Hattie McDaniel*, *Guntersville*, and *Huntsville II* made train service possible. (George Barnett.)

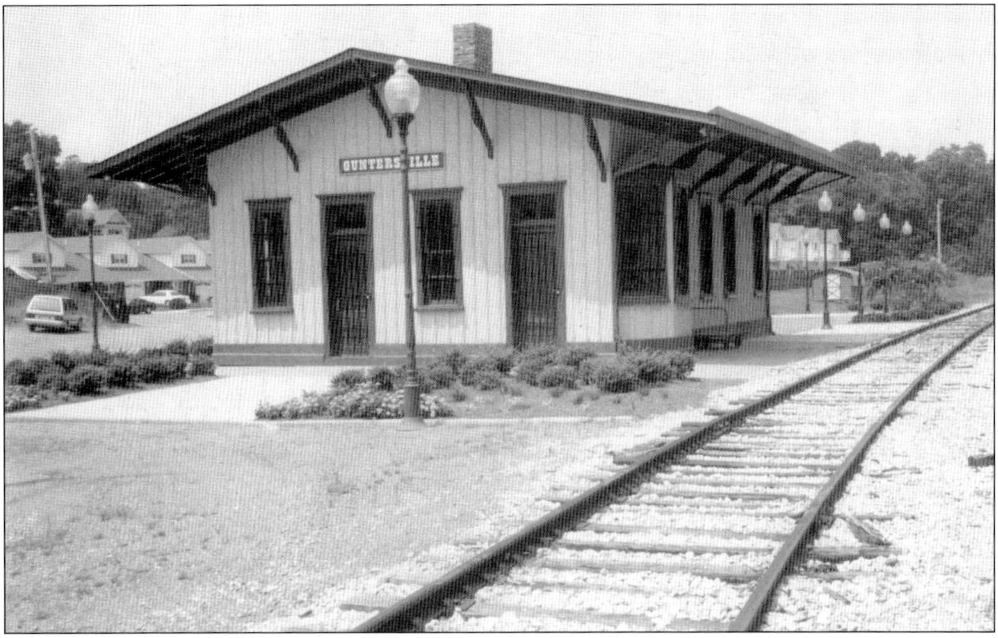

Several hundred people jammed into this depot on June 26, 1911, when three-time presidential candidate William Jennings Bryan's train stopped here. Introduced by the Honorable John Lusk, Bryan launched into a brief oratory. Bryan returned to Guntersville on April 12, 1918, and gave a speech at the courthouse. Today, the depot is a museum that contains numerous photographs, paintings, and artifacts. (*Advertiser-Gleam.*)

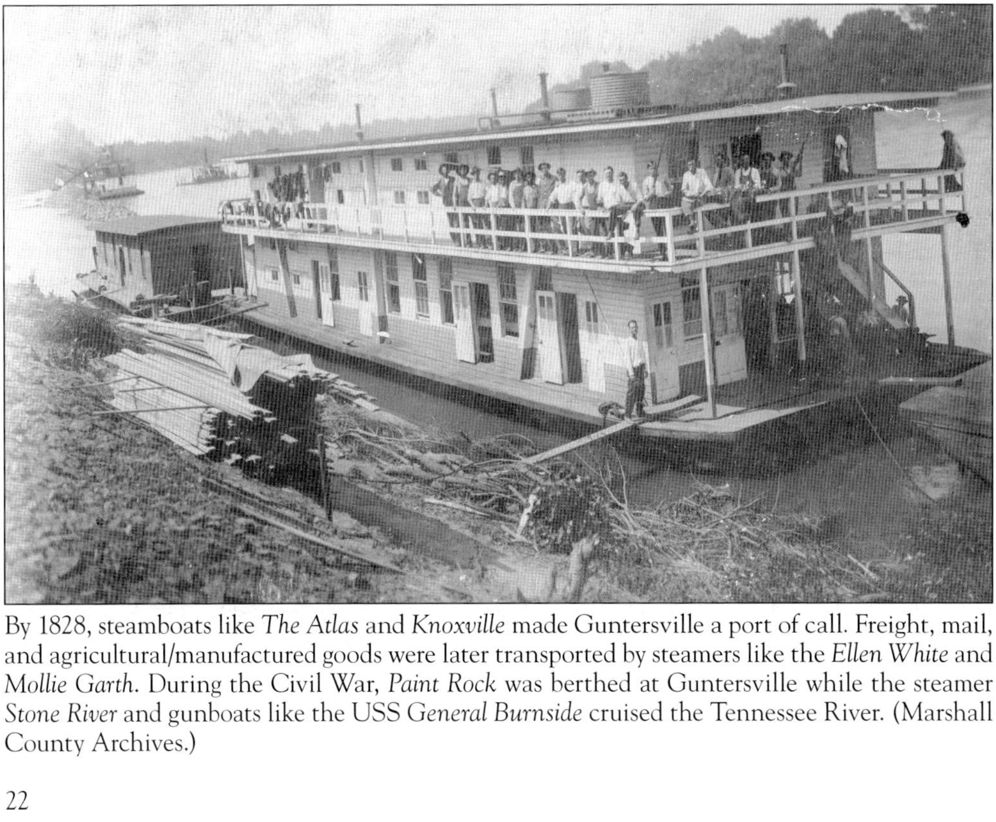

By 1828, steamboats like *The Atlas* and *Knoxville* made Guntersville a port of call. Freight, mail, and agricultural/manufactured goods were later transported by steamers like the *Ellen White* and *Mollie Garth*. During the Civil War, *Paint Rock* was berthed at Guntersville while the steamer *Stone River* and gunboats like the USS *General Burnside* cruised the Tennessee River. (Marshall County Archives.)

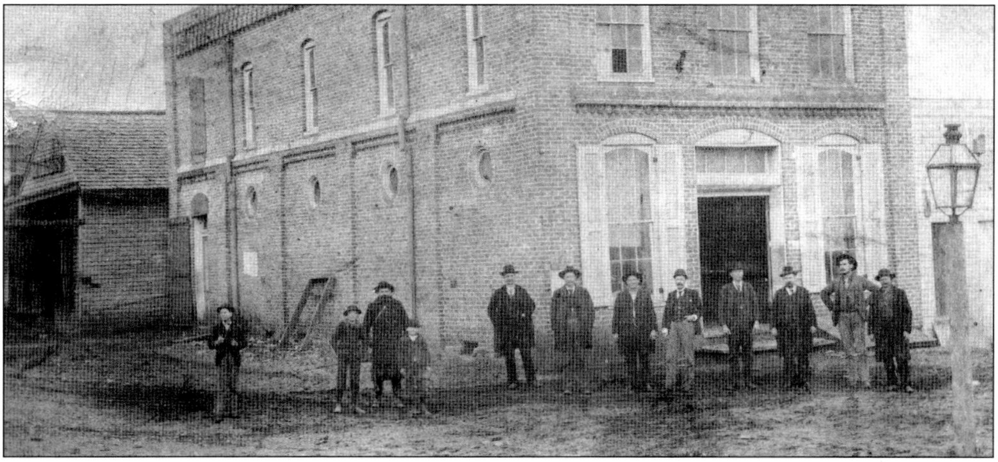

In 1885, twelve streetlights were added to Broad Street and Blount Avenue for the cost of $60. Shown are, from left to right, Burton Gilbreath, Kirby Winston, Gum Wells (sheriff), Gad Winston, two unidentified, John Gilbreath, Emmett Gilbreath, Joe Lattimer, and Montgomery Gilbreath. At left is the law office of John G. Winston. (Marshall County Archives.)

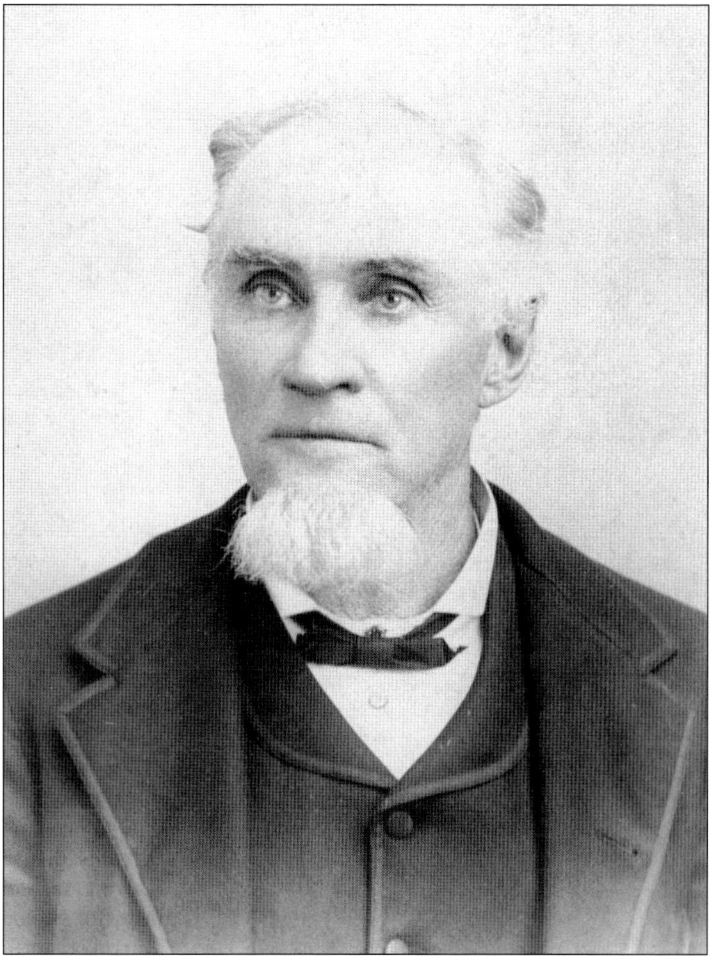

Col. James Sheffield (shown) led the 48th Alabama Infantry, ran for governor in 1882, and killed Dr. William May in 1890. Sheffield blamed the doctor for his daughter Andrew's opioid addiction and her act of arson on a neighbor's house. Andrew was committed to Bryce State Mental Hospital. Her letters were later published in *The Letters of a Victorian Madwoman*, edited by John Hughes. (Marshall County Archives.)

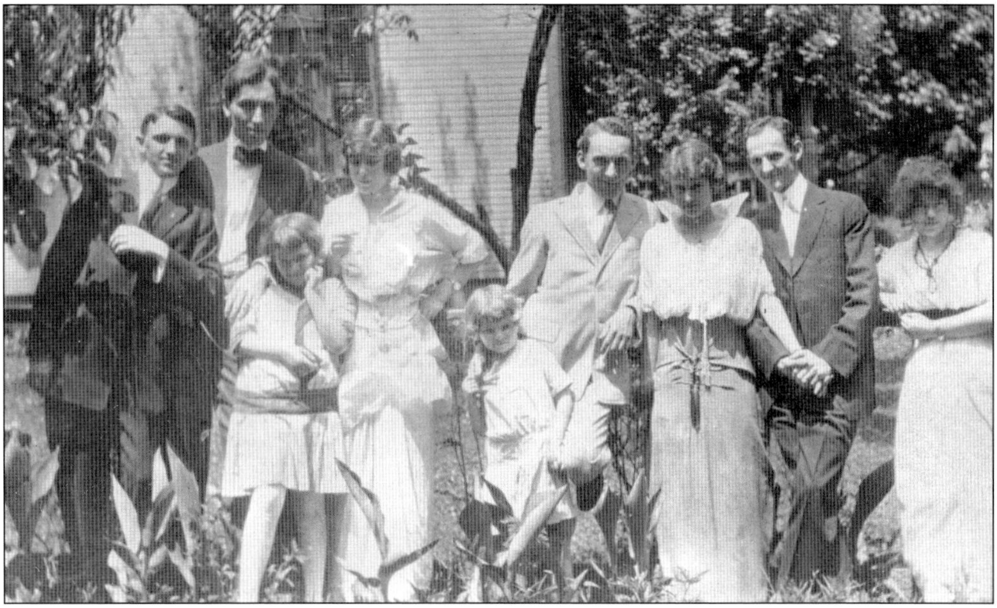

In small cities like Guntersville, social life revolved around relatives, friends, and neighbors. In this convivial photograph are, from left to right, Wood Throckmorton, Owen Hulsey, Sara Thomason, Mary Julia Street, Mary Miller Thomason, Mack Killcrease, Clara Duncan, Grover Bryant, and unidentified. Throckmorton owned a drugstore, Hulsey operated a mercantile, Killcrease practiced law, and Bryant worked as a banker. (Marshall County Archives.)

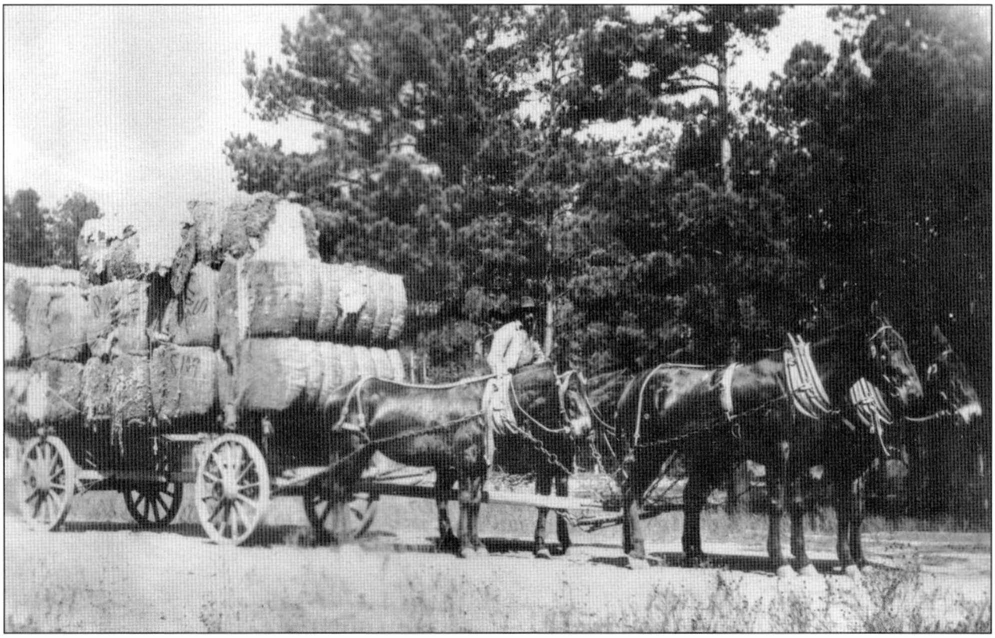

The wagon in this picture shows bales of cotton headed to market. Farmers, taking into account production costs like fertilizers, poisons, and gin expenses, prided themselves on having the greatest yields. Overproduction often caused prices to plummet. In the late 1920s, the First National Bank of Guntersville encouraged farmers to cut cotton production and grow more food crops. (Marshall County Archives.)

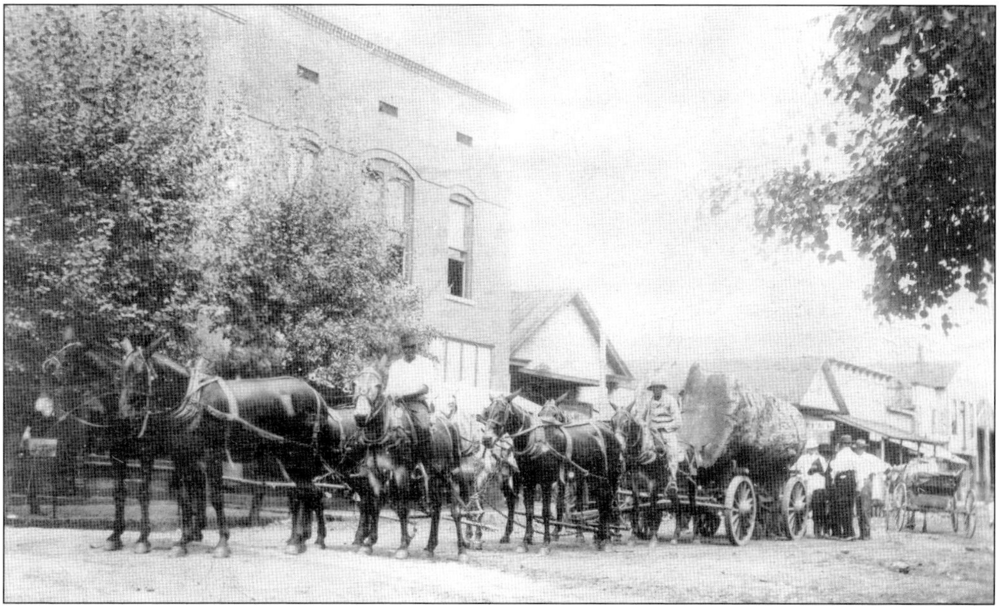

This undated photograph shows an eight-mule team with unidentified teamsters and a log cut from Erwing Grizzell's property. The background businesses include W.G. Henry's Store at left, Thomason Drugs, David Jordan's office, and the post office. Harvesting timber contributed to industries like Wyeth City's Woodenware Company and Standard Basket Factory. (Marshall County Archives.)

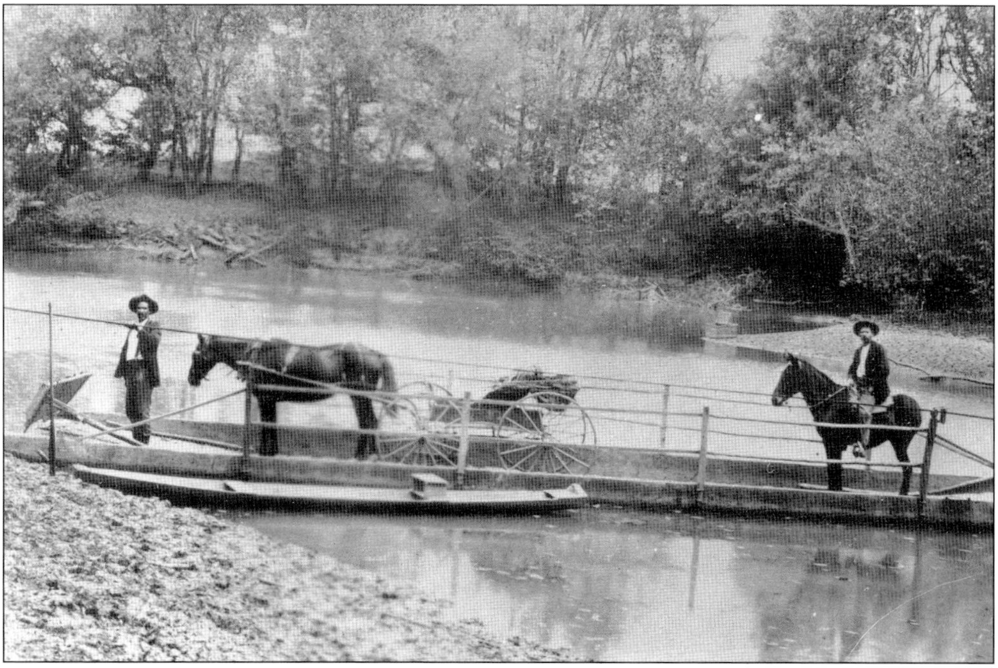

Until bridges became standard in Guntersville, people depended on ferries. Traveling from home to town and moving goods required the use of a ferry. Humans, wagons, carriages, and livestock had to load and unload, wait for space, and pay to be conveyed from one side of the river to the other. This image shows two unidentified men on a ferry. (Marshall County Archives.)

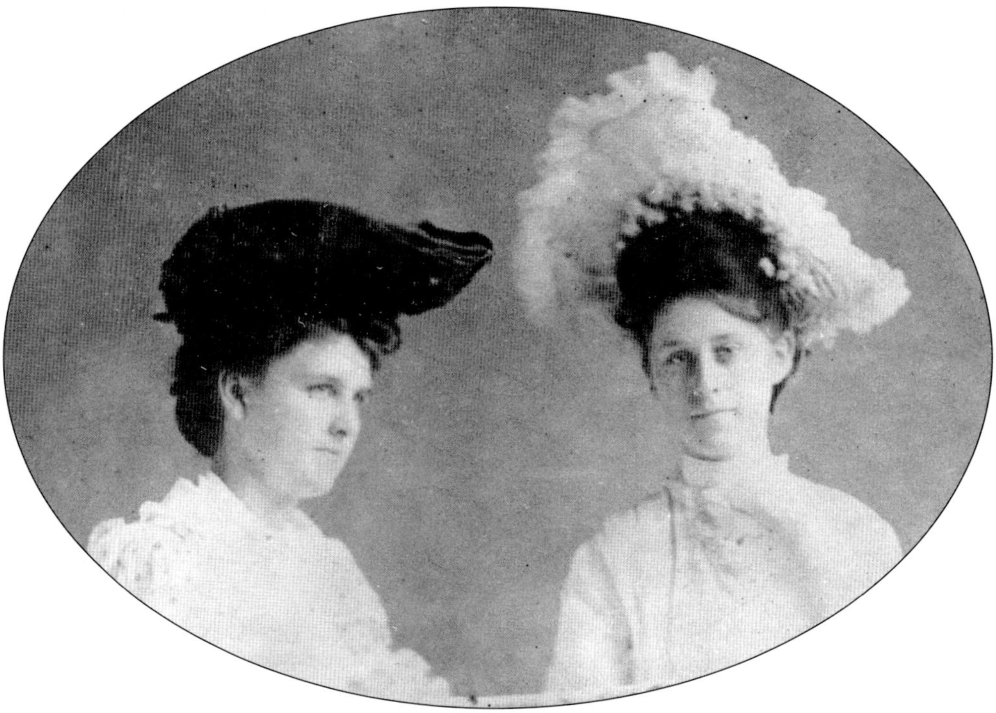

Pictured are Birdie Hooper (left) and Eula Jordan (right). Birdie, the daughter of A.R. and Lucinda Hooper, is best remembered for her work with the Church of Christ. She married Charles Kennamer. When Kennamer was appointed US attorney in 1921, the family moved to Montgomery. The daughter of Mattie and William "Bill" Jordan, Eula married Powell Alves. (Marshall County Archives.)

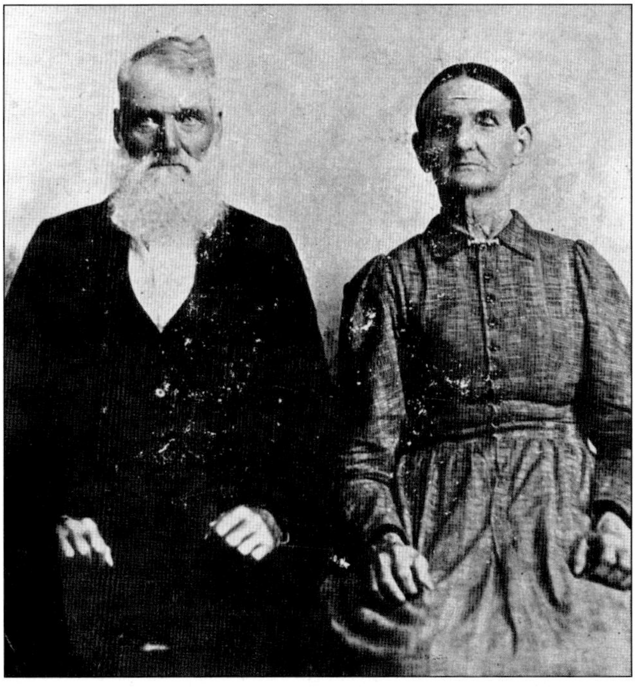

Shown are Newton and Peggy Sheffield. Originally from Paulding, Georgia, the couple raised a large family in Guntersville. Their children were Sara (married to Jim Cooley), Emily, Amanda (married to Frank Edmonds), Elizabeth (married to Joseph Donaldson), Harriet (married to Rev. Ary Weems), Newton J. (married to Martha Warren), and Elijah (married to Dollie Yielding). Newton and Peggy relocated and died in Milam County, Texas. (Pete Sparks.)

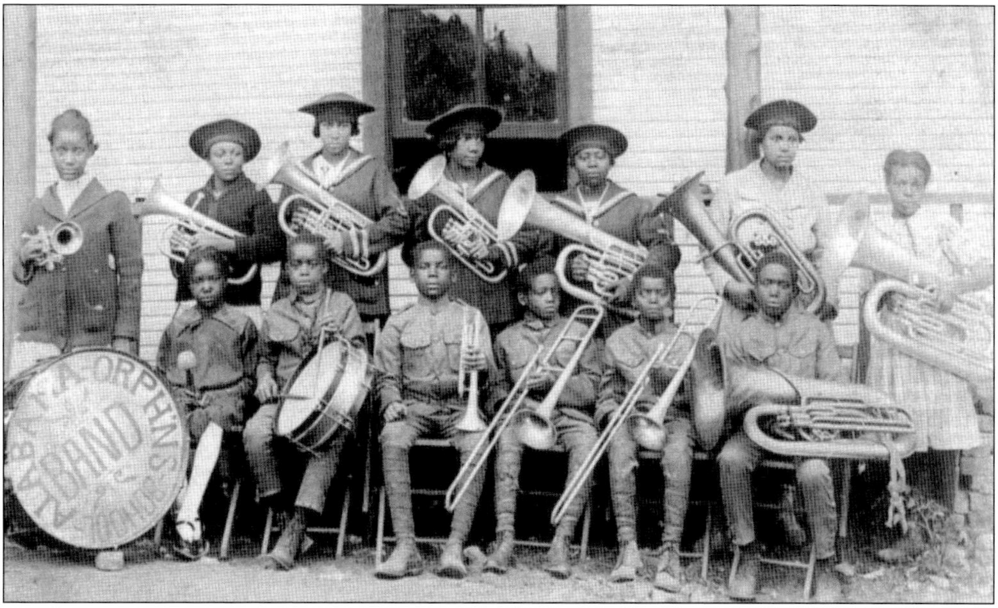

In the early 1910s, Rev. J.W. Blount established a school for orphaned Black children near Huntsville, Alabama. He encouraged a love of music in his pupils by forming a band in which they could develop and grow their talents. Dubbed the Alabama Orph'ns School Band, the group performed statewide, from Guntersville to Montgomery. At its peak, Blount's school had 40 students. (Huntsville–Madison County Public Library.)

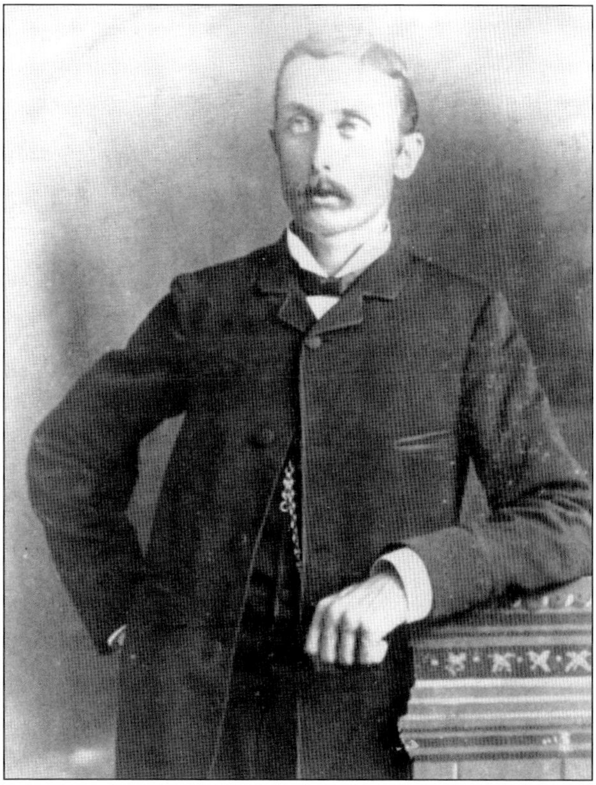

In the mid-1880s, Albert Gallatin Henry Jr. (shown) was listed as the only millionaire in Alabama. His father Albert Gallatin Sr. and grandfather Hugh farmed, operated a store, and established an innovative system of credit for farmers to pay when crops were harvested. Securing goods from New York, they advertised merchandise ranging from farm supplies and patent medicines to crockery, clothing, and jewelry. (Marshall County Archives.)

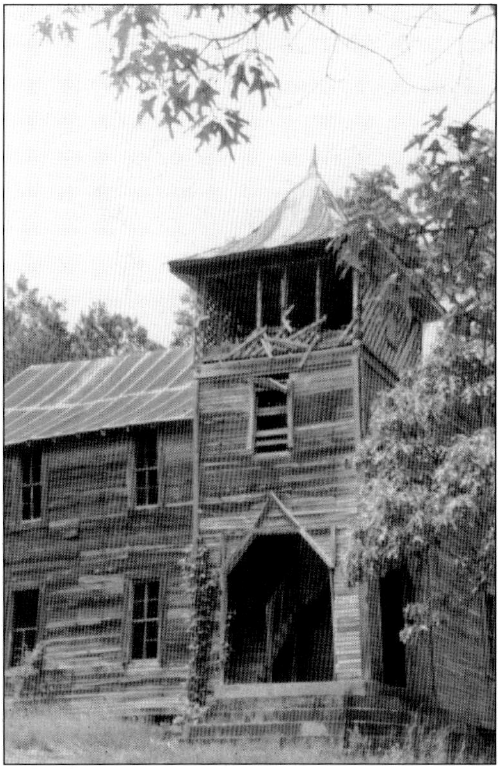

This two-story building, pictured around the 1960s, reflects the remains of a Black Masonic lodge at Wakefield (Five Points). Also used as a church, the building had a Masonic emblem on the front with hewn pews inside facing an altar. Wakefield was once known for Robbins' Spring and a racetrack. In 1966, its one-teacher school closed, and the students were reassigned to Guntersville. (Salmon Library, University of Alabama in Huntsville.)

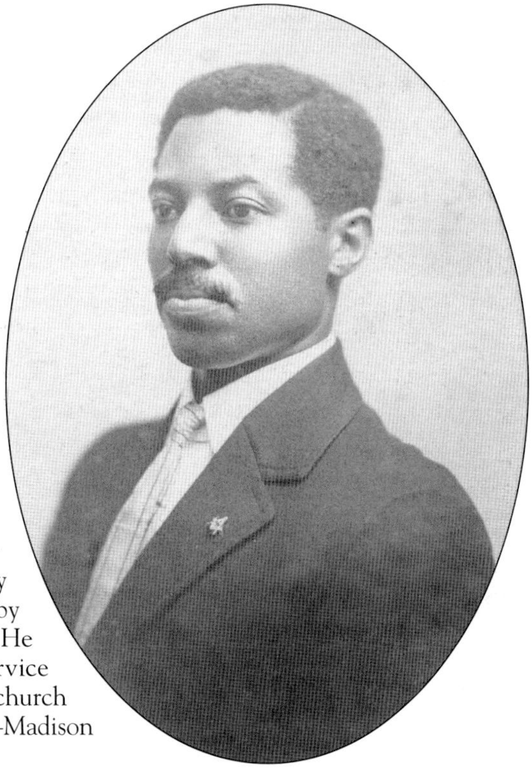

Pictured is Benjamin Franklin Moore, who operated a business on Blount Avenue. Active in the Livingston Chapel African Methodist Episcopal Church, he funded a sanctuary for the church on Taylor Street. For approximately 40 years, Moore opened church services by ringing a bell to call members to worship. He was recognized for his philanthropy and service as superintendent of the Sunday school, and church members called him "Mr. Frank." (Huntsville–Madison County Public Library.)

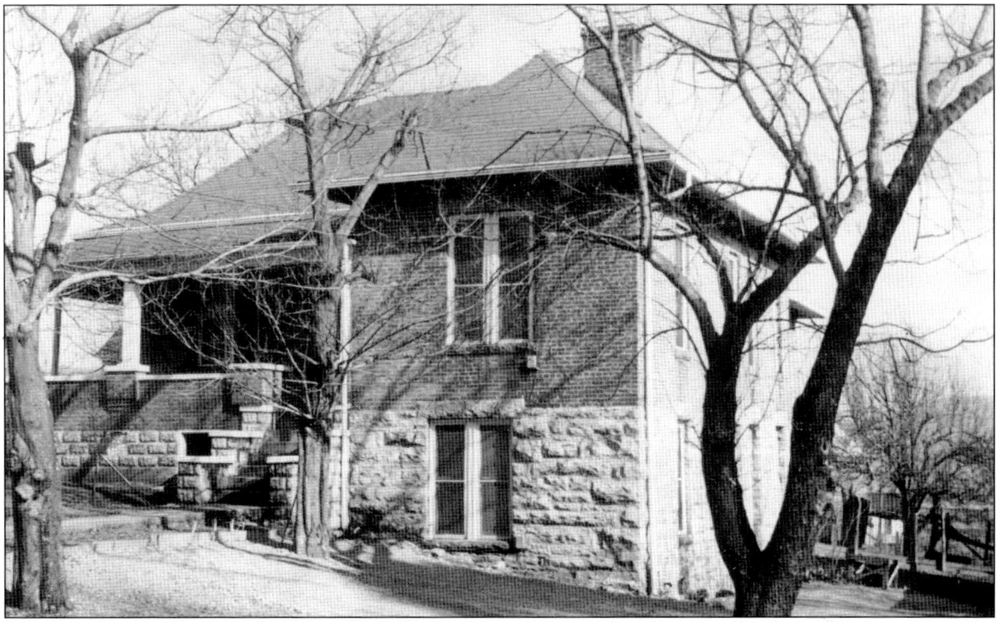

This residence on Blount Avenue once served as the Marshall County jail. In 1907, Bob Watts, convicted of murdering Jackson "Purd" Winkle, became the last man legally hanged in the county. Sheriff John Lewis was the last sheriff to work in this building. (Salmon Library, University of Alabama in Huntsville.)

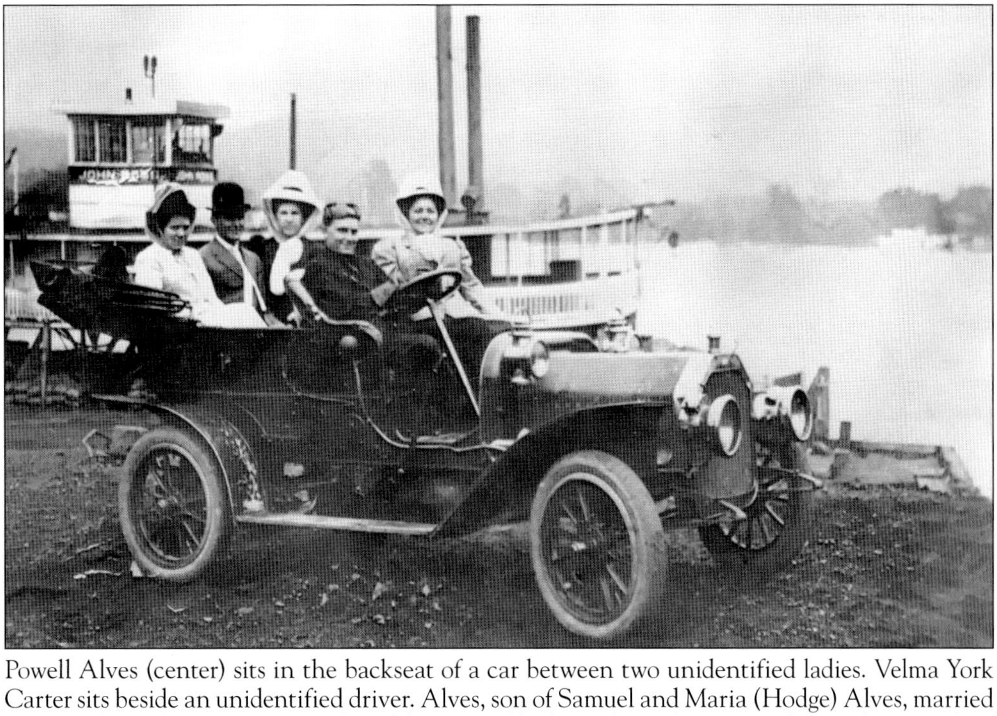

Powell Alves (center) sits in the backseat of a car between two unidentified ladies. Velma York Carter sits beside an unidentified driver. Alves, son of Samuel and Maria (Hodge) Alves, married Eula Jordan. The 1920 Census listed him as a blacksmith in the automobile industry. Alves established a plumbing company on the east side of Broad Street (Gunter Avenue) between Worth and Ringold Streets. (Marshall County Archives.)

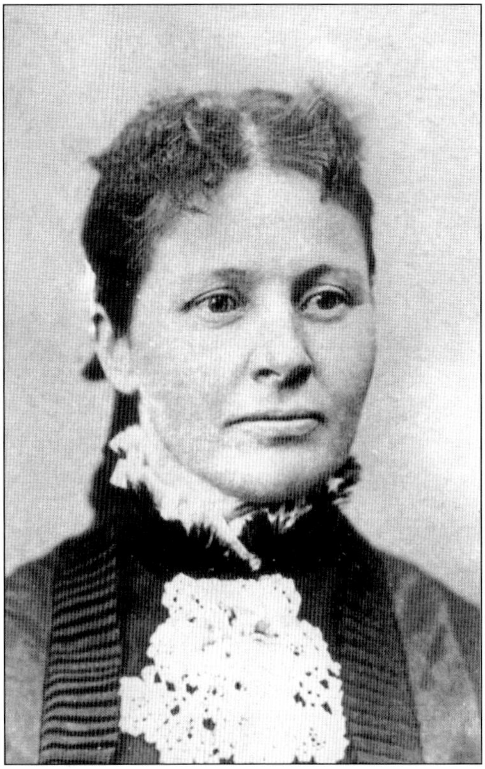

Around 1888, the Wyeth City Land Development Company offered land for the construction of churches. In response, the Church of Christ, which had been meeting in private homes, constructed a building on Broad Street (now Gunter Avenue) at a cost of $1,175. Shown is Permelia "Puss" Moore, who, with Cora Gilbreath, Birdie Hooper Kennamer, and Sallie Ratcliff Seibold, organized many of the church's activities. (Marshall County Archives.)

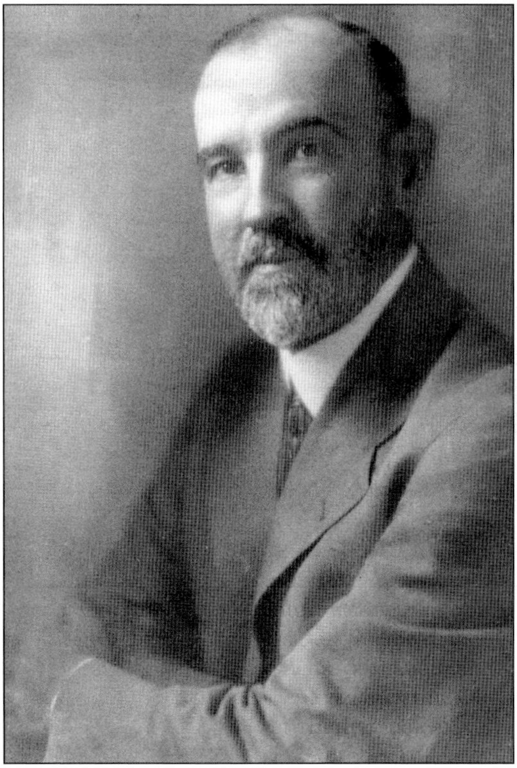

The son of probate judge Thomas Atkins Street, Oliver Day Street (shown) deserves special recognition for his historical articles on and maps of Marshall County. Street was honored as an original trustee of the Alabama Department of Archives and History. A lawyer, he served as a US district attorney for northern Alabama for seven years and as special assistant for the state attorney general. (Marshall County Archives.)

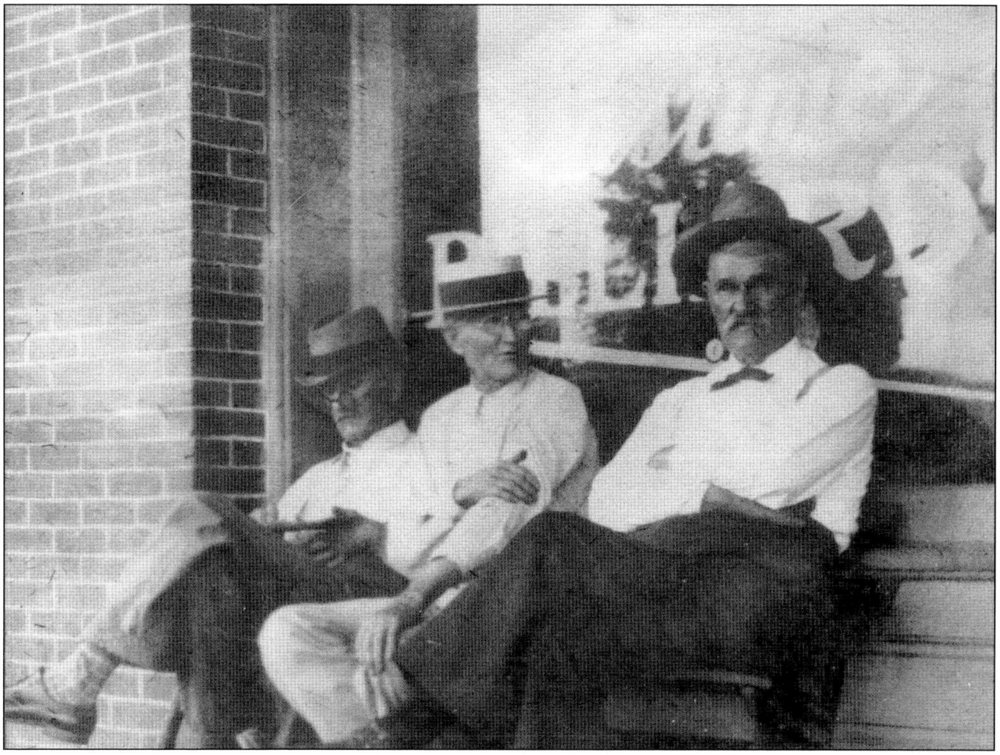

Enjoying sun and conversation outside Pastime Billiards at Guntersville in 1935 are Green B. Seibold (left), John W. Starnes (center), and William "Bill" Jordan. Seibold had worked in retail with a grocery store business, while Starnes and Jordan had farms at Claysville and Manchester, respectively. (Marshall County Archives.)

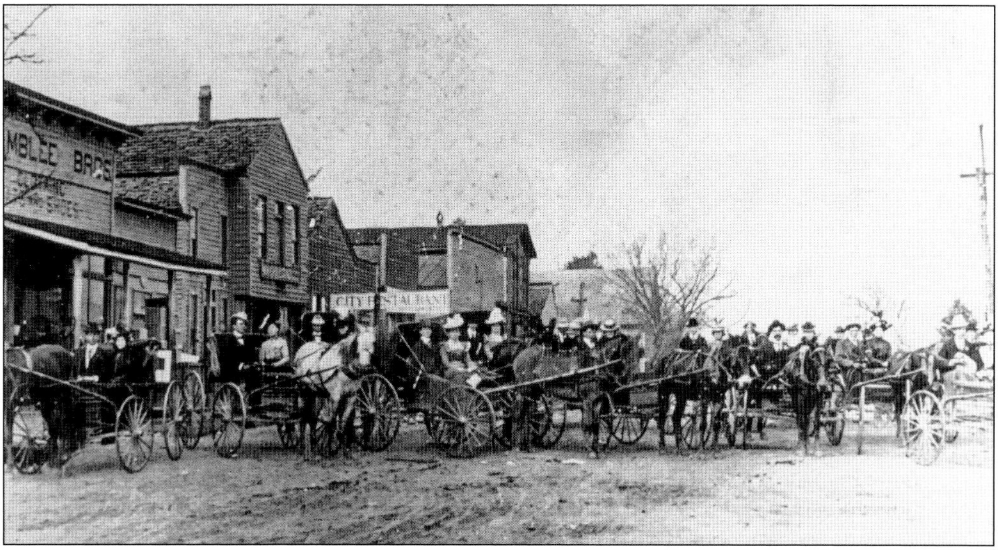

This wedding party, pictured around 1900, gathered on Broad Street (now Gunter Avenue) about a block north of Taylor Street. In 1889, a telephone line was established from Scottsboro, and in 1892, a telegraph system was added to the depot. These additions greatly improved communications for the residents of Guntersville. (Marshall County Archives.)

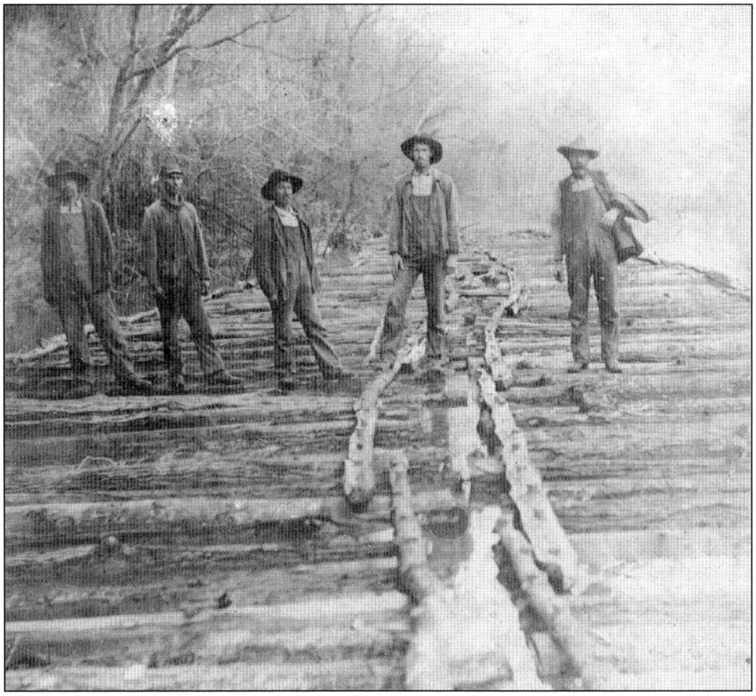

This image shows the importance of the lumber industry in Marshall County. These unidentified workers, all employed by George Washington Stewart, cut down trees, transported them to the Tennessee River, and then "walked" them downstream to a sawmill. The Ross-Graden Lumber Company, which still exists today, probably purchased this lumber. (Pete Sparks.)

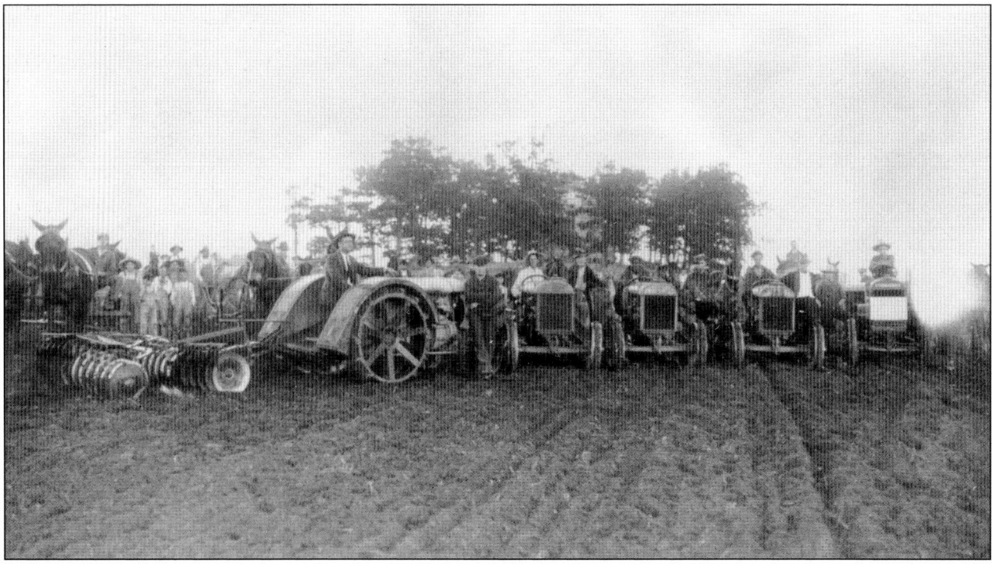

Fordson Tractors advertised that one of its machines could handle the work of 12 mules with only one driver. This undated picture, taken at Warrenton, shows volunteers participating in a community project to raise cotton. The money from the cotton sales went into a fund to build a new school. Time, labor, supplies, and equipment were donated to construct Warrenton School. (Marshall County Archives.)

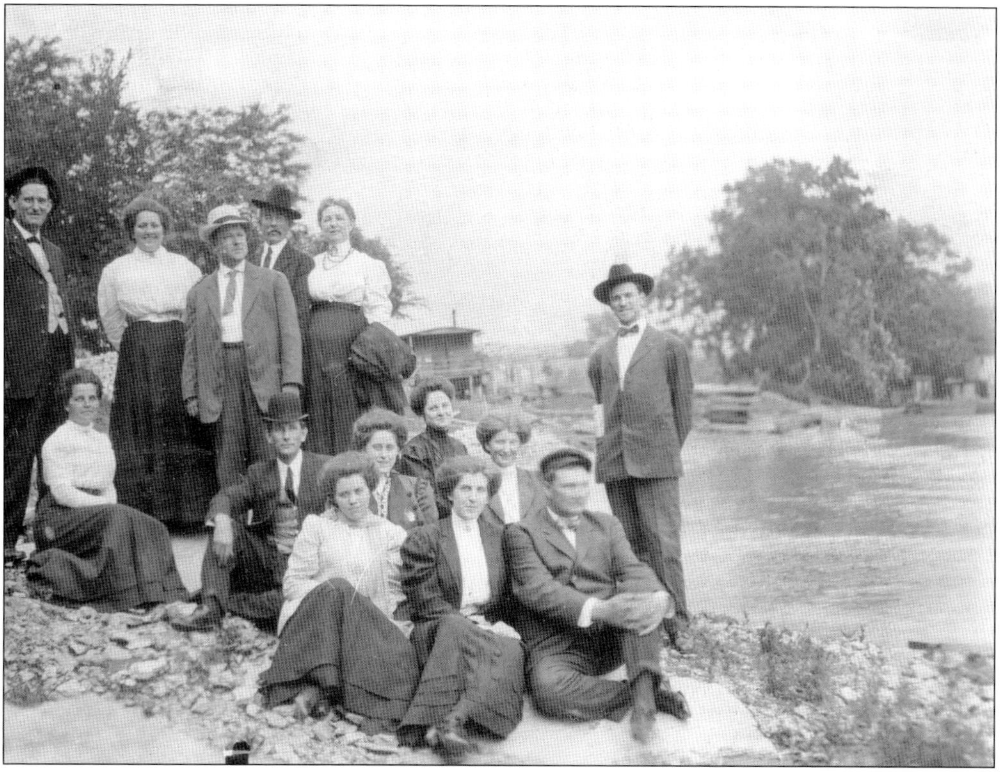

Pictured here are, from left to right, (first row) Lola Luther, Flora Long, Jim McIntyre, and Dee Isbell (standing); (second row) Sophie Timmons Jordan, Ed Roden, Bessie Bryant, Eula Jordan Alves, and Mamie Seibold McIntyre; (third row) D.C. Jordan, Velma York Carter, John Carter, J.D. Holt, and Dena Hays Holt. (Marshall County Archives.)

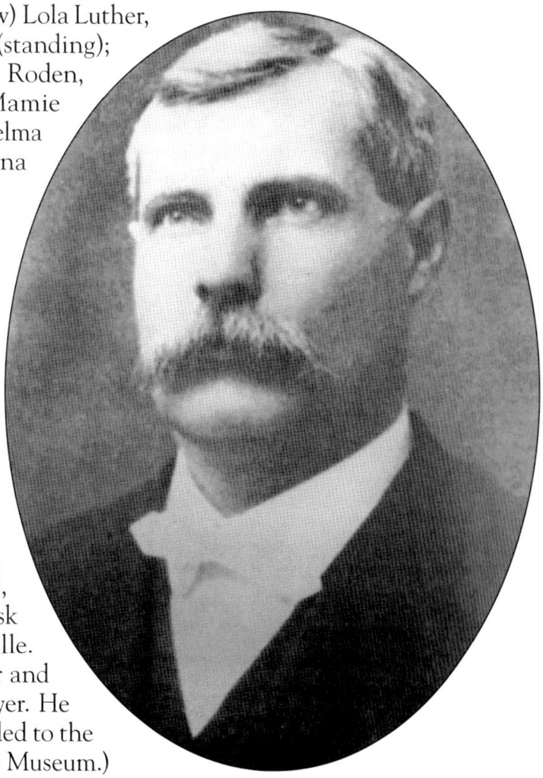

John Alexander Lusk (shown) constructed a new brick building for Lusk and Bell in 1895, sparking the beginning of the Lusk and Lusk law firm, the oldest business in Guntersville. During his career, Lusk served as a solicitor and gained a reputation as an outstanding lawyer. He continued working despite an accident that led to the amputation of one of his legs. (Guntersville Museum.)

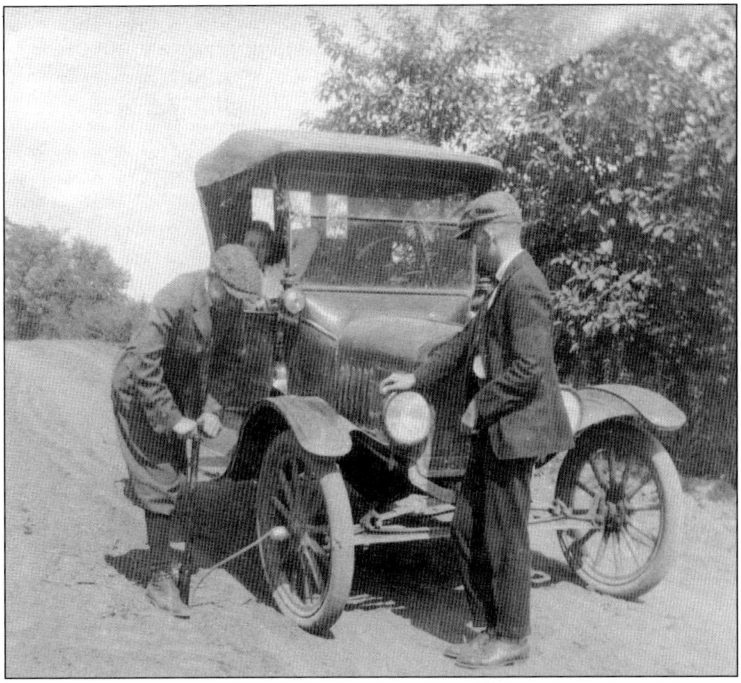

John H. Carter Jr. (left) and Harry Throckmorton (right) are shown repairing a tire in 1917. While in France during World War I, Throckmorton sent a cablegram home and found that the telegrapher knew Guntersville because it was the only city in the world with that name. After the war, Throckmorton opened a pharmacy in Tuscumbia, while Carter worked for the Guntersville electric board. (Marshall County Archives.)

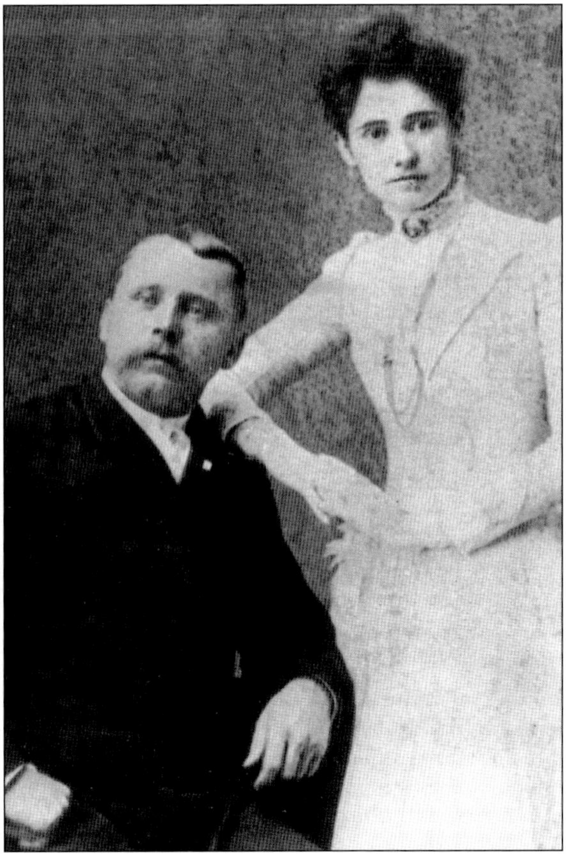

Thomas L. Farrow came to Guntersville, established a general store, and built a cotton warehouse. His first wife, Belle Cochran, died in 1900 during a period of widespread illness. In 1908, Farrow married Margarette Lusk (pictured at right with Farrow), daughter of Dr. Lorenzo and Mary Emma Lusk. In 1901, Farrow, an alderman, and Robert Bell unsuccessfully offered to donate land to move the depot from Wyeth City to Guntersville. (Marshall County Archives.)

Seated in the center is James "Jim" Cooley, the eldest son of John Richard and Lydia Cassie Kirkpatrick Cooley of Manchester. He is pictured with five of his children. Shown are, from left to right, Lizzie, Jim, Bob, John, and Ida. Cooley outlived three of his four wives—Sara Sheffield, Sally Wood, and Flora Thompson. He was survived by his fourth wife, Dora Hunkapiller. His son Crawford died in World War II. (Pete Sparks.)

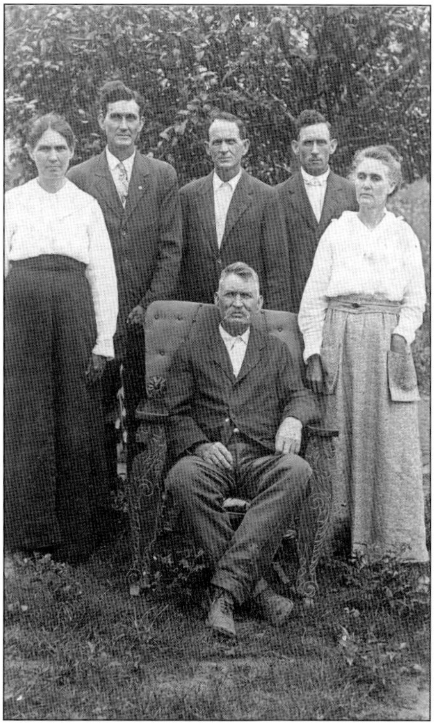

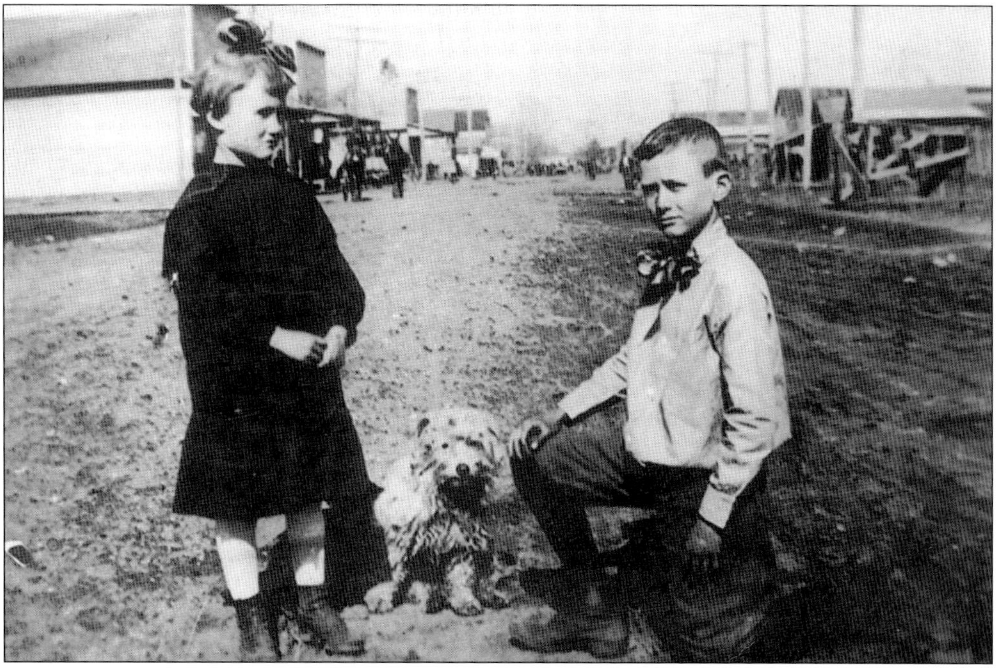

This 1915 photograph of an unpaved Guntersville street shows Hazel Moon (left) with her brother Earl. In 1933, Hazel married John Columbus Oaks. In 1930, Earl (1910–2000) worked as a soda clerk in a drugstore. Ten years later, he worked for an electric company, then served in the Navy during World War II. In 1947, he and his father, Walter, opened the Moonglo Motel and Café. (George Barnett.)

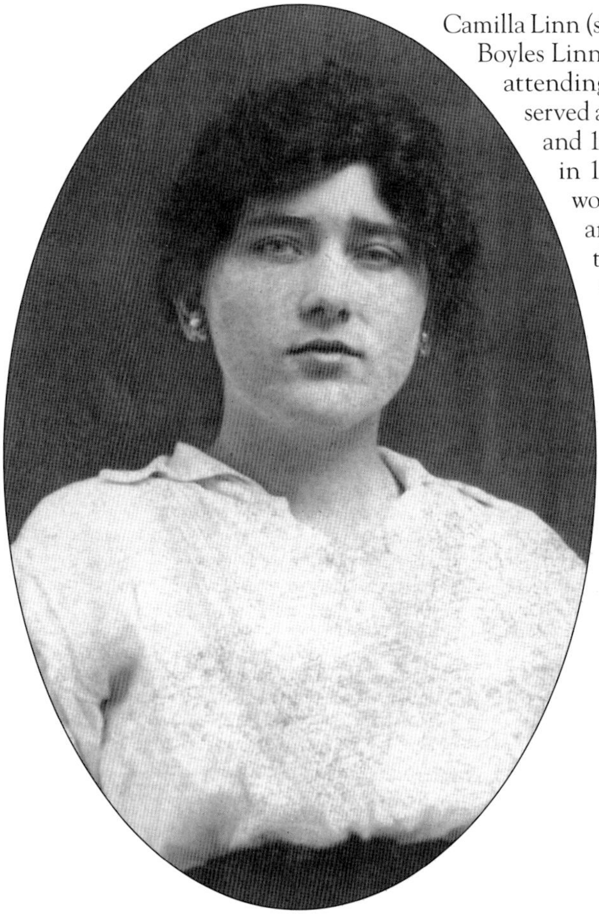

Camilla Linn (shown), daughter of William and Annie Boyles Linn, taught school in Guntersville. After attending Peabody College in Nashville, she served as a principal at Gadsden between 1925 and 1927. Linn married Dr. William Rosser in 1927 and moved to Birmingham. She worked in the Parent-Teacher Association and belonged to women's auxiliaries for the State of Alabama and Jefferson County. (Rosser Papers, Lister Hill Library, University of Alabama at Birmingham.)

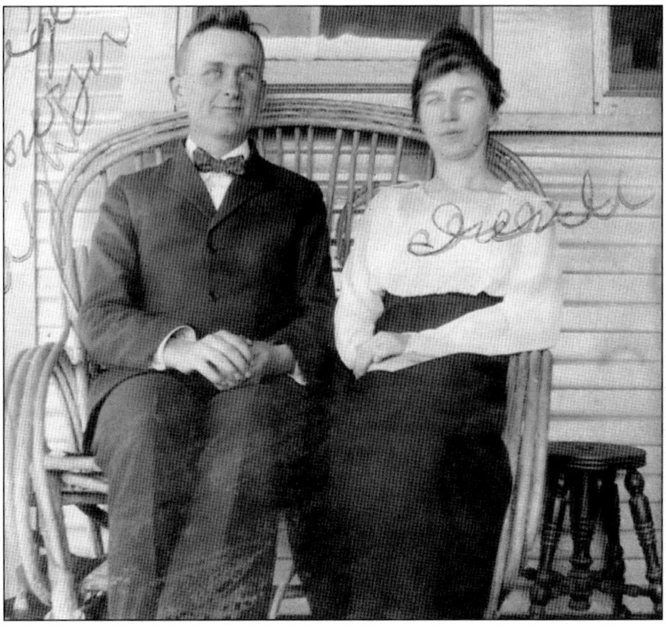

This image shows Thomas Harvey Wright (left) with Irene Linn around 1920. Wright graduated from the University of Alabama law school in 1916 and formed a partnership with lawyer William C. Rayburn. In 1921, Wright married Hattie Jackson, who had taught at Marshall County High School. Wright's sister Bessie Wright taught with Irene at Guntersville Elementary School. (Rosser Papers, Lister Hill Library, University of Alabama at Birmingham.)

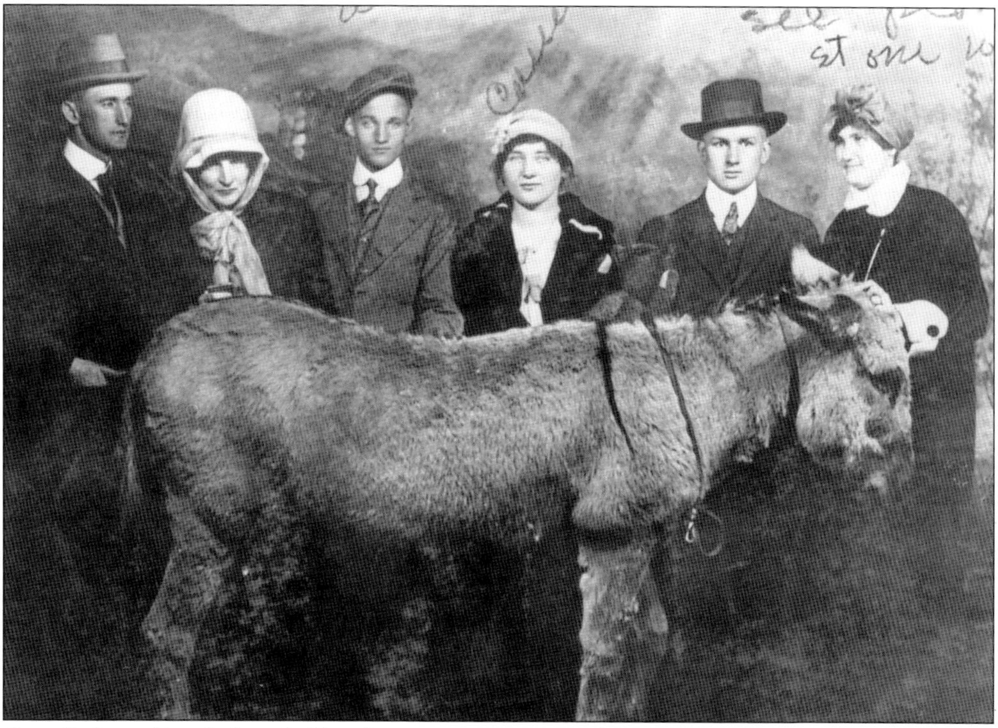

Camilla Linn (fourth from left) is shown enjoying a social occasion with an unidentified group. Linn and her two sisters, Irene and Fannie, taught at Guntersville's elementary school with Prof. R. Lee Barnes. This c. 1916 image appears to be from a county fair that was held at Guntersville. Camilla saw her first airplane at the fair. (Rosser Papers, Lister Hill Library, University of Alabama at Birmingham.)

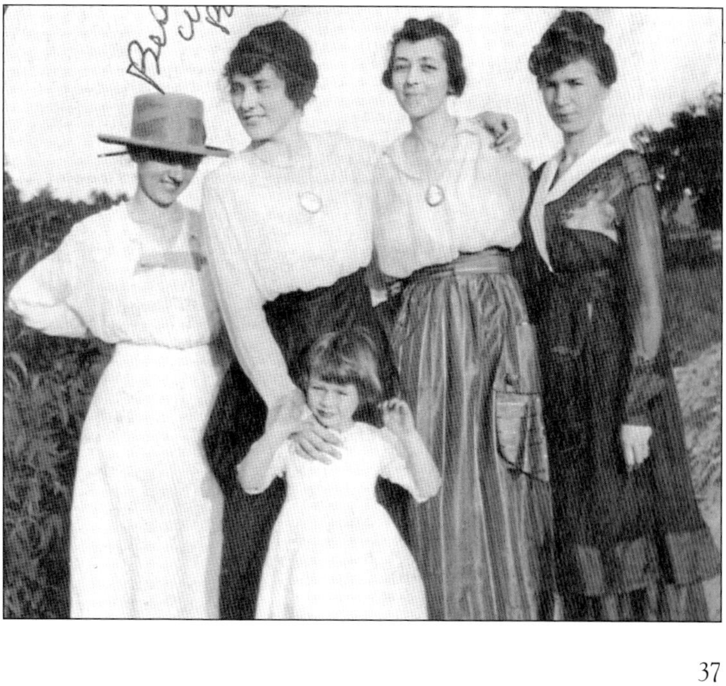

Pictured are, from left to right, Bessie Wright, Camilla Linn, unidentified, and Irene Linn, along with an unidentified child. Fannie Linn and Ethel Reed joined them later. Irene and Camilla moved to Gadsden, where the latter became a principal. Camilla and Irene attended summer school at Peabody College. (Rosser Papers, Lister Hill Library, University of Alabama at Birmingham.)

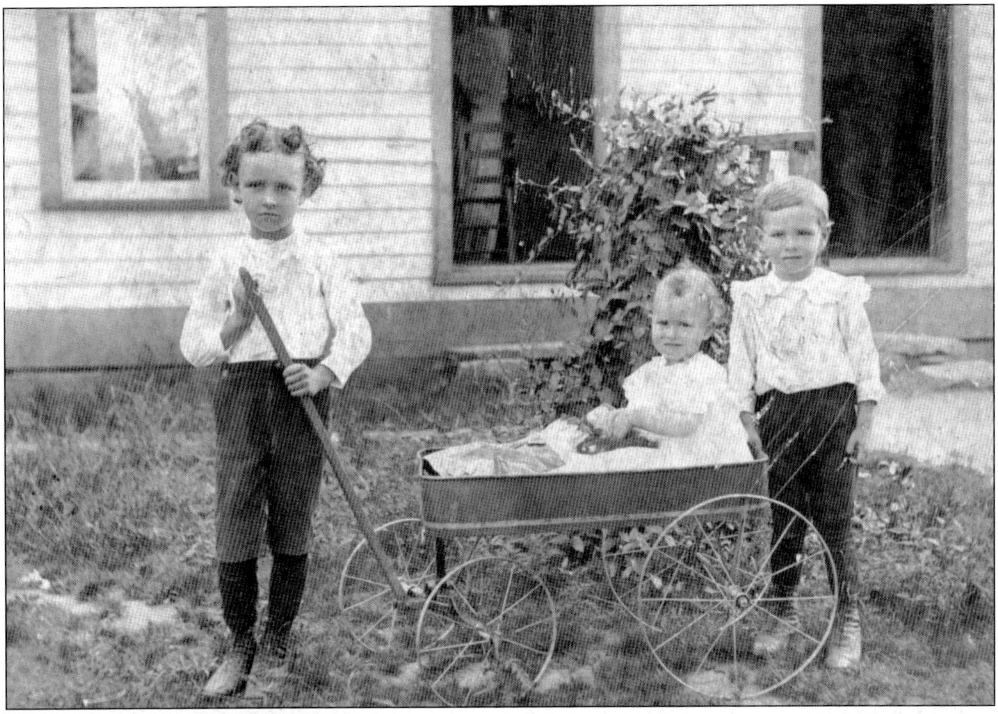

The children of George Washington and Bessie Stewart—William Stickles, Ilene Stewart (in wagon), and Charles Stewart—are shown at the Seibold house on the northeast corner of Blount Avenue and Scott Street. Ilene married Ferrell Sparks and had four children—Stewart "Johnny," Wallace "Joe," Julian "Pete," and Rhodora. (Pete Sparks.)

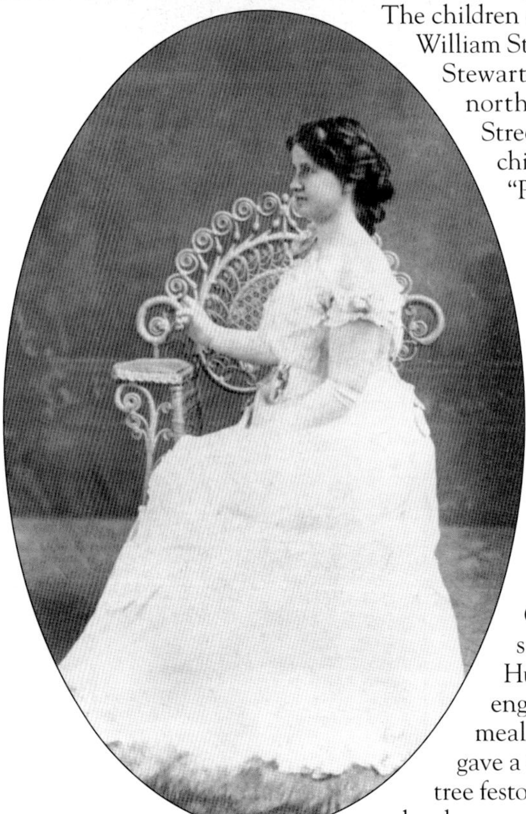

Mary Caius Fennell (shown), daughter of Caius and Mattie Foster Fennell, was a local socialite. Mary became engaged to Owen Hulsey. In 1915, Leila Lusk hosted the couple's engagement party, which included a six-course meal and theater entertainment. Edna Bradford gave a Christmas social for the couple with a festive tree festooned with gifts. For many years, Hulsey ran a hardware store in Guntersville. (Larry Smith.)

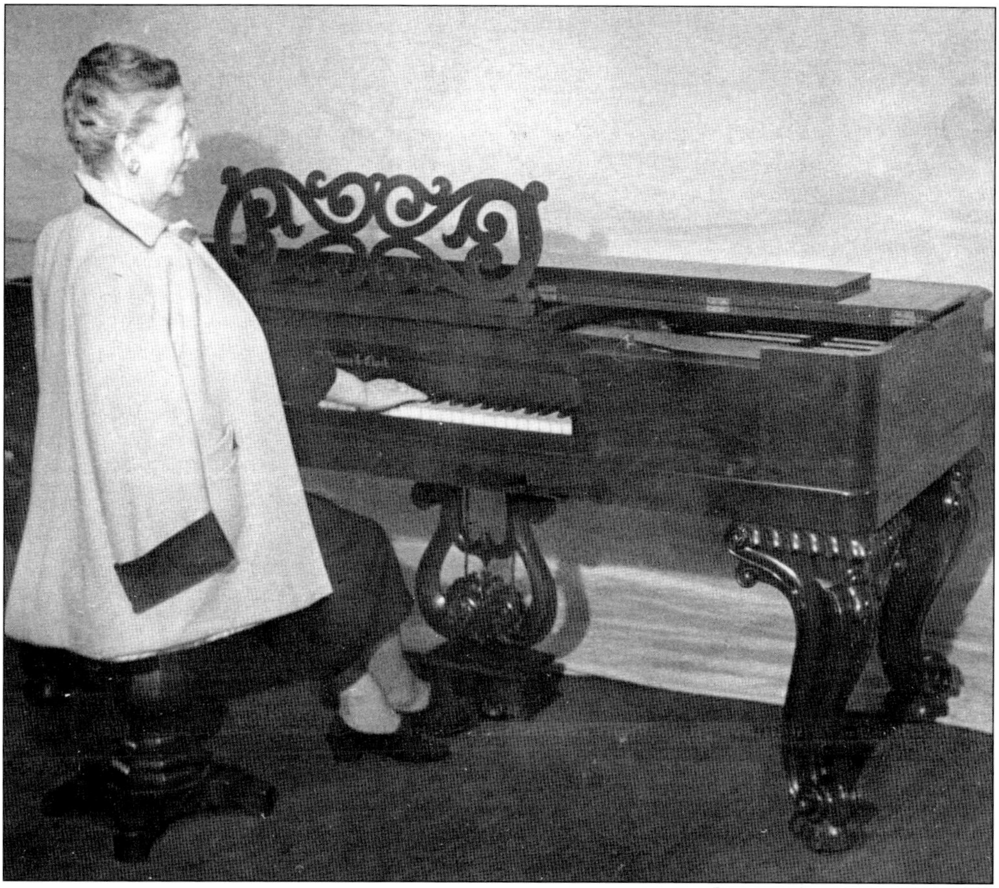

Erin Fennell (shown), daughter of Caius and Mattie Foster Fennell, married Sam Henry Jr. in 1904. Erin was the pianist—a position inherited from her mother—at First Methodist Church. In 1920, she promoted a drive to buy the stained-glass windows for the church. Erin and her sister Mary donated an heirloom Foster family piano (shown) to the Arlington Historic House (Mudd-Munger House) in Birmingham. (Marshall County Archives.)

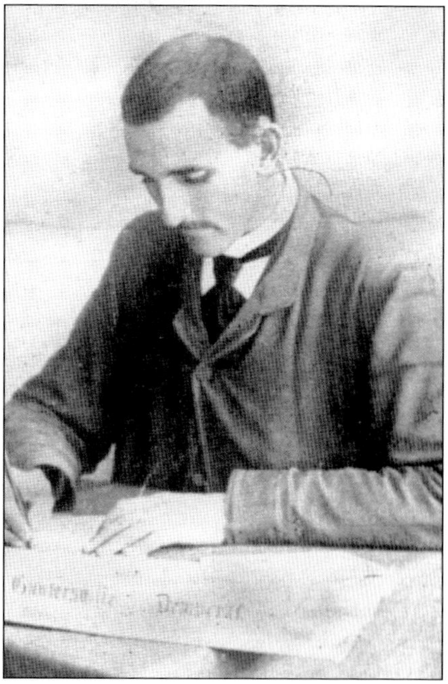

Pictured here is Edwin O. Neely, the distinguished editor of the *Guntersville Democrat*, who came to Guntersville in 1887. Hoping to improve local infrastructure, he pledged money for a bridge in 1888. He and his wife, Lois Peck, had three children: Ethel, Carl, and Albert. One of Neely's 1895 maps is frequently used by local historians. Neely died in 1902. (Marshall County Archives.)

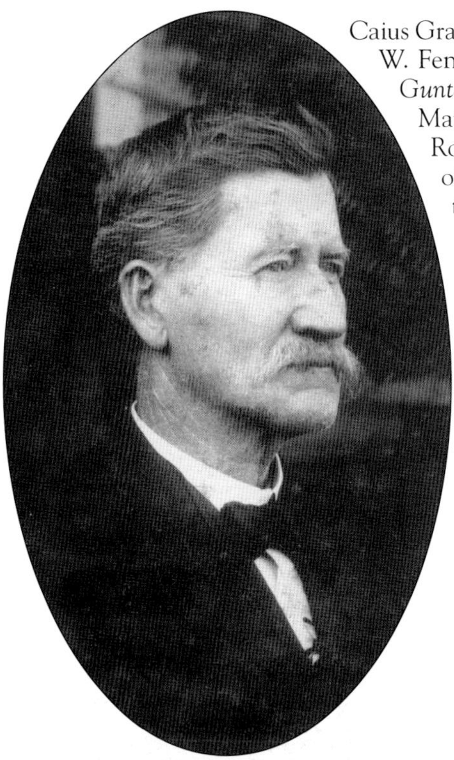

Caius Grattan Fennell (shown), the youngest son of Dr. James W. Fennell and Matilda Allison, owned and edited the *Guntersville Democrat* from 1903 until 1928. He married Mattie Foster, and the two had three children: Erin, Robert, and Mary. In 1909, Caius was elected president of the Alabama Press Association. He became one of the first Guntersville residents to own a Studebaker. (*Advertiser-Gleam.*)

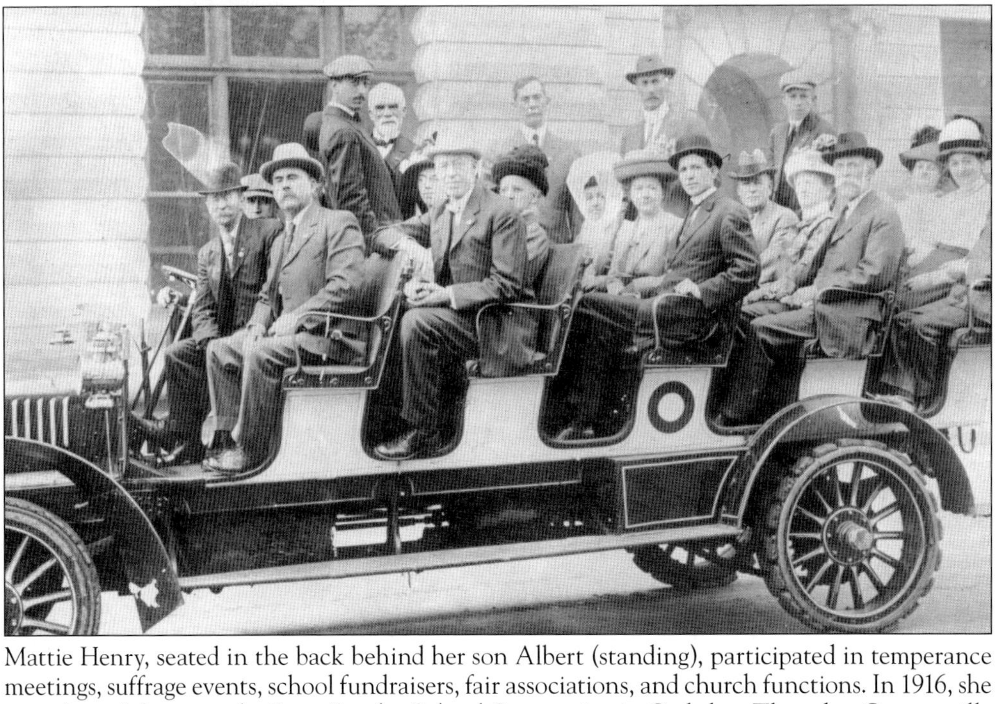

Mattie Henry, seated in the back behind her son Albert (standing), participated in temperance meetings, suffrage events, school fundraisers, fair associations, and church functions. In 1916, she served as a delegate at the State Sunday School Convention in Gadsden. The other Guntersville delegates included W.E. Roden, Mae Hodges, G.R. Givens, Mary Foster, Mack Killcrease, and Emma Fricke. (Marshall County Archives.)

Two

Residents, Scenes, and Events

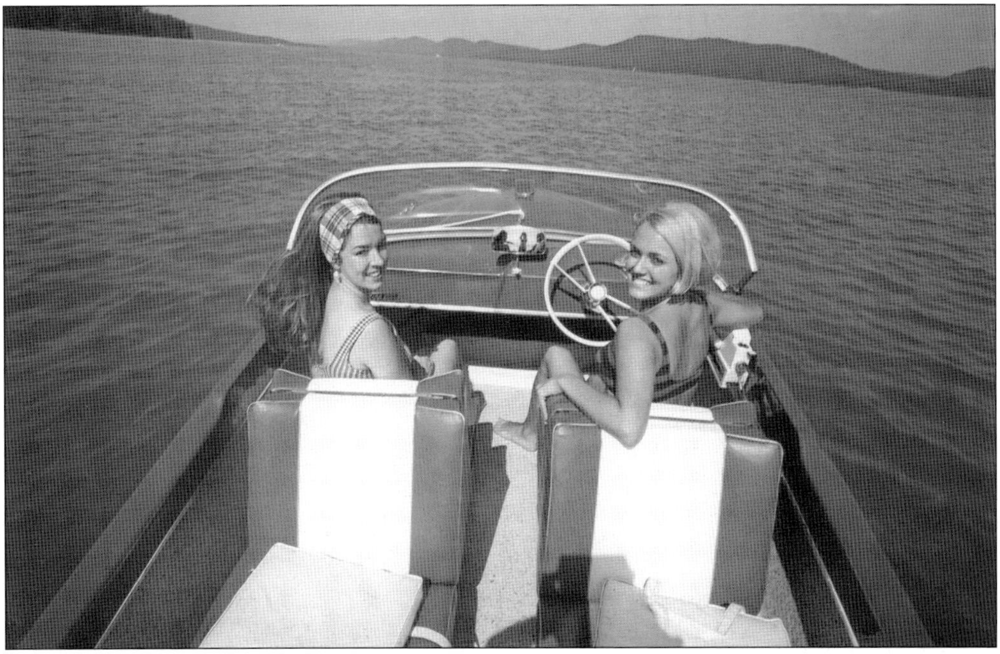

In this promotional photograph, Nancy Rhe Mason (left) and Milla McCord are shown enjoying the beauty of Lake Guntersville. Mason, daughter of Robert and Rhe Mason, earned a degree in education from the University of Alabama, co-owned a mortgage company in Atlanta, directed the Guntersville Museum, and currently owns a cattle farm. The daughter of Cullen and Olga McCord, Milla garnered prestige as Junior Maid of Cotton, Miss Channel 13, alternate Miss Guntersville Lake, and 1966 Auburn homecoming queen. She earned a master's degree in audiology, married Tom Sachs, and had two children, Cord and Tegan. In her current position as assistant to mayor Leigh Dollar, she continues to play a role in encouraging Guntersville's growth and development. (Tennessee Valley Authority.)

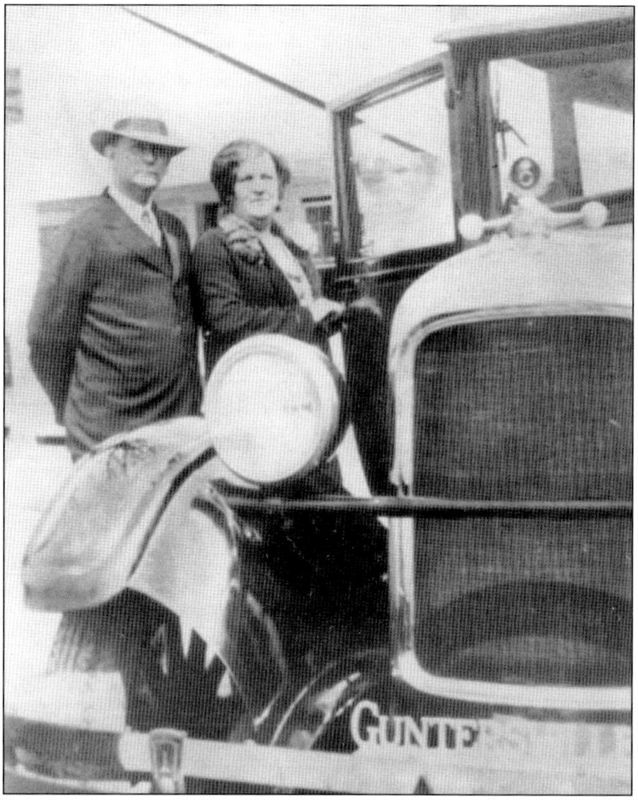

William Edward "Ed" Roden and his wife, Willie Belle Roden, are shown beside an automobile around the time of their marriage in 1929. A salesman, Ed was the son of John and Martha Roden; Willie's parents were W.C. and Sophronia Story. Willie's first husband, riverboat captain Arthur Rains, died in 1926. Ed was once photographed with the riverboat wheel that is displayed at the Guntersville Museum. (Marshall County Archives.)

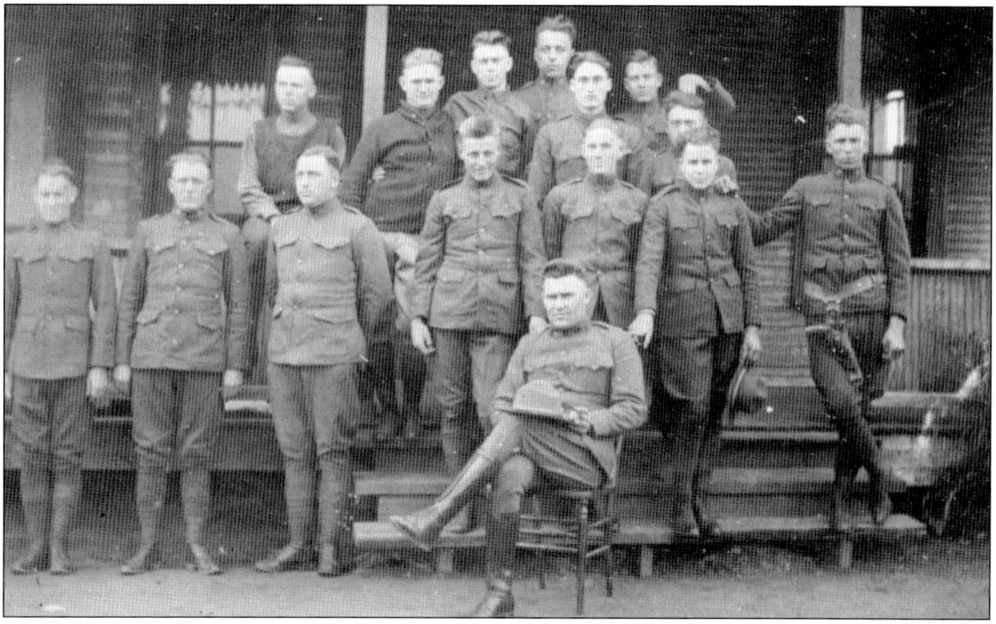

Company L, 167th Infantry, served 18 months in France. Pictured are, from left to right, (first row, seated) Burley Hamil; (second row) Clarence Hix, Pete Hill, Hubert Walls, Eugene Whitaker, John Bright, Royce Means, and Slim Kemp; (third row) Herchel Berry, John Cummings, Talmadge Alexander, Dewey Bolton, Albert Ridgeway, Sam Walker, and ? Miller. (Marshall County Archives.)

Charles Williams (shown) was among the Black recruits from Guntersville who served in World War I. The others were James Bailey, Charles Boykins, Sim Boykins, Murray Coles, Tom Ellis, Anderson Erskine, John Garth, Will Graves, Herman Hampton, John Hampton, John Henry, Alf Horton, Ed Horton, Jim Horton, Percy Jones, Charles Jordan, George Love, Jesse Lovelady, Ernest Montgomery, Henry Montgomery, Burton Moore, Frank Moore, Will Moore, Johnson Pinkerton, Marion Ross, and Jesse Wilam. (Huntsville–Madison County Public Library.)

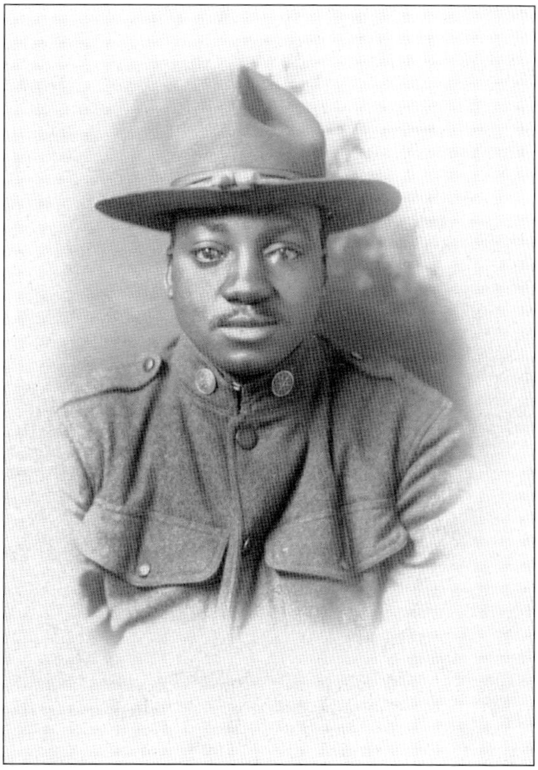

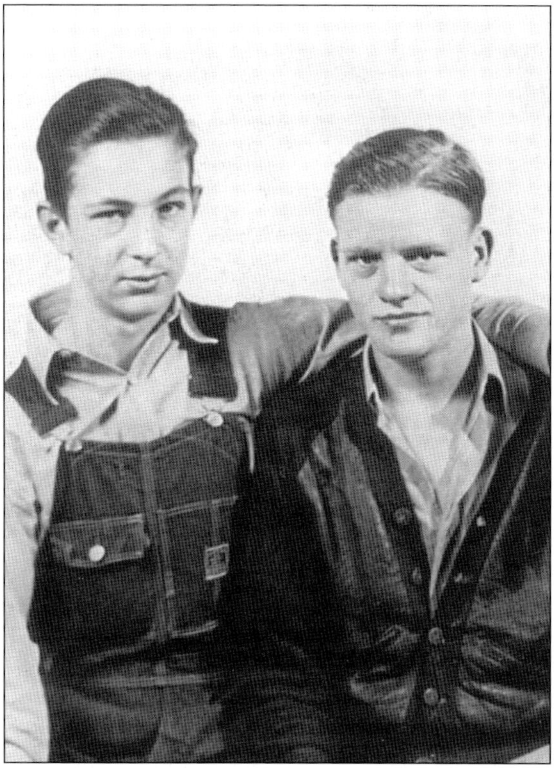

Kenneth Hubble (left) and Hubert "Cotton" Harris (right) served in the military during World War II. Hubble, son of Sant and Fannie Hubble, operated a store and became manager of Brindlee Waterworks in 1968. Harris, son of Toomer and Ruth Harris, worked at a service station. When he joined the Navy, he saw 13 months of continuous sea duty. In August 1961, Harris died in an automobile accident. (George Barnett.)

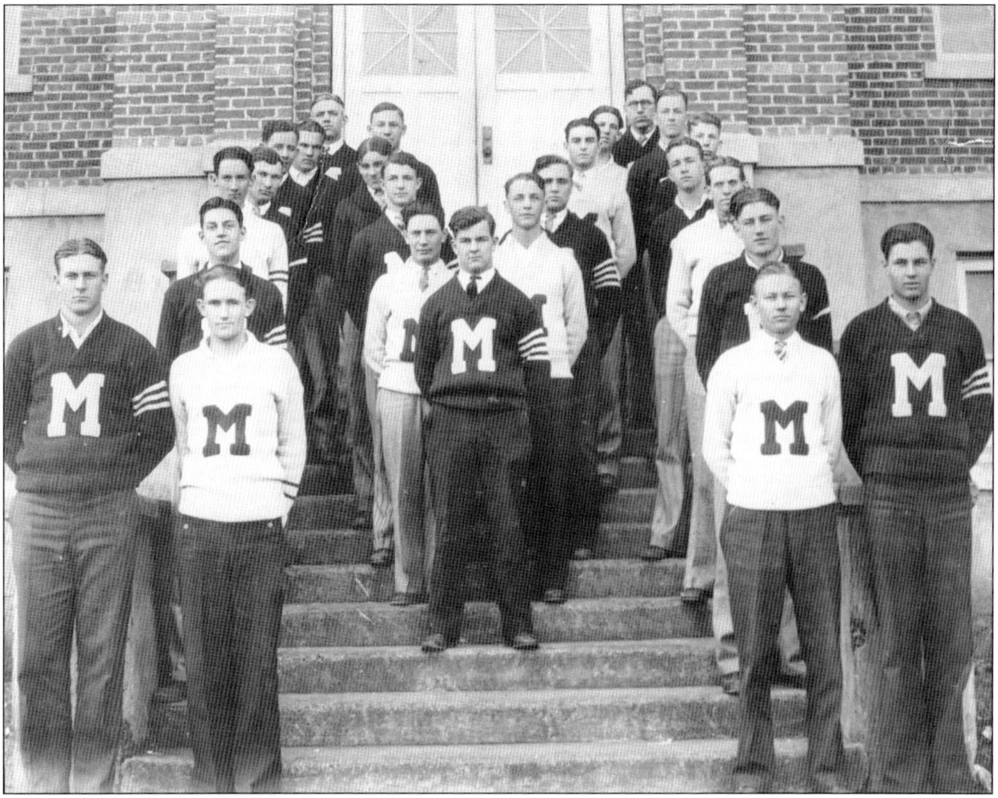

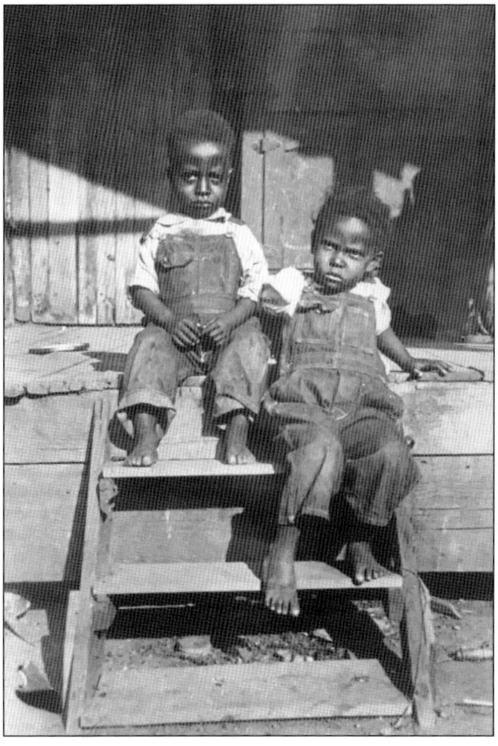

The Marshall County High "M" Club members shown here in 1927 are, from left to right, Washington Bennett, Lee Barnard, Mack Moss, Bryan Williams, Watson Hooper, Fred Roberts, Johnnie Segers, John Meeks (coach), John Walls, Buddy Roberts, Joe Creel, K.L. Rogers, R.B. Norrell, Nevada Whitten, Herschel Beard, Bob Latimer, George Adams, Dexter Hovater (principal), Raymond Wedgeworth, ? Williams, Robert Mason, Harold Huddleston, Grady Huckaby, Ray Barnard, and "Hippockets" Woods. (Nancy Gilbreath Graham.)

Jennie Taylor (1926–2010; left) and James Otis Moore (1919–1958) sit on the steps of their grandparents' home on Railroad Avenue. Their mothers, Irene Reed Harris and Gertrude Reed Moore Logan, respectively, were the daughters of Jerry and Mollie Reed. Moore lived and worked his entire life in Guntersville except during World War II. Taylor married Frank Hundley, moved to New York, and raised four sons and six daughters. (George Barnett.)

Ruth Smith (left) is shown babysitting with Betty Taylor in the 1930s on Hill Avenue at the home of Dono and Loree Taylor. A retired teacher, Taylor is the director of the Marshall County Archives, which houses photographs, marriage records, obituaries, family files, newspapers, census data, probate/civil court records, and microfilm. The original volunteers at the archives included Taylor, Margene Black, Lindy Hard, Jo Goss, and Rosemary Darnell. (Betty Taylor.)

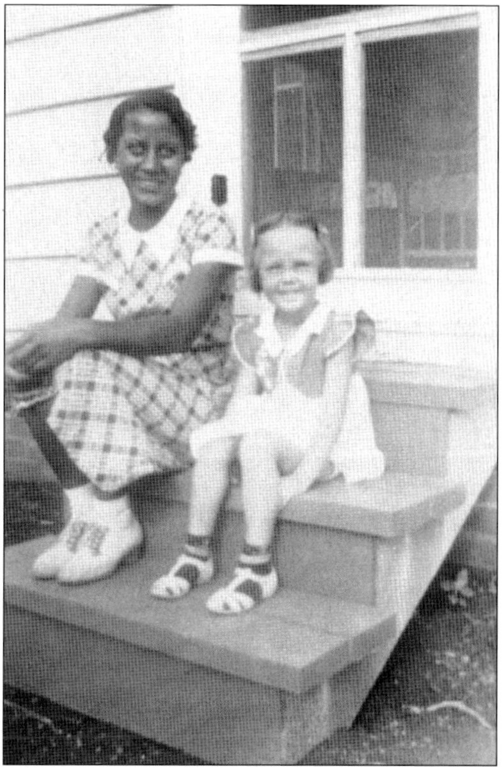

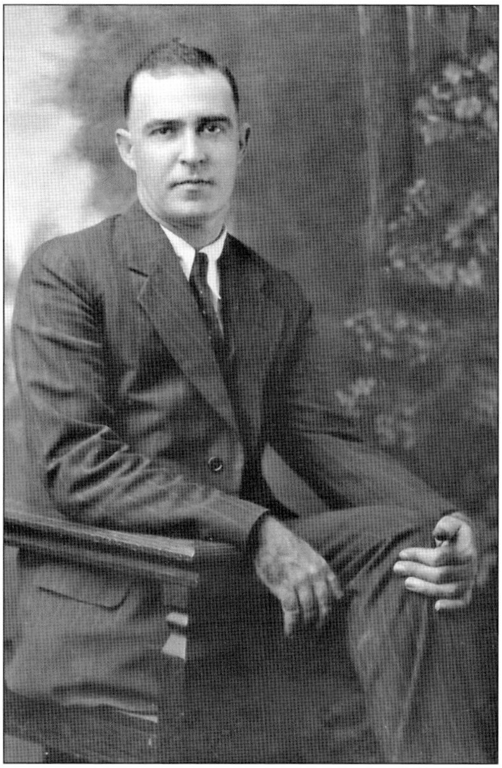

Quintus "Dono" Taylor (1899–1943) worked as a brakeman for the railroad and as deputy sheriff of Marshall County. He served as sheriff from 1935 to 1939 in a time when individuals were not allowed to be reelected for consecutive terms. In 1943, Taylor had a fatal automobile accident while driving home from his fishing camp. He was survived by his wife, Loree, and their children, Buddy and Betty. (Betty Taylor.)

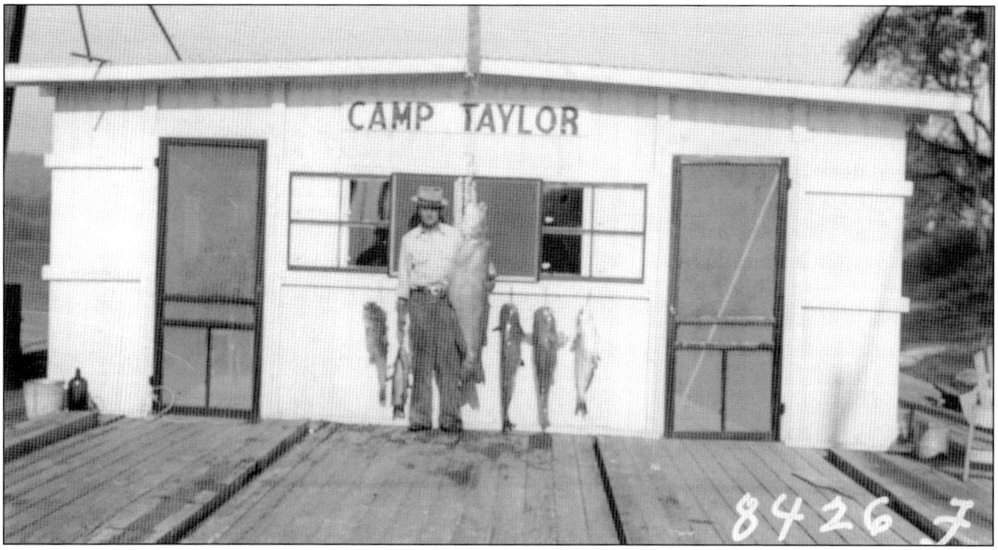

Camp Taylor (shown) was located on Fearn Creek just below the TVA Guntersville Dam. Located on the north side of the river, the camp was operated by Dono and Loree Taylor. The camp offered boat rentals, bait, and river access. After Dono's death, Loree operated the facility until the late 1940s, when Glenn Vaughn acquired the lease and renamed it Vaughn's Fishing Camp. (Alabama Department of History and Archives.)

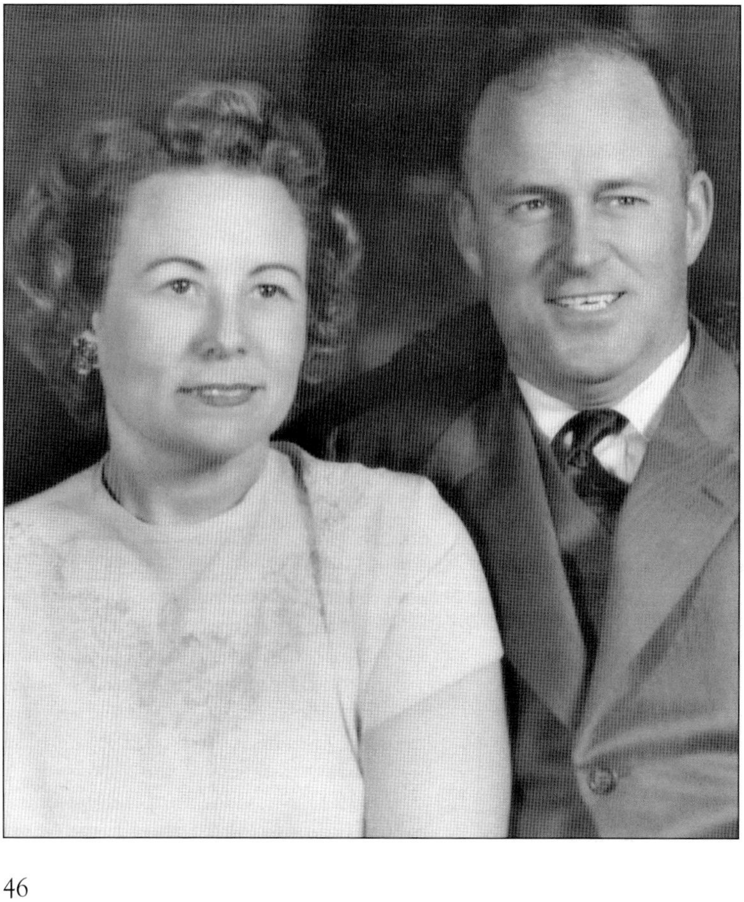

The son of Jim and Mary Pritchett Boyles, Zeke Boyles (shown with his wife, Eva) served as sheriff of Marshall County from 1939 to 1947 and in 1951. Chief deputy Washington Bennett, Boaz chief of police Leonard Floyd, and Boyles were killed while serving a warrant on farmer Aubrey Kilpatrick, who also perished in the altercation on May 17, 1951. An estimated 5,000 people attended Boyles's funeral and burial. (Betty Taylor.)

This is Mary Jane Edwards, the daughter of William and Ellen Fearn Edwards. She married Ernest Montgomery in 1917. After serving in the military, Ernest worked on a transfer boat for the railroad. The couple lived in a house on Carlisle Avenue. Their elder daughter, Callie, earned a degree from Alabama State College. (Marshall County Archives.)

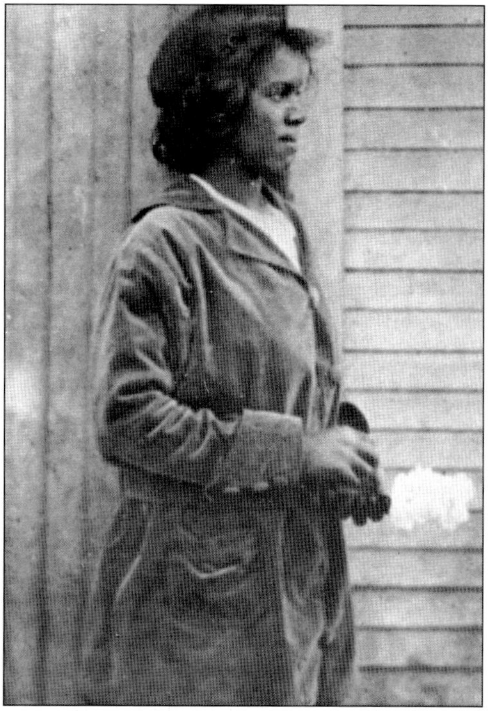

On June 13, 1946, the Nashville, Chattanooga & St. Louis Railroad launched a diesel electric tugboat, the MS *Guntersville*. Sponsor Lynn Hurn is pictured at the ceremony. Jan Albert served as maid of honor. Lynn and Jan's mothers, Pocahontas Albert and Rosa Hurn—along with Wright Ross Sr. and a host of 75 people from Guntersville—traveled to Decatur for the event. Other guests included dignitaries and railroad personnel. (Betty Taylor.)

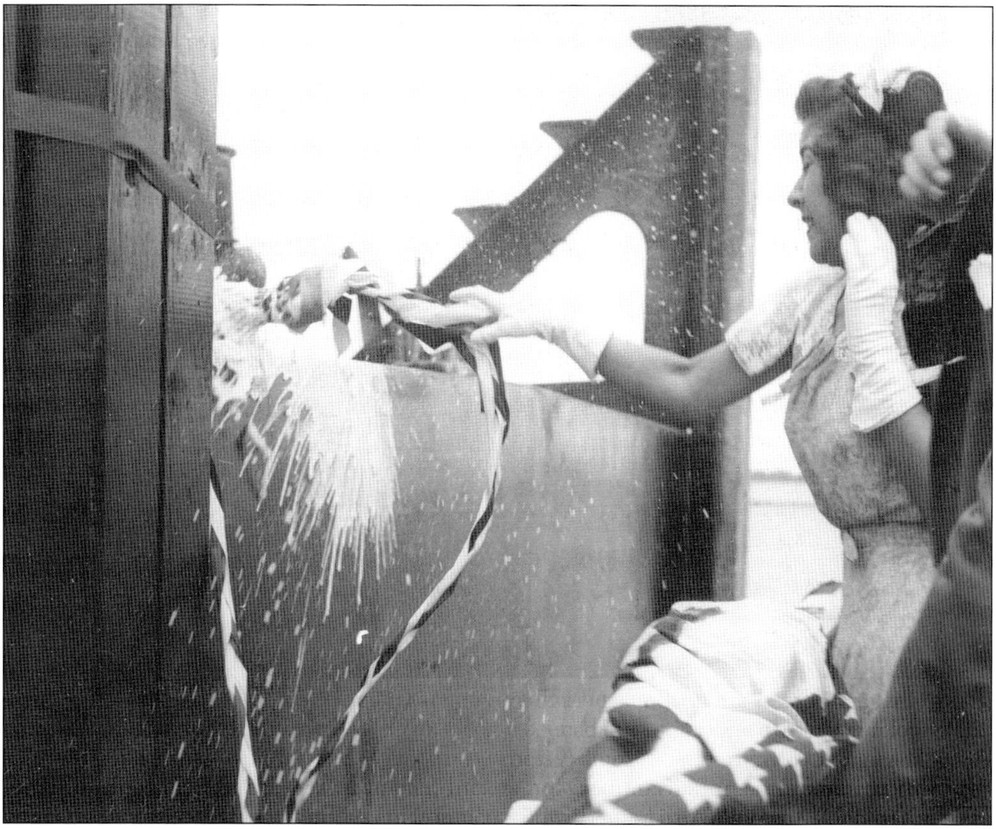

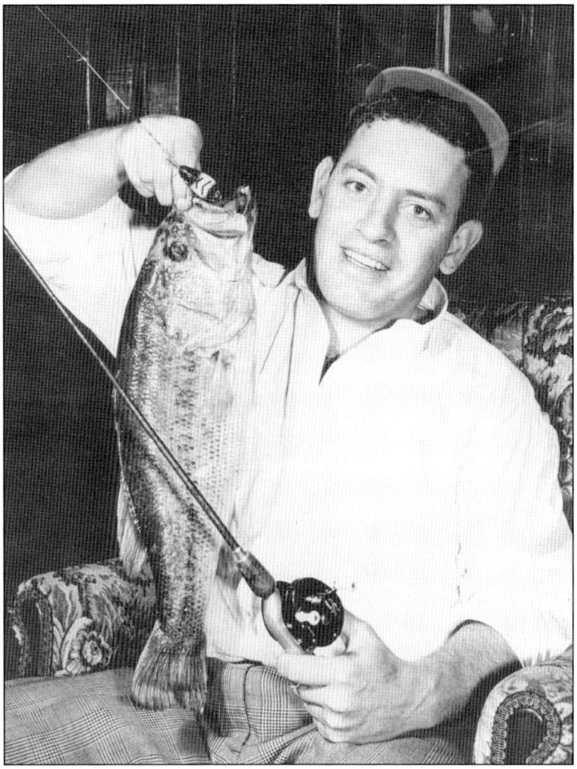

Jess Alston "Pete" Duncan Jr. loved hunting, fishing, and boating. The first drum major at Marshall County High School, Duncan interrupted his education to serve in World War II. After finishing high school in 1947 and a stint at the University of Alabama, he sold sporting goods and real estate, operated marinas at Guntersville City Harbor, and worked for two years as a police dispatcher. (Marshall County Archives.)

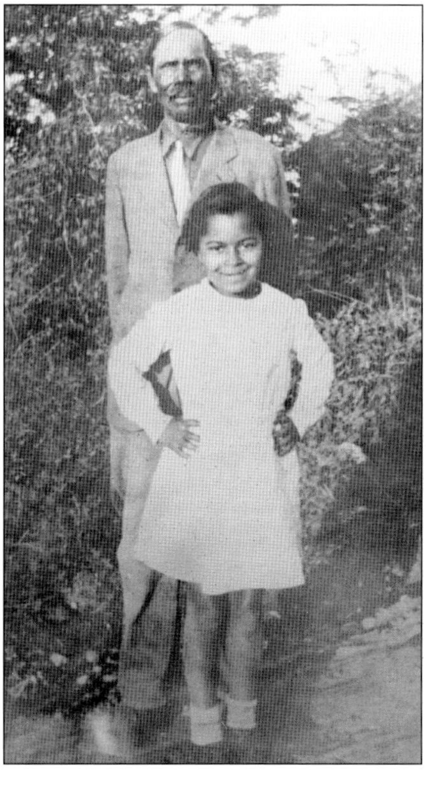

The daughter of Ernest and Mary Jane Edwards Montgomery, Ruby Montgomery is shown with her grandfather Bill Edwards. In 1955, she graduated from Alabama Agricultural and Mechanical College with accolades for being one of the first Black citizens from Guntersville to earn a college degree. She taught at Lakeview School, married Joseph Greene, and moved to Cleveland, Ohio, where she continued her teaching career. (Marshall County Archives.)

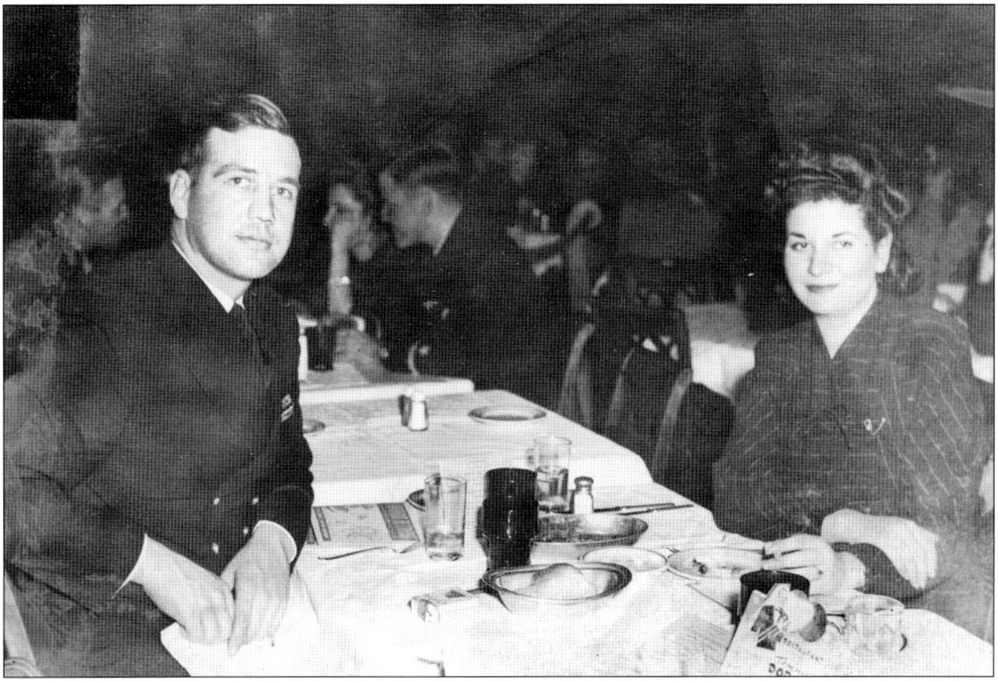

In the Navy, Jack McGowin (shown with an unidentified friend in New York) was on the USS *St. Louis* on December 7, 1941, at Pearl Harbor and aboard the USS *Missouri* at Tokyo Bay on September 2, 1945, at the formal surrender of Japan. On a dare in 1947, McGowin jumped from Guntersville's 58-foot-high George Houston Bridge but failed to surface. (Betty McGowin Jones.)

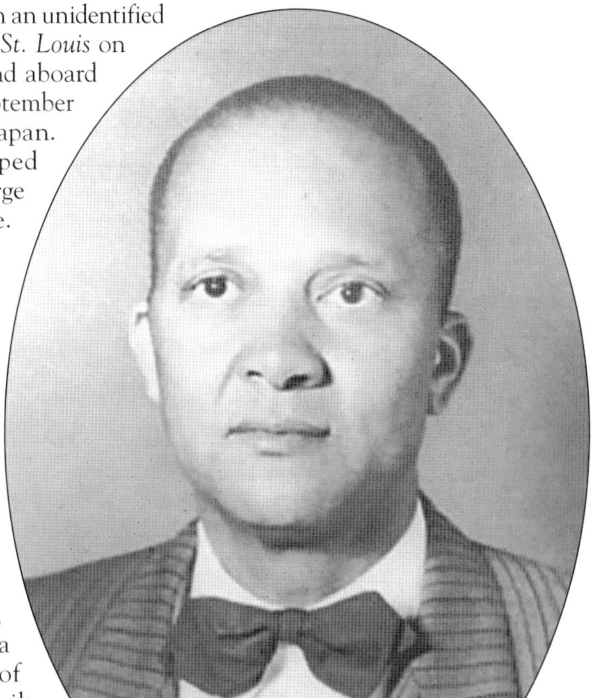

In 1940, Roosevelt Williamson (shown), who held a master's degree from Alabama State College, became principal of Lakeview School, which had been built to serve Black students in Marshall County. When Williamson died in an accident in 1967, 600 people attended his funeral at town hall. A park located on the old school property was named for Williamson. (Guntersville Museum.)

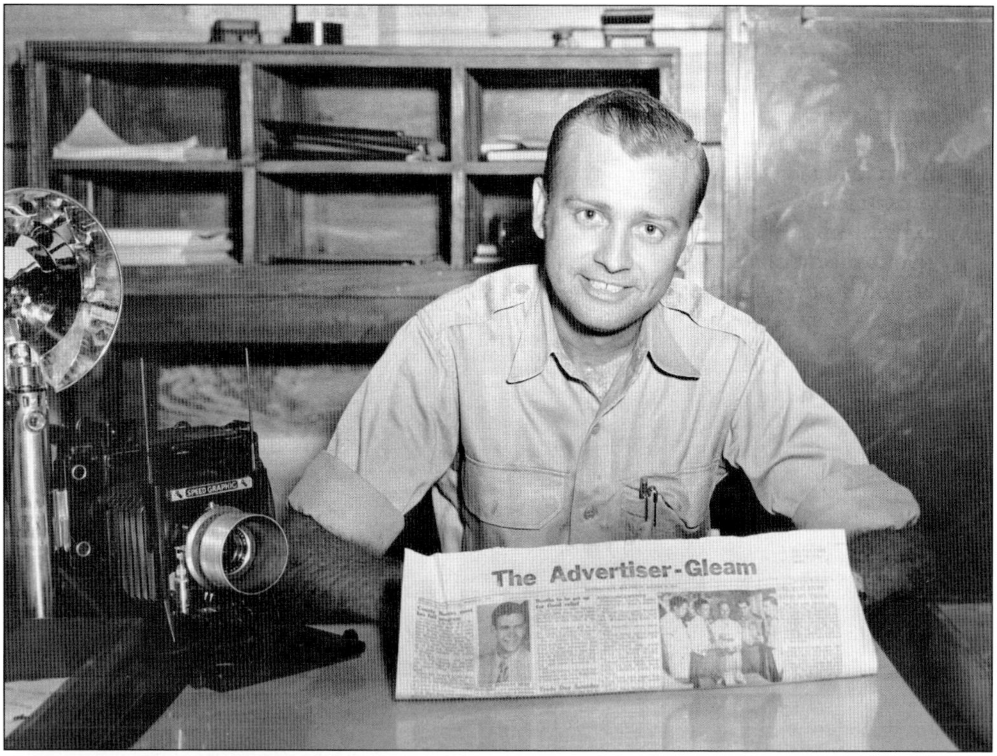

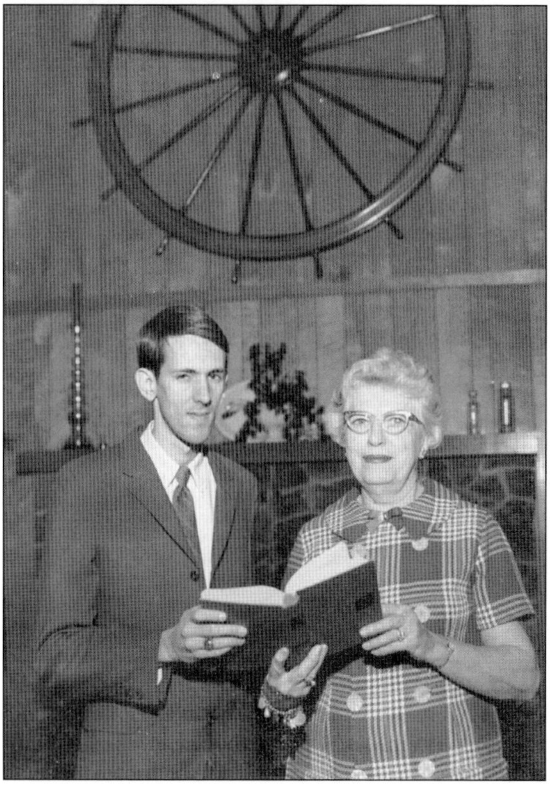

The son of Arthur and Sarah Cagle, Bill Cagle (1925–2010) began his photography career in the late 1940s following his naval service in World War II. During the Korean War, he served in the Air Force. Stationed in Texas, Cagle documented a tornado that destroyed downtown Waco in 1953. Cagle is pictured with a copy of the *Advertiser-Gleam* sent by his wife. By airmail, its arrival took seven to eight days. (Marshall County Archives.)

Katherine Duncan (right) is pictured with Larry Smith, her coauthor for the book *The History of Marshall County*. Duncan had a passion for researching the history of Guntersville. She worked for the *Advertiser-Gleam* and taught special education. The daughter of Thomas and Mattie McKinstry, Katherine married Jess Duncan in 1925. She and Jess had one child, Jess "Pete" Duncan Jr. (Marshall County Archives.)

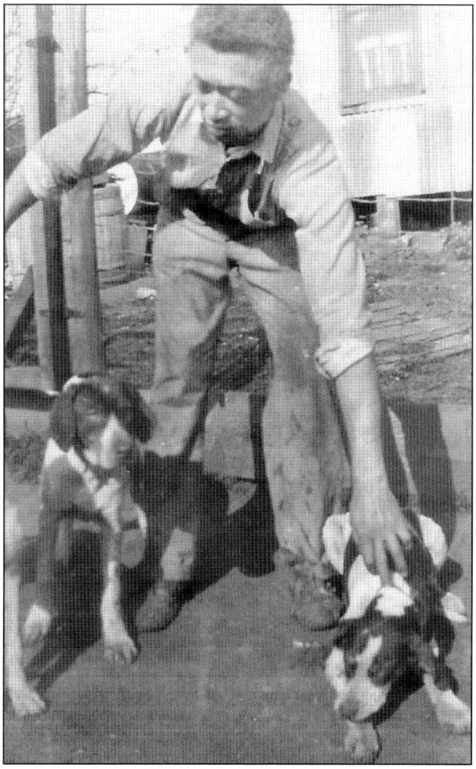

Emmett Smith (shown) was responsible for police dogs during the administration of Sheriff Dono Taylor. Smith and his wife, Isabell, lived with their three children—Mary, Nelson, and Ruth—on Railroad Avenue until the construction of the TVA Guntersville Dam, after which they moved to Taylor Street. Smith also worked as a gardener and handyman while his wife cooked at the county jail. (Betty Taylor.)

In this 1967 photograph, Boy Scouts troop 173 of Guntersville is pictured with US representative Bill Dickinson (center). Over the years, this Boy Scouts unit completed many beneficial projects. One of the most innovative involved contracting with farmer Donald Bevill to plant 15,000 seedlings at 4¢ per tree to earn $600. The endeavor taught them forestry and wildlife management. (Alabama Department of Archives and History.)

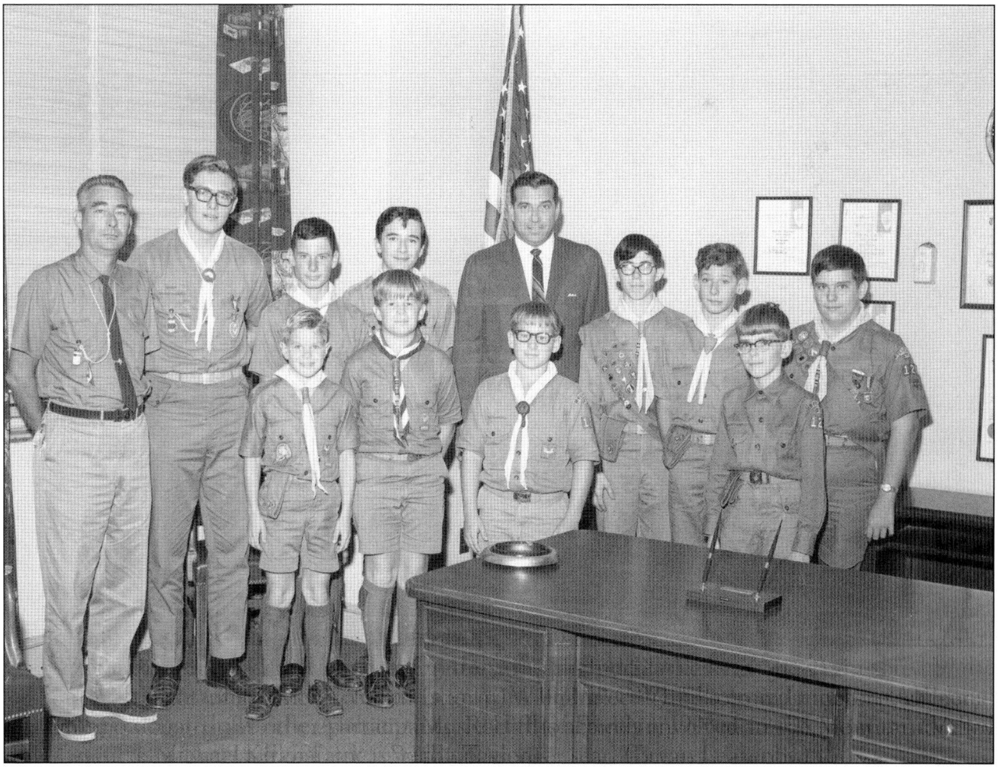

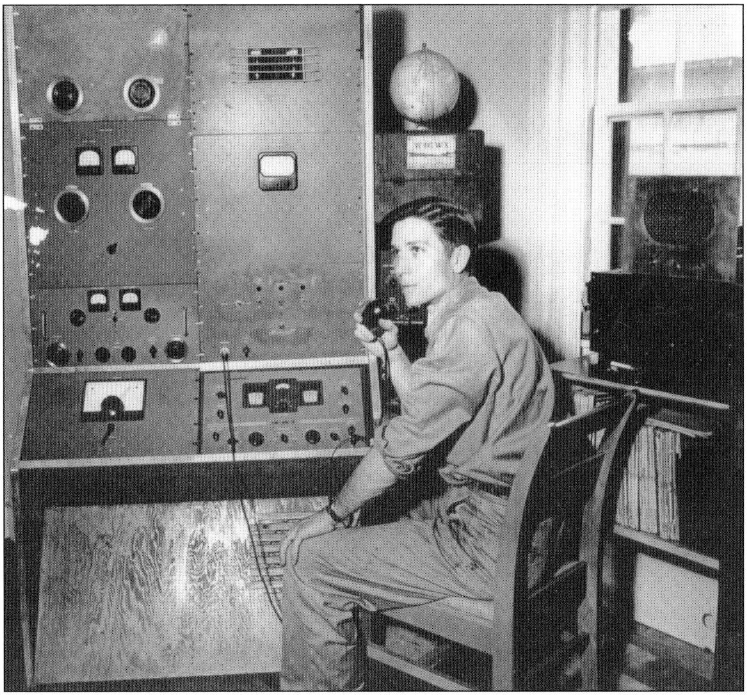

Kenneth McCormick is shown with his radio transmitter, which was the first licensed amateur device (W4GWXX) in Guntersville. McCormick worked as a radio and television repairman. From sweeping a fix-it shop as a teenager to excelling in radio school during World War II, he was grounded in new technology. McCormick and Bill Harris compiled photographs for the historical society. (Marshall County Archives.)

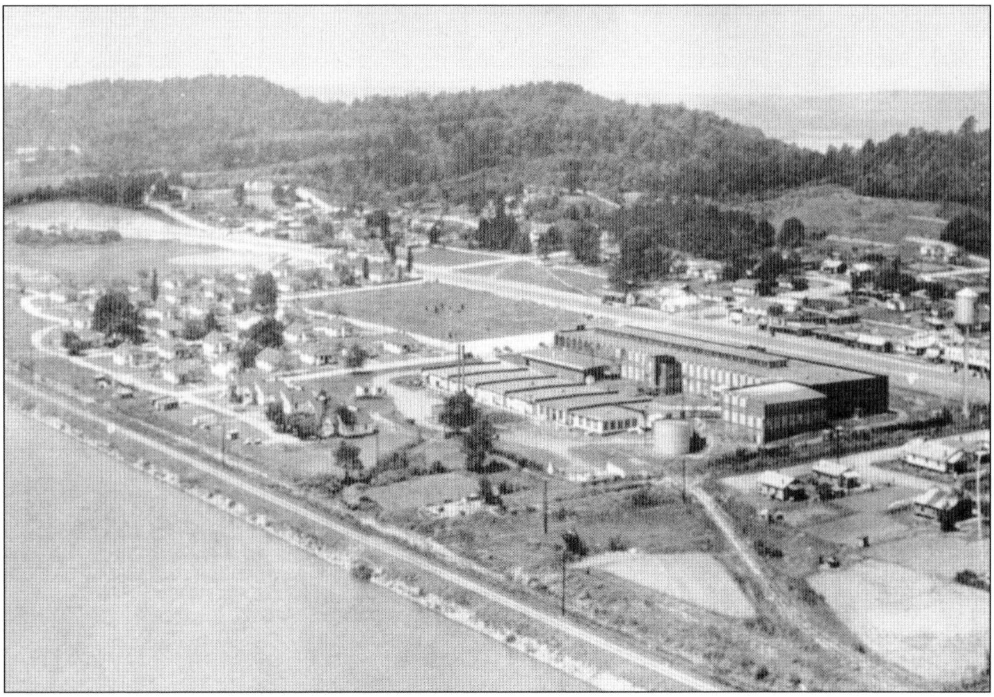

This cotton mill began as the Saratoga Victory Mills in 1928 and went through a series of owners, changing its name to Julia Cade Mills and then Lakeside Mills. Its workers were among the first to participate in the 1934 national textile strike. Comprising 160,000 square feet over nine acres, the facility is listed in the National Register of Historic Places. It is now the home of Mike's Merchandise and Crazy Cazboy's. (Mike Jones.)

Bill Yancy (right) is shown with coach Bucky Pitts on the football field. An announcer for WGSV, Yancy hosted a show called *Let's Go Fishing.* In 1978, he reported a record of 18 crappie, weighing 42.5 pounds, that were caught by Jimmy Manley and Larry Sutton. The fish averaged two pounds, six ounces, with the largest topping the scales at three pounds. (Marshall County Archives.)

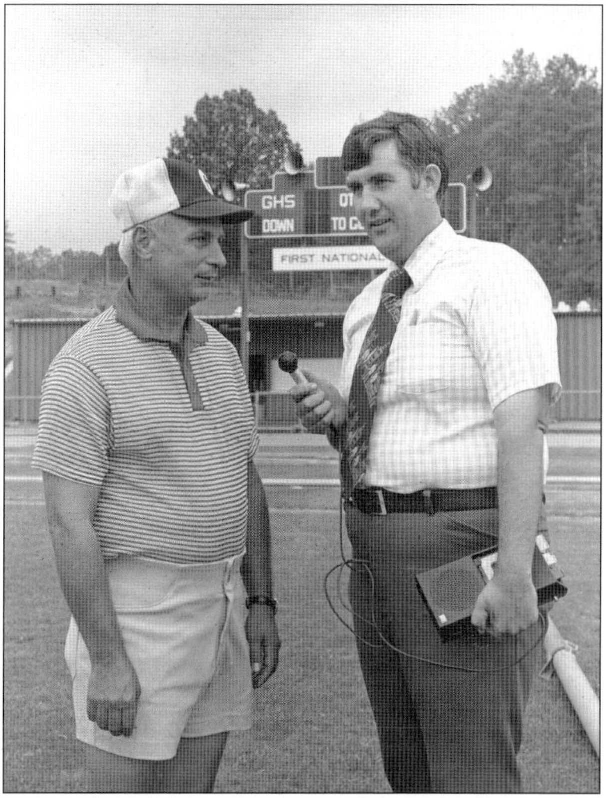

On Christmas Eve, Lake Theatre owner Bill Harris (standing in the aisle at right) provided a free movie for the children of Guntersville. Packing the building, the kids relished the entertainment. Their parents no doubt appreciated Harris's generosity, as it afforded them shopping time. Harris's wife, Dora, manned the ticket booth and always knew who was 12 years old or younger. (Guntersville Museum.)

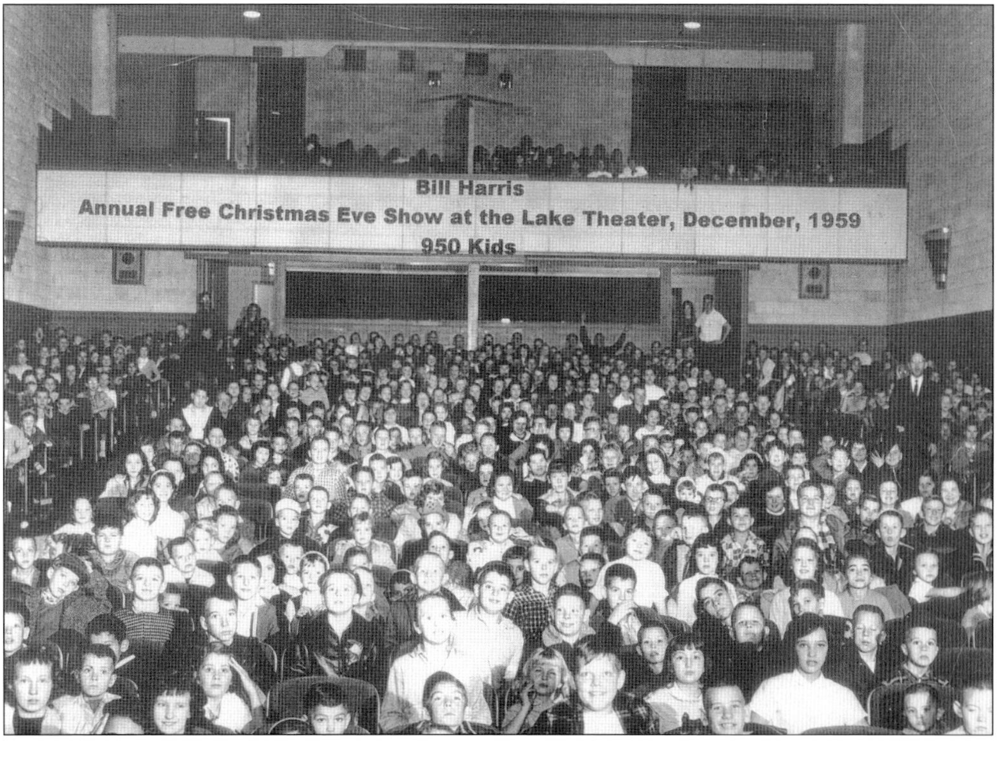

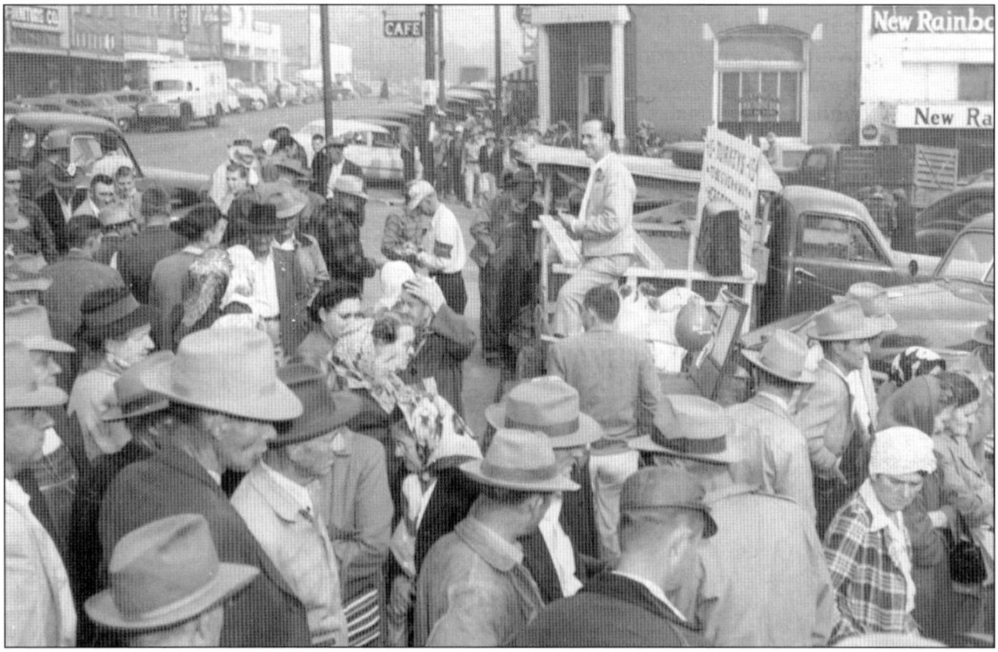

Sponsored by Guntersville's merchants, monthly trade days generated large crowds in the 1950s because of cash drawings of $500 or more. People came early and stayed late for entertainment like rummage sales as well as prizes and raffles run by nonprofit organizations like the Jaycees. This unidentified man sold raffle tickets for a drawing to win turkeys; the raffle items varied, often depending on donated merchandise. (Marshall County Archives.)

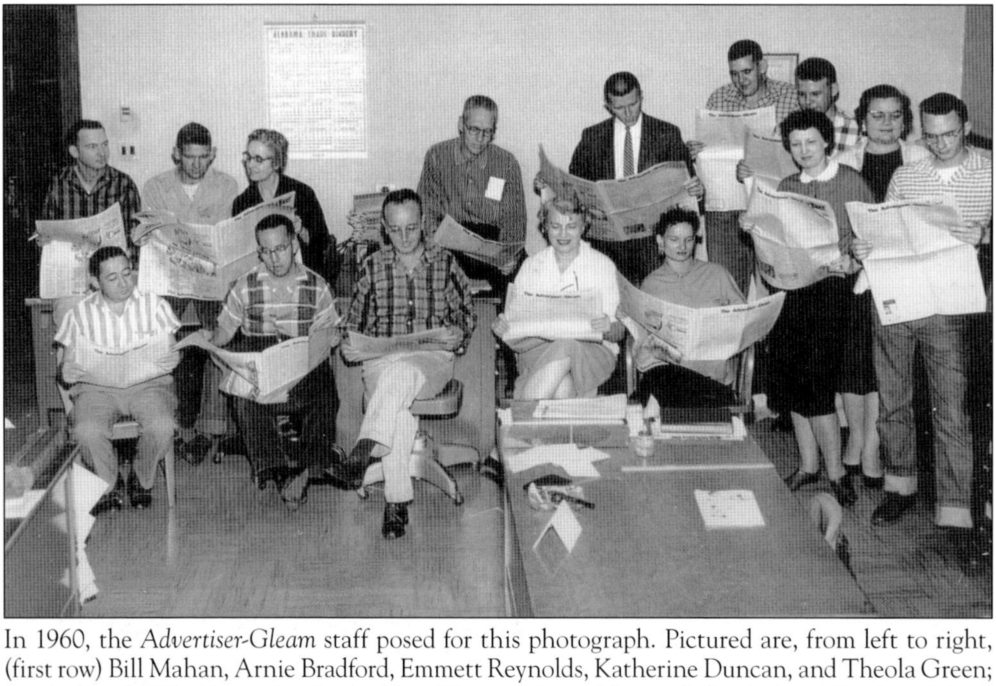

In 1960, the *Advertiser-Gleam* staff posed for this photograph. Pictured are, from left to right, (first row) Bill Mahan, Arnie Bradford, Emmett Reynolds, Katherine Duncan, and Theola Green; (second row) Billy Grant, Bo Artis, Alice Harvey, Porter Harvey (editor), Don Woodward, Neil Dispennett, L.C. Mitchell, Glema Hall, Mary Rouse, and Freeman Elliott. (*Advertiser-Gleam.*)

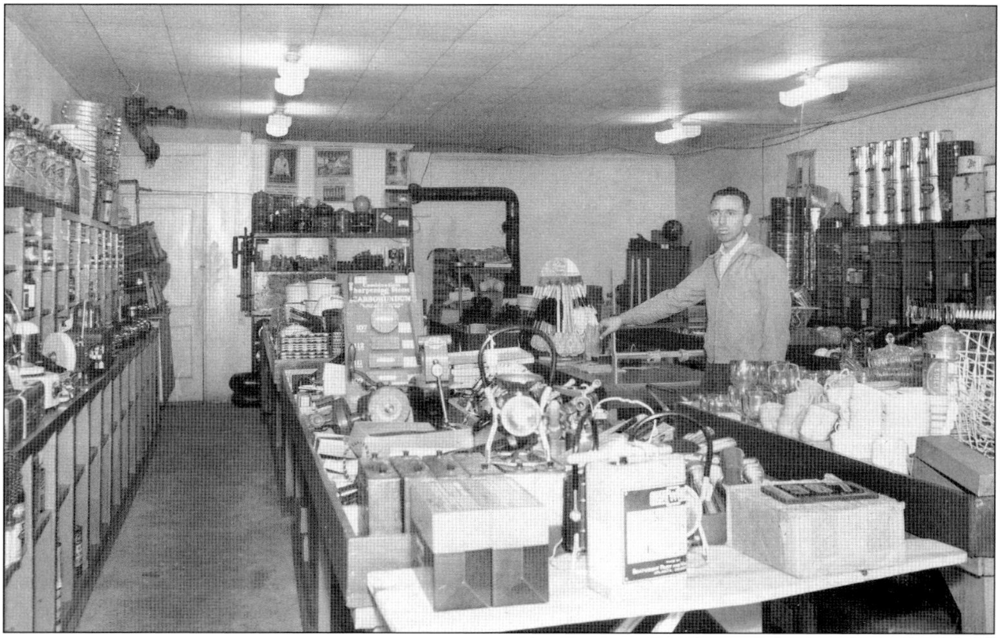

Paul Taylor (shown) operated a hardware store in Guntersville for 36 years, worked at the chamber of commerce, and served on the city council. At the First Methodist Church, Taylor held positions like Sunday school superintendent, trustee, and building committee member. Taylor and his wife, Dorothy, sang in the church choir for 45 years and with a family quartet. He developed the Andrew Jackson subdivision. (Marshall County Archives.)

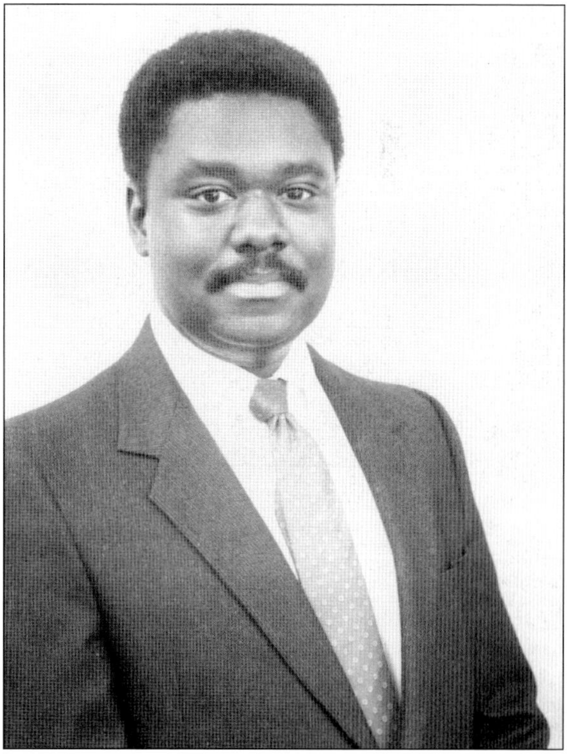

At 15, Claude Hundley III, the son of Claude and Hattie Hundley, washed dishes at Vaughn's Catfish Café. In 1984, he earned a law degree from the University of Alabama. He practiced law in Guntersville before moving to Huntsville. In 2011, Gov. Robert Bentley appointed him to Madison County's district court. In 2018, Gov. Kay Ivey selected him as a circuit judge for the 23rd Judicial Court. (*Advertiser-Gleam*.)

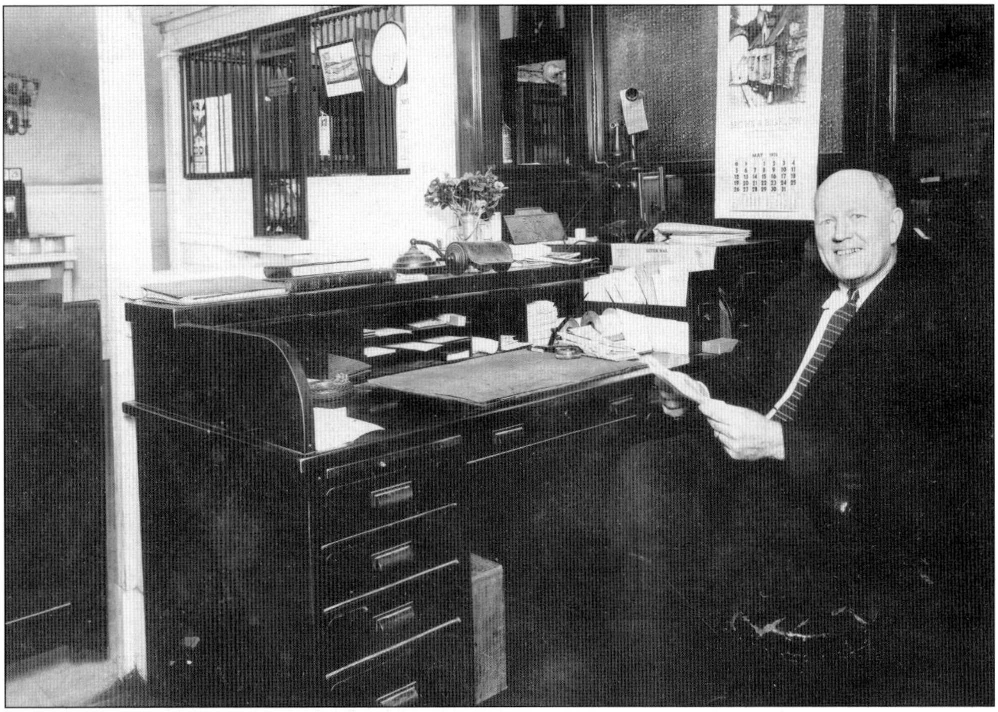

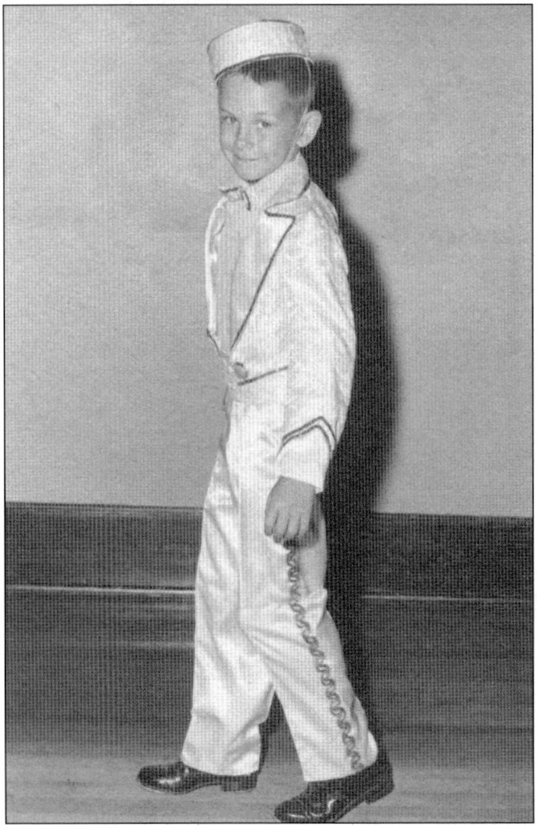

In 1920, John Pearson Willis arrived in Guntersville to clerk at the First National Bank. He became president in 1932 and advanced to become the chairman of the board of directors in 1966. When he died in 1980, his vast accomplishments included civic improvements and memberships in military and fraternal orders. He married Marilym Lusk and reared three children—Ida Will, John Jr., and Mary. He is pictured here in 1935. (Huntsville–Madison County Public Library.)

Jimmy Hindman is shown demonstrating his dancing skills at a recital around 1956. A registered pharmacist, Hindman graduated from Auburn University in the early 1970s and operated a drugstore in Guntersville until 1987. He also had a lengthy tenure as a member of the Guntersville City Council until 1989. Hindman enjoys reading, studying history, and spending time with his wife, Nancy, and their family. (Marshall County Archives.)

The lighthouse at Powell's Harbor stands off Highway 227 near the Wayne Farms Feedmill. The picture was taken from the highway looking toward Veterans' Bridge. Howard Powell Sr. and his son Howard Powell Jr. owned and operated a sand/gravel business for two generations. Their former home at 300 Gunter Avenue is on the Alabama Register of Landmarks and Heritage; most recently, it housed the Mountain Valley Arts Council. (Buddy Taylor.)

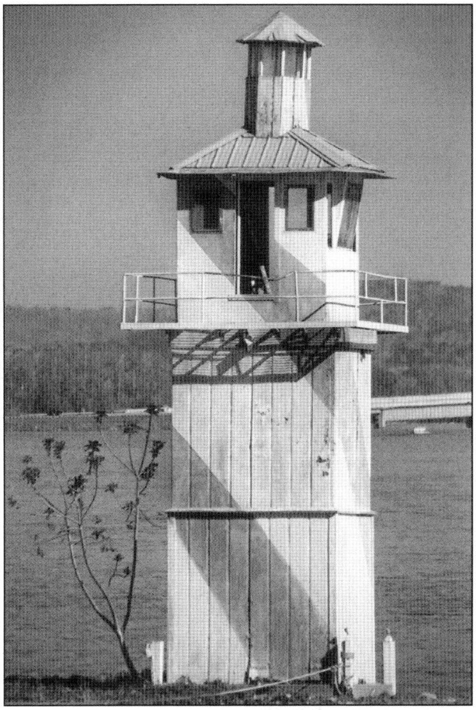

Born in Illinois, Lloyd Wilson Darnell (shown in 1985) managed the Mueller fire-hydrant factory for 24 years. The plant at Albertville employs 500 people and manufactures 400 hydrants per day. Before Darnell's retirement in 2000, the site produced its two-millionth fire hydrant. Lloyd and his wife, Rosemary, have lived in Guntersville since 1976. They reside at Buck Island and attend the Church of Christ. (*Advertiser-Gleam.*)

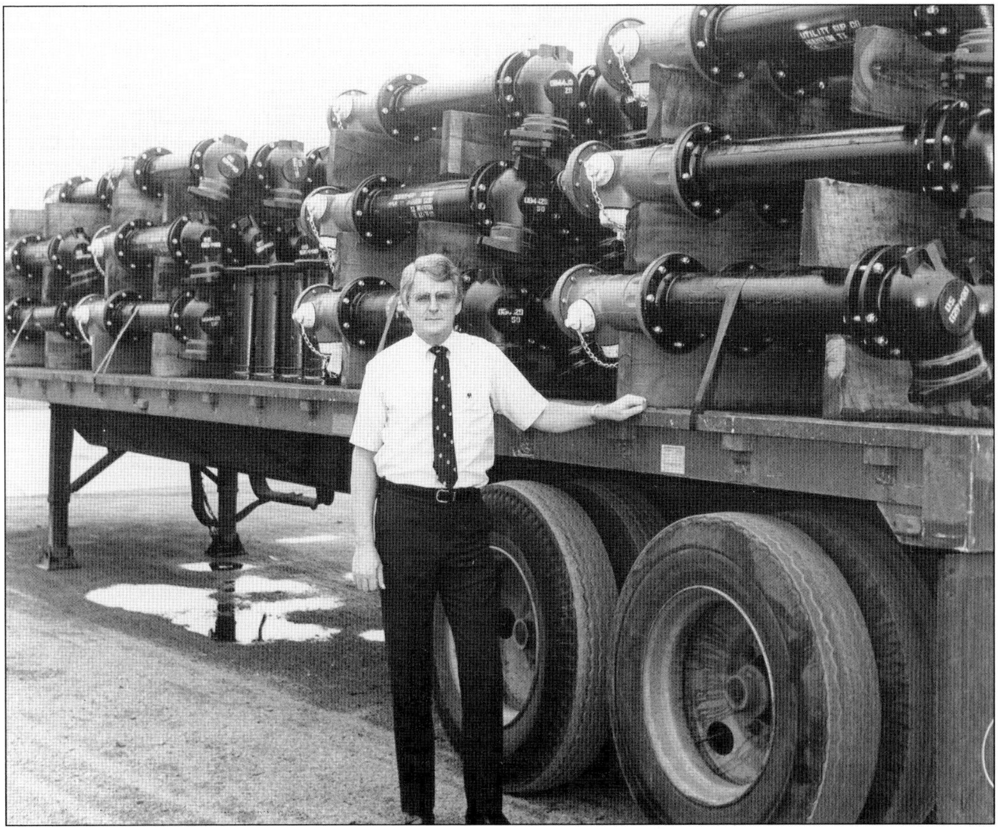

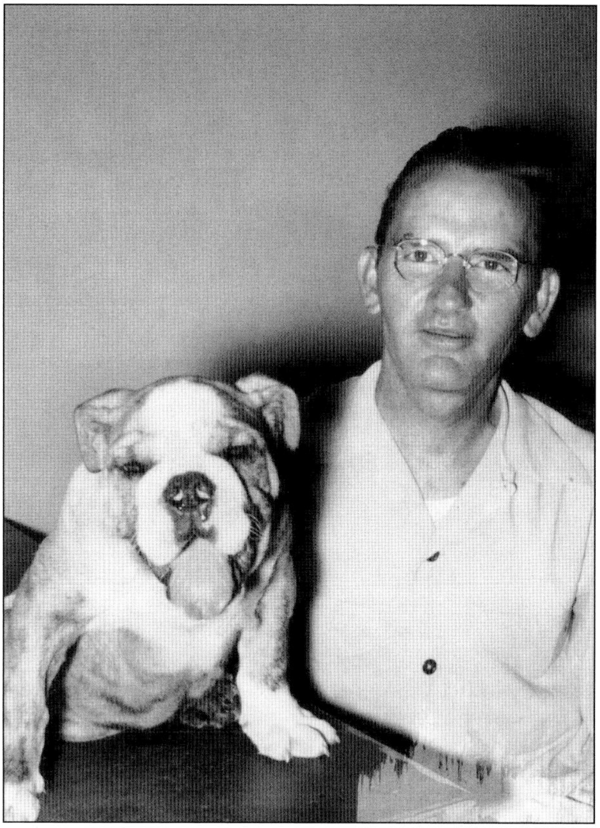

Bill Harris is pictured with one of his many bulldogs. In 1963, he and his wife, Dora, adopted Pretty Boy, their sixth English bulldog. The four-month-old pedigree had placed first in a Memphis kennel club show. Bill quipped, "We never have made our dogs mind. They make us mind." (Marshall County Archives.)

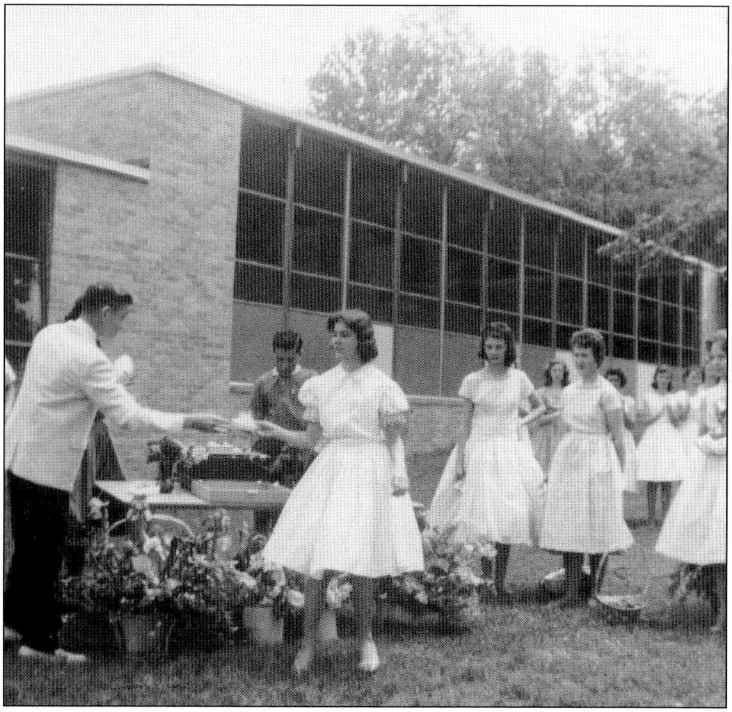

In 1959, Carlisle Park School (pictured) opened with fifth-, sixth-, seventh-, and eighth-graders in attendance. This picture shows a May Day celebration directed by the teachers, especially Nellie Waldrop. From left to right are Dale Collins, Randy Troup, and Lisle Hipp with unidentified girls watching. Guntersville Middle School, adjacent to this site, was constructed in the early 2000s to replace the older facility. (Authors' collection.)

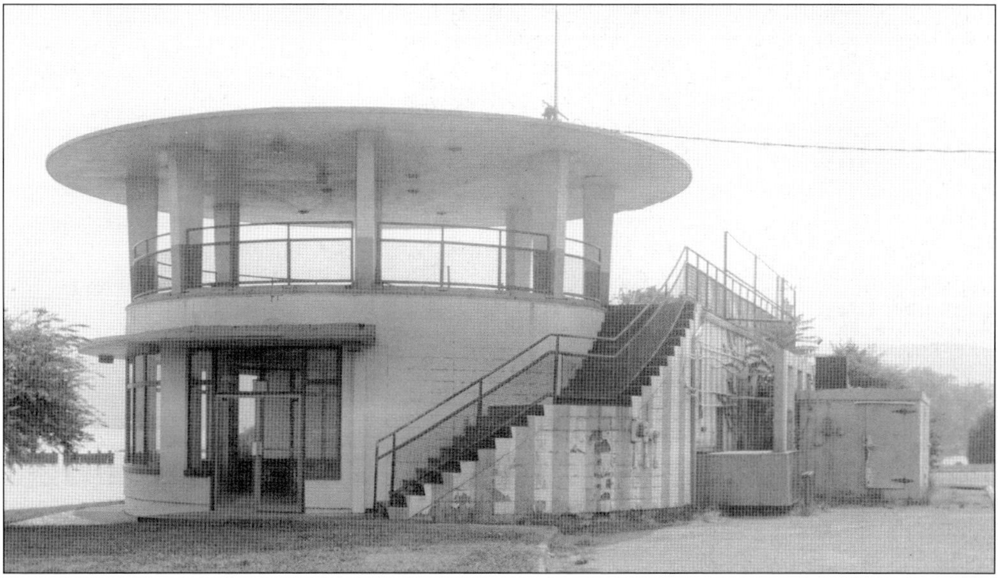

Pictured is the Harbor House, a popular restaurant in Guntersville for 35 years. Following a nautical theme, designers arranged public dining in a rounded area, with the kitchen and lounge toward the middle, private rooms in the rear, and a rooftop space for spectacular views of the harbor and lake. Actor Alan Hale Jr. once dined at the Harbor House. The building was torn down in 2003. (Buddy Taylor.)

In May 1959, members of the Colony Garden Club met to weed flower beds at the city boat dock. The organization had funded and planted Floribunda roses as a community service project. Shown are, from left to right, Virginia Hunter, Martha Nell Johnson, and Gene Clark. Virginia McGowin took the photograph. Behind them is a sign advertising the Harbor House. (Marshall County Archives.)

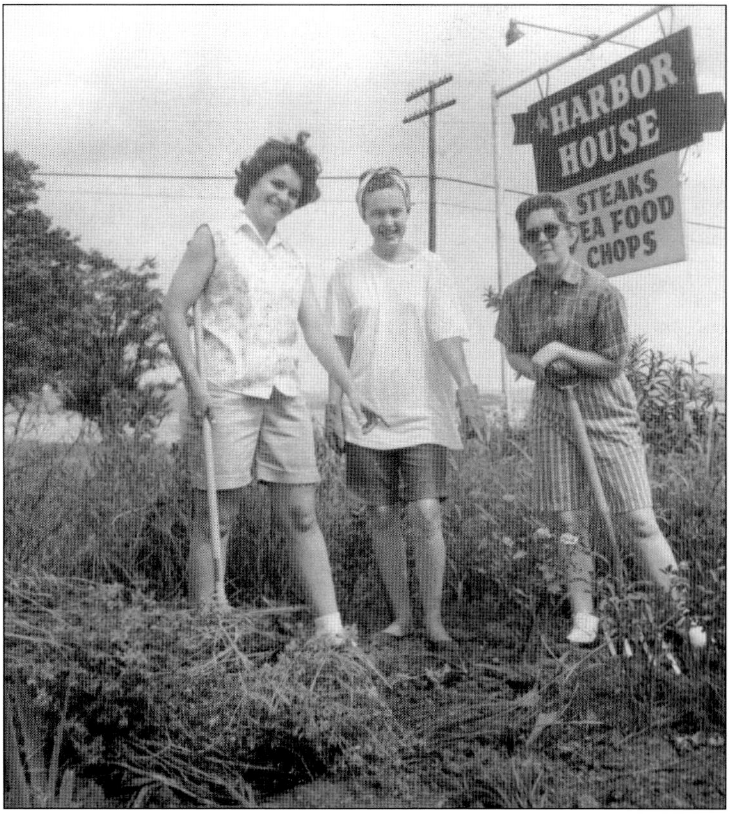

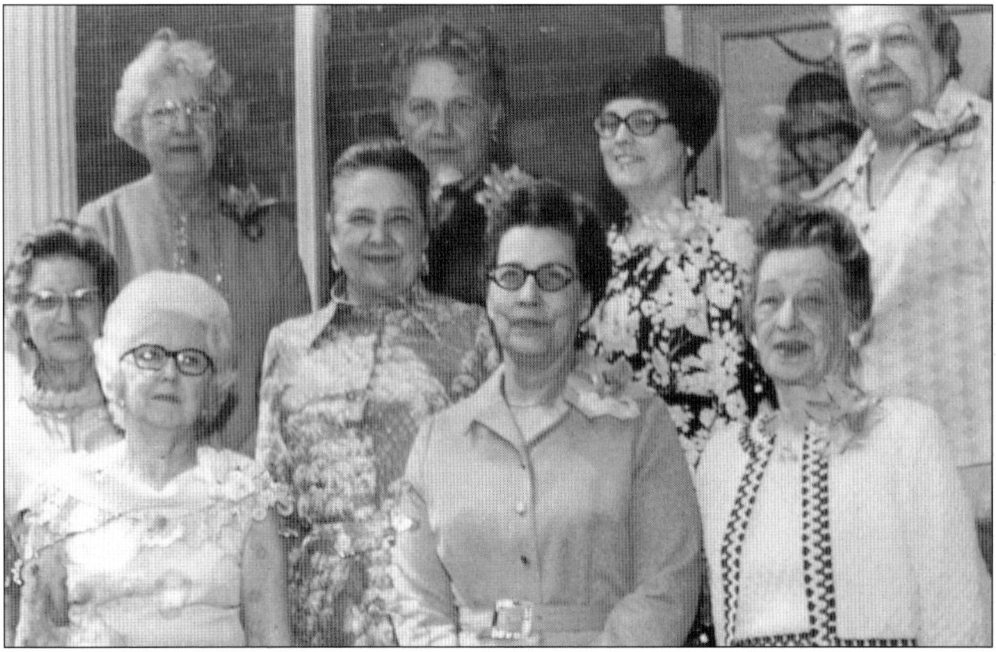

Pictured here are (first row) Arrie Crabtree, Ruby Gilbreath, Truda Ragsdale, Elna Cowen, and Mary Julia Ross; (second row) Katherine Duncan, Elizabeth Lusk, Elsie Brown, and Zona Brown. They served at the 1975 golden anniversary reception for John and Marilym Willis, where more than 400 friends and family celebrated on Easter Sunday. (Gail Smith Ingrum.)

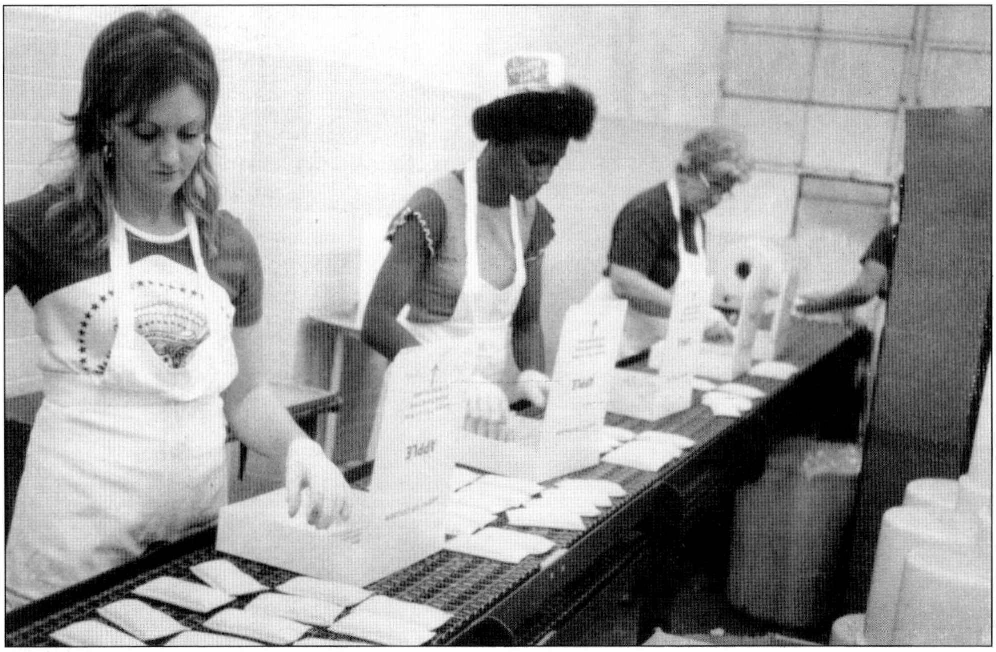

Pictured are, from left to right, Hubble Bakery employees Brenda Troxel, Mary Gurley, and Bernice Cornelius. The bakery made 200 pies at a time, preparing roughly three tons of pies in a year. In 1975, Troxel signed a petition soliciting the State of Alabama to add guardrails on the East Lake Causeway. (Marshall County Archives.)

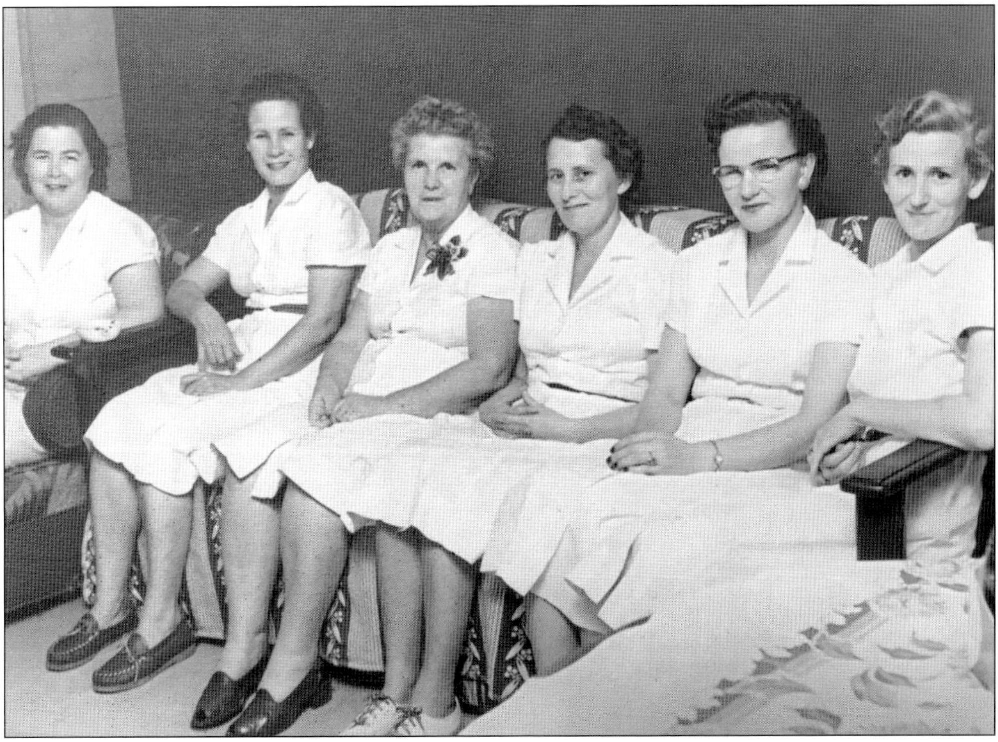

These Hubble Bakery workers are, from left to right, Nova Jean Moon, "Bill" Atchley, ? Rainwater, Jewell Brewer, Edna Foster, and Opal Troup. The bakery operated until 1981. Owner Ray Hubble explained that his company had lost money for more than three years. Facing greater competition, he reduced employees and limited truck routes before gradually going out of business. (Marshall County Archives.)

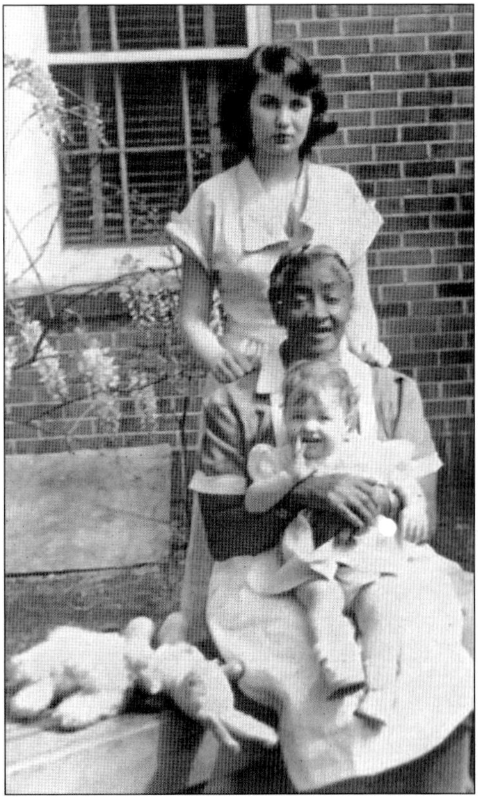

Seated in the yard at the J.P. and Marilym Willis home is Lillie Moore with baby Gail Smith, daughter of Ida Will Willis and Claude Herbert Smith, on her lap. Standing behind them is Bertha Kernachan. A cook for more than 50 years in the Lusk-Willis homes, Moore, known as fun-loving and kind, enjoyed taking photographs and created an array of amazing images, which are available to view at the Huntsville–Madison County Public Library. (Gail Smith Ingrum.)

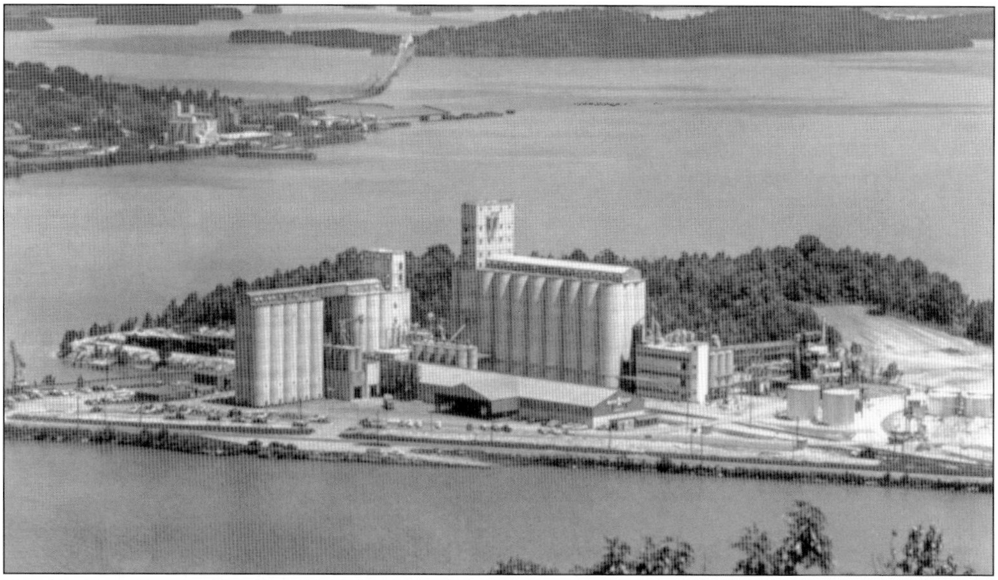

The Ralston Purina Feed Mill held its grand opening on June 1, 1957, with approximately 16,000 people present. Ticket-holders toured the new facility and enjoyed entertainment by Roy Acuff, Minnie Pearl, the Duke of Paducah, and the Smoky Mountain Boys. Pearl told the crowd that she flirted with Thomas Martin (mayor), Clarence Porch (chair, chamber of commerce), and Arvel W. Todd (Alabama's Commissioner of Agriculture and Industries). (Marshall County Archives.)

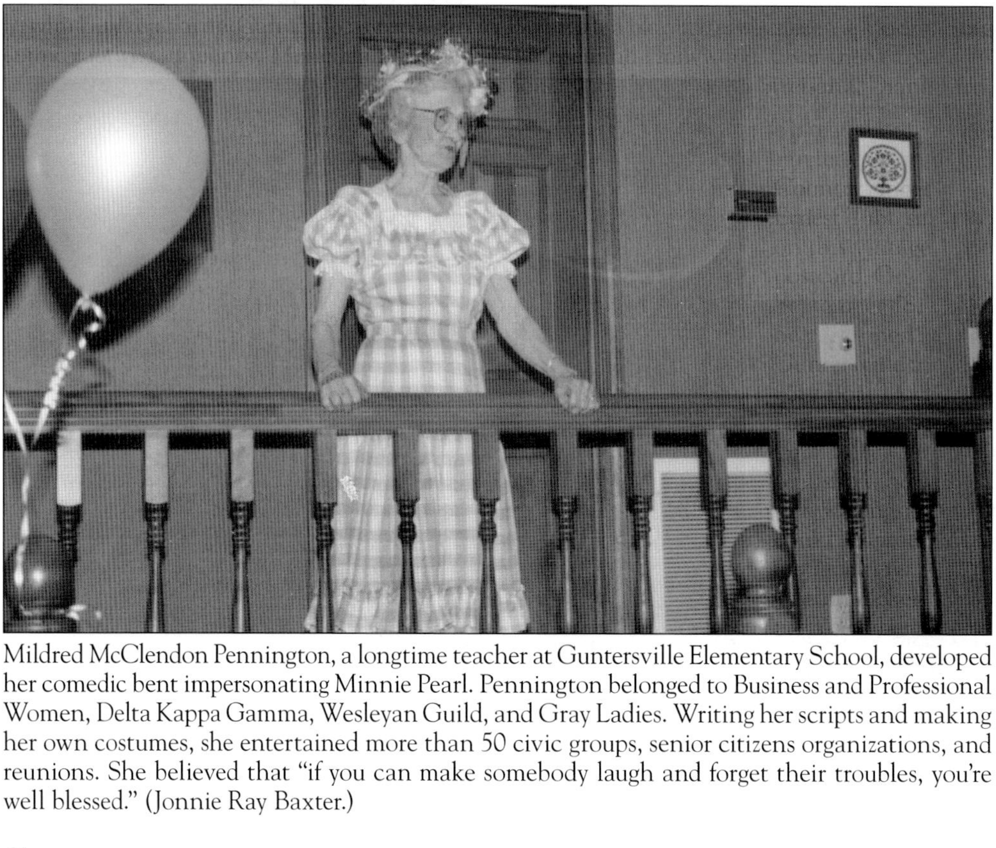

Mildred McClendon Pennington, a longtime teacher at Guntersville Elementary School, developed her comedic bent impersonating Minnie Pearl. Pennington belonged to Business and Professional Women, Delta Kappa Gamma, Wesleyan Guild, and Gray Ladies. Writing her scripts and making her own costumes, she entertained more than 50 civic groups, senior citizens organizations, and reunions. She believed that "if you can make somebody laugh and forget their troubles, you're well blessed." (Jonnie Ray Baxter.)

Wright Ross Sr. (shown) saw Halley's Comet in 1910, shared kinship with Andrew Lytle, and married Mary Julia Street. In 1920, Ross and Joe Graden founded the Ross-Graden Lumber Company, which celebrated its 100-year anniversary in 2020. Wright's sons Wright "Pete" Ross Jr. and Oliver Street "Buddy" Ross, as well as successive grandsons, have led the building materials company. (John Ross.)

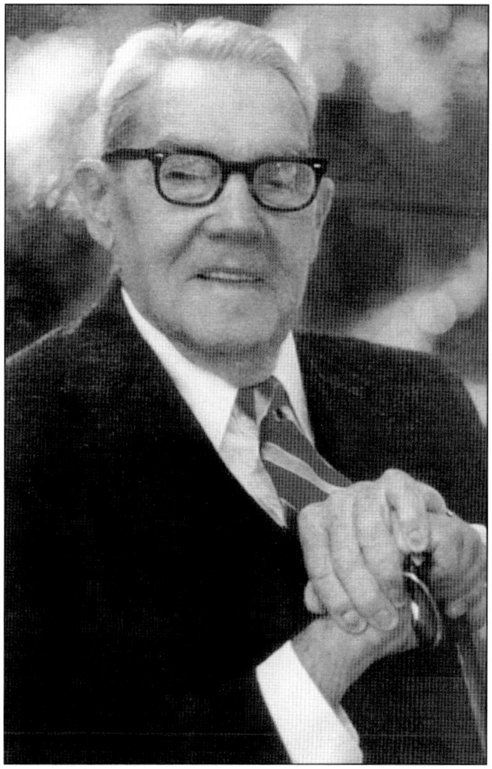

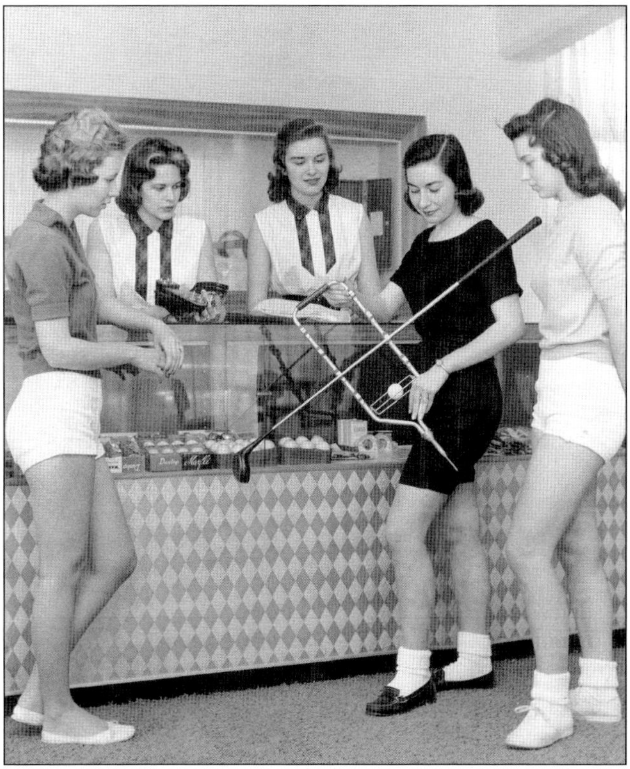

These ladies are viewing merchandise at the Val Monte Shores resort golf shop around the late 1950s. Pictured are, from left to right, Linda Adams, Sarah Jane Mabrey, Mary Ruth Manning, Billie Jean Barnard, and Dorothy Jo Oaks. The nine-hole course was the first one in Alabama to have underground irrigation. Three of the holes were lighted to allow for night play. (Marshall County Archives.)

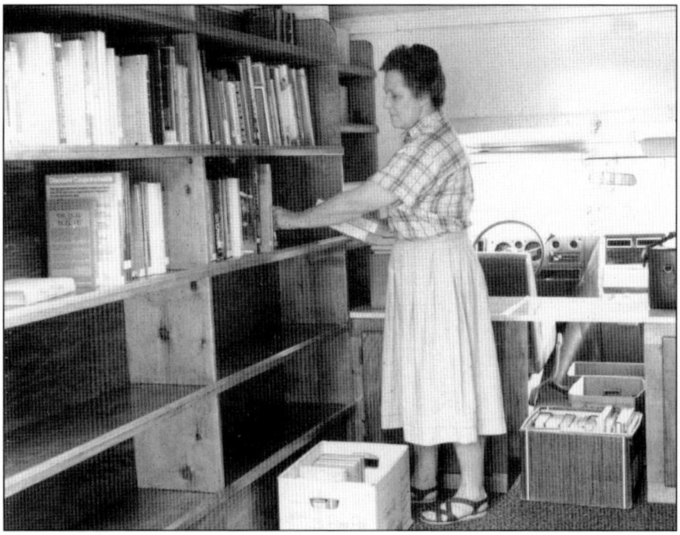

This is Lorene Hubble, who, for over 16 years, manned the bookmobile for Marshall County's Library Board. In the days before e-books, the bookmobile service provided a lifeline. To deliver reading material to 14 rural communities, five nursing homes, and numerous day care centers, Hubble checked out 1,000 to 1,200 books per month. Some of her regular patrons ordered as many as 20 books every other week. (*Advertiser-Gleam.*)

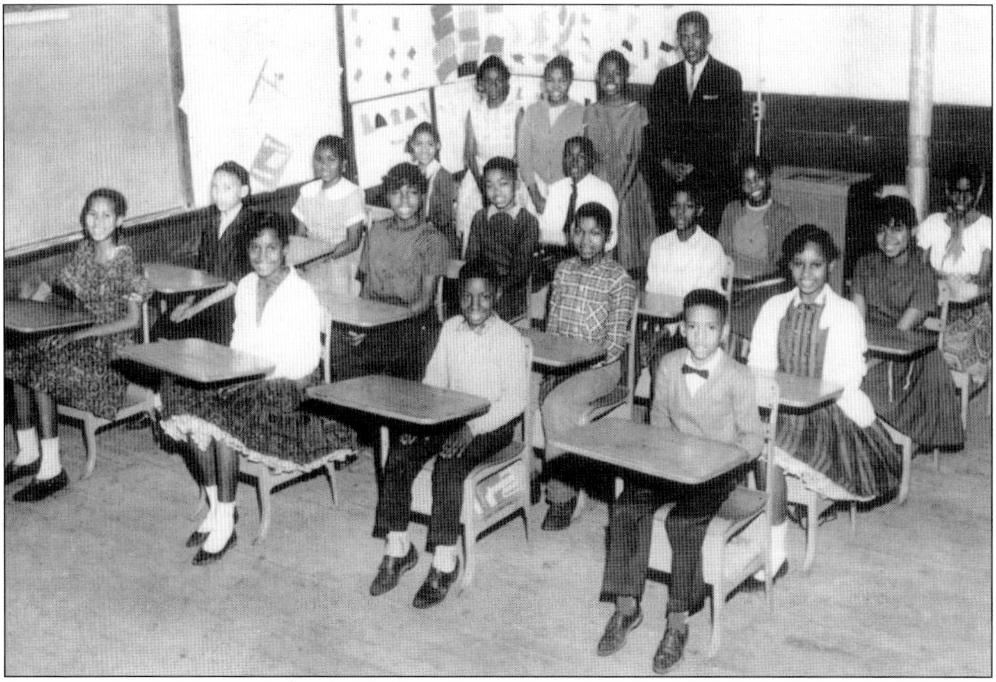

This undated photograph shows teacher James Horton with his class at Lakeview School. Lakeview opened in 1940, and on May 1, 1942, Corene Huff became the first graduate. Roosevelt Williamson became the principal in 1940 and offered guidance until his death in 1967. Adolph Scissum then served as principal. Lakeview School closed in 1968, and the building burned down in 1974. (*Advertiser-Gleam.*)

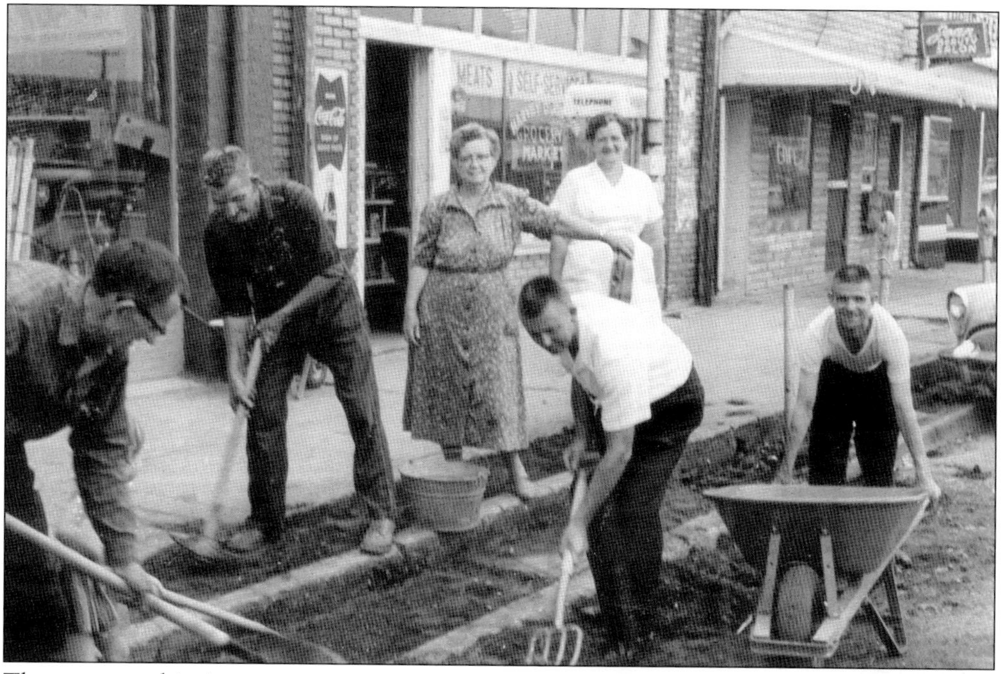

The stores on this street in South Town are Joan's Beauty Shoppe, Dot's Café, Harvey D. Johnson's Grocery Store, B & B Hardware, and Perkins's Furniture and Appliance. In this 1961 photograph are, from left to right, Buddy Brazelton, Cody Nelson, Prudie Ward, Lloyd Chandler, Alice Scott, and Jughead Godwin. They are preparing for the placement of a concrete slab between the street and sidewalk. (Buddy Taylor.)

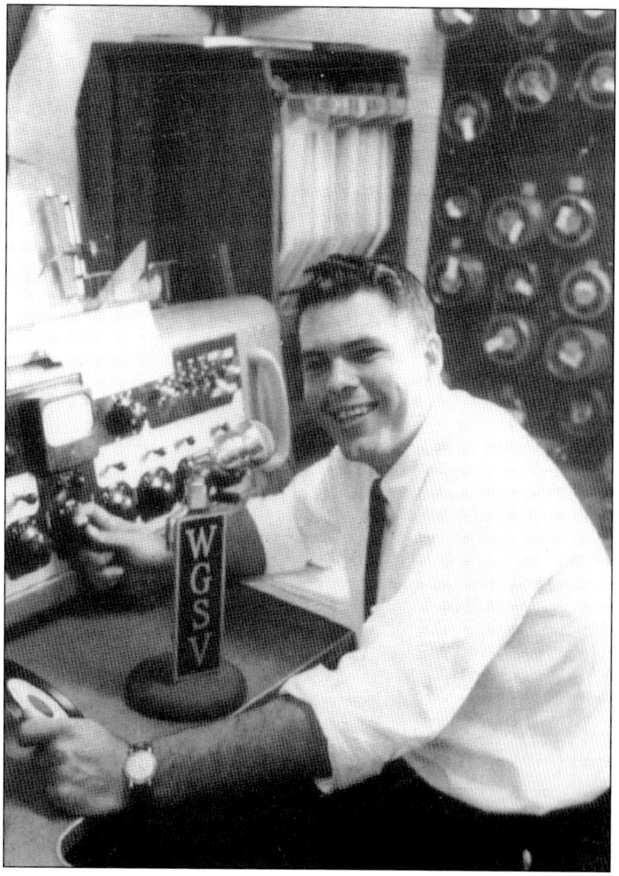

Bruce Underwood has worked in the broadcasting business for more than 50 years. To quote one WGSV listener, Underwood has always been "like a breath of springtime" for the residents of Guntersville. He arrives at work by 4:30 a.m. and begins his three-hour show at 6:00 a.m. Underwood describes himself as a "jack of all trades." (*Advertiser-Gleam.*)

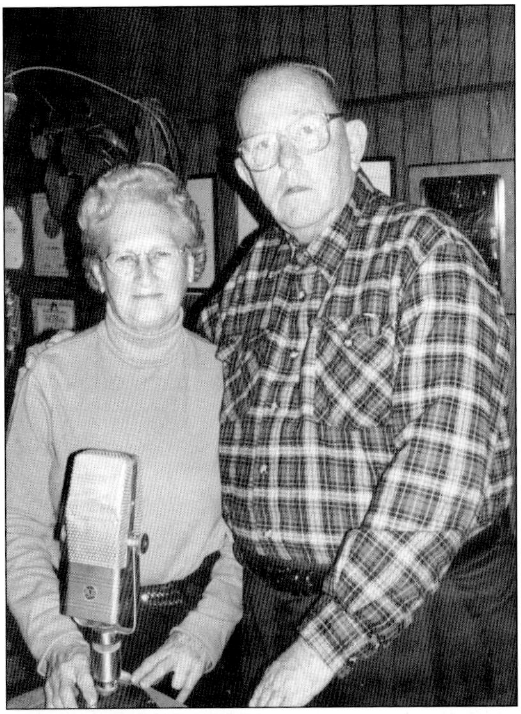

Ruby Dee and Radford Carter were noted radio announcers primarily for WTWX in Guntersville. The duo played gospel music in the mornings and Nashville-style music at night. Radford's early show *Cabin on the Hill* was especially popular. The couple emceed for gospel concerts and fundraisers. "Ruby Dee and Radford C." were the grand marshals for the Guntersville Christmas parade in 1981. (*Advertiser-Gleam.*)

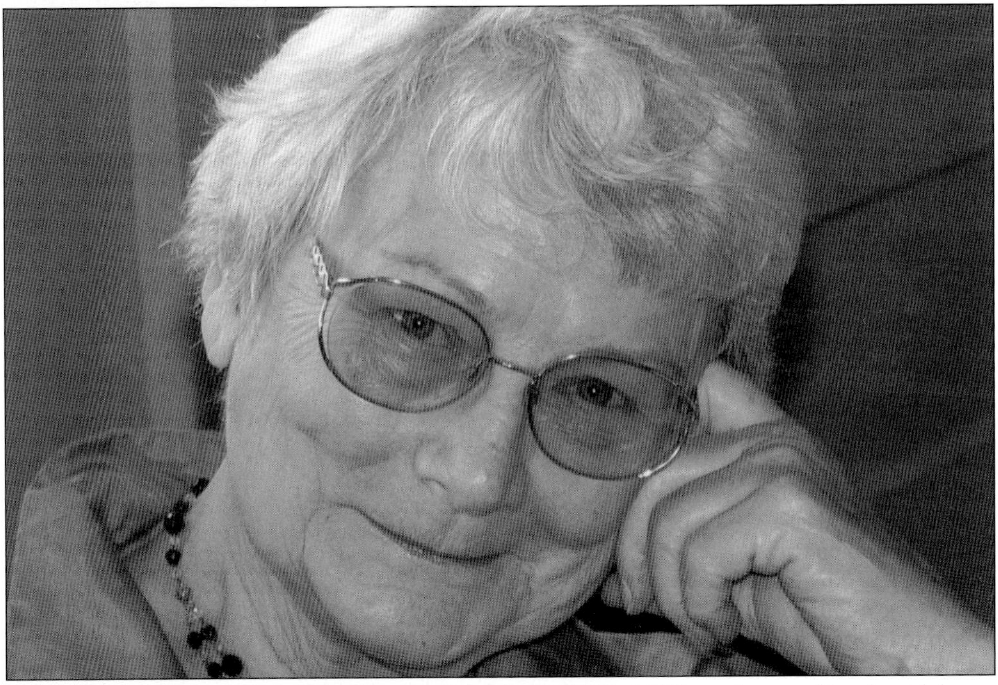

Founder of the Whole Backstage Theatre, Dot Moore (1933–2013) was honored by the Alabama State Council for the Arts with the 2009 Lifetime Achievement Award. A teacher, she formed the Teen Club when a 1968 automobile accident claimed the lives of Mike Jennings, James Tedder, and Steve Moshkoff. When the Teen Club began performing plays, she persuaded the city to use the old Guntersville Elementary School as a venue. (*Advertiser-Gleam.*)

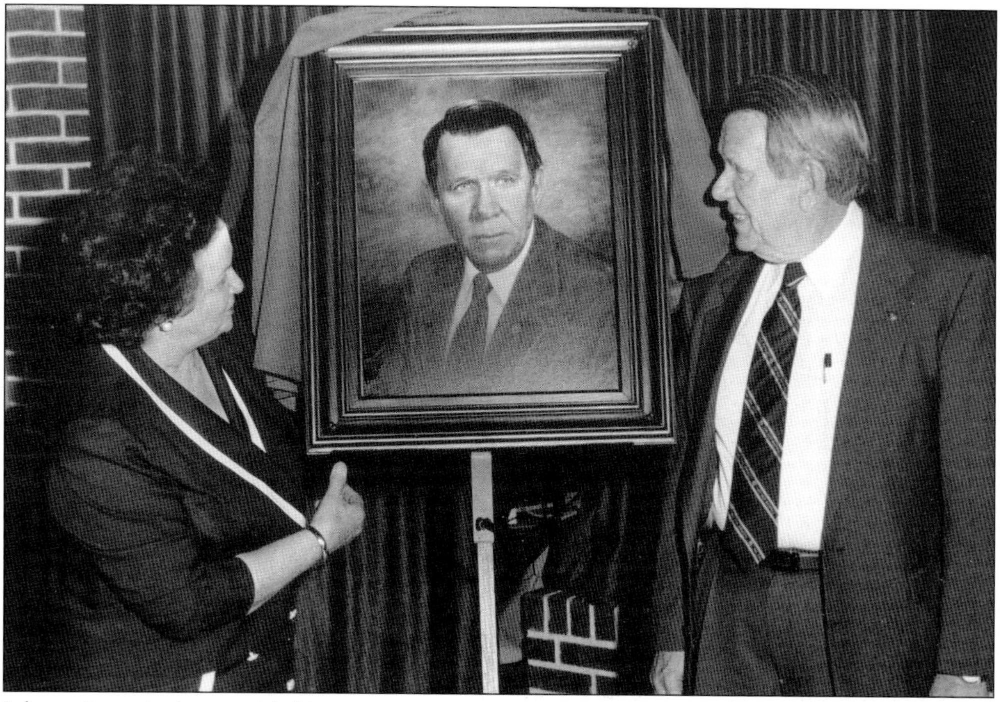

Johnny Long is shown with his wife, Mary Lynn. The son of Sam and Lillian Long, trumpeter Johnny served over 30 years as director of bands for Troy State University. In 1987, he became president of the Alabama Bandmasters Association. In 1994, Guntersville mayor James Townson declared the week of April 6 "Johnny Long Week." In 2011, *CBS Evening News* conducted a piece on Johnny's life. (*Advertiser-Gleam.*)

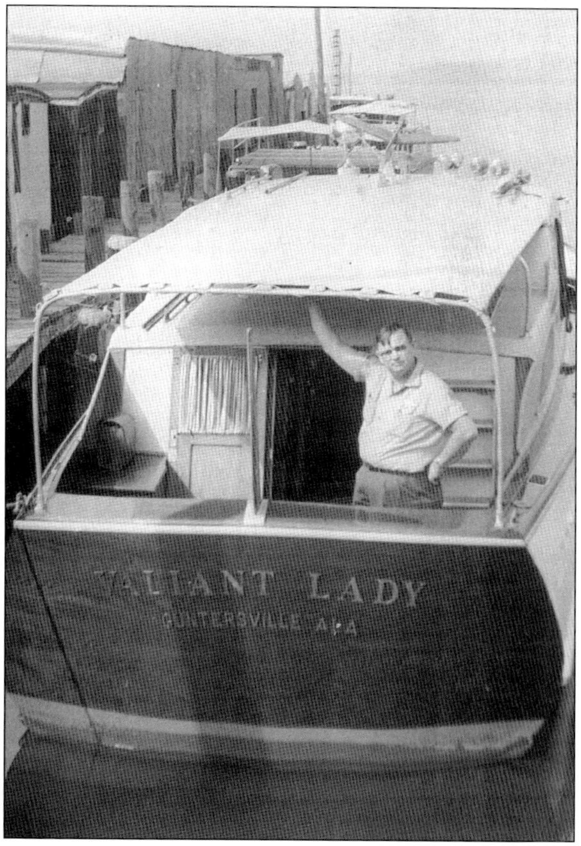

In a 1959 drawing held by the Cosmopolitan Club, Sheriff Warren Jones won a 14-foot fiberglass boat. He then traded it for a 17-foot aluminum boat. In this 1962 photograph, Jones poses with the cruiser *Valiant Lady*, a 25-foot-long vessel with a 90-horsepower Chrysler motor. Pundits joked that wrongdoers should be forewarned that Sheriff Jones was ready for water pursuit. (George Barnett.)

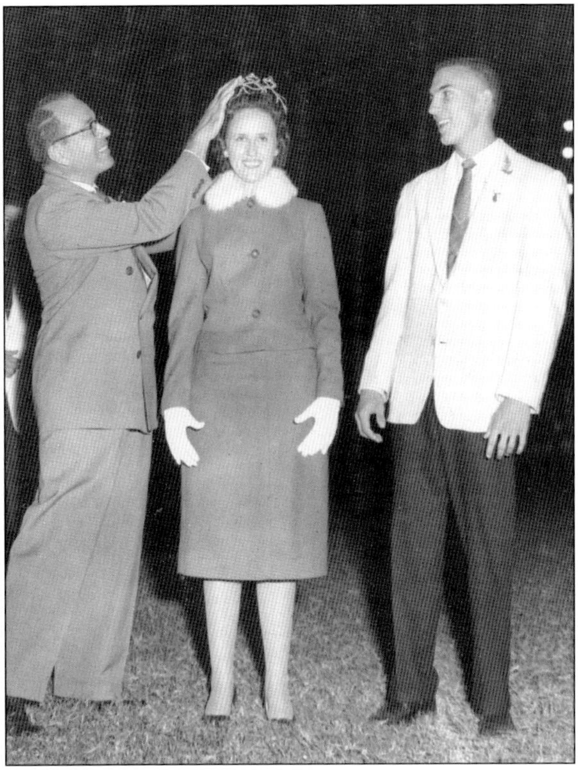

Dallas Briscoe, principal of Marshall County High School, is shown crowning Glenda Buchanan as the 1959 homecoming queen. Buchanan's escort Carl Wisener is at right. Supporting attendants were Kathleen Manning, escorted by Don Ryan, and Middy Speir, escorted by Johnnie Smith. Wisener eventually became a principal and later superintendent of Morgan County. (Marshall County Archives.)

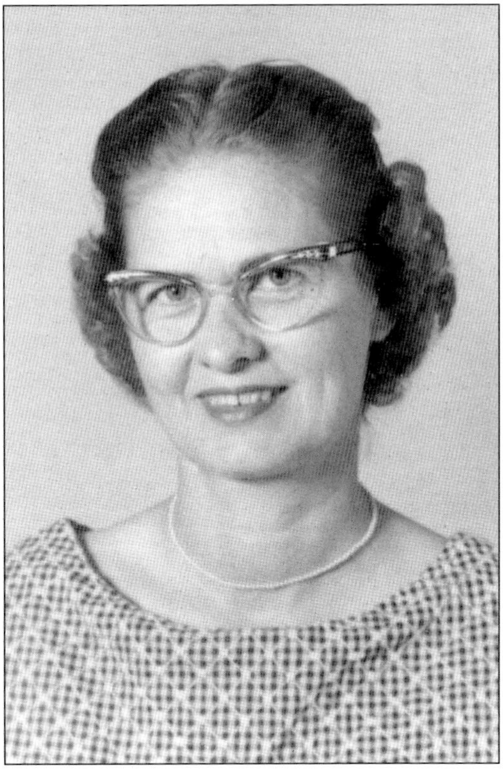

Born in 1918, Edith Street Hallman, shown here around 1962, died in 2019. She graduated from Jacksonville State University, married Charles Hallman, and taught school for 30 years. When she retired in 1975, she and her husband opened the Charles Hallman Realty Company. In 2013, Edith was recognized as the oldest active member of the First Baptist Church. The children of Edith and Charles are Vicki, Becky, and Lucy. (Authors' collection.)

In 1998, workers at the Marshall County Health Department threw a retirement reception for Emma Breedlove. Breedlove worked at the department for 17 years as a health service aide. She had worked at City Hospital, Boaz-Albertville Hospital, and in private home care. At the reception, she expressed her plan to stay active and continue helping others. (*Advertiser-Gleam.*)

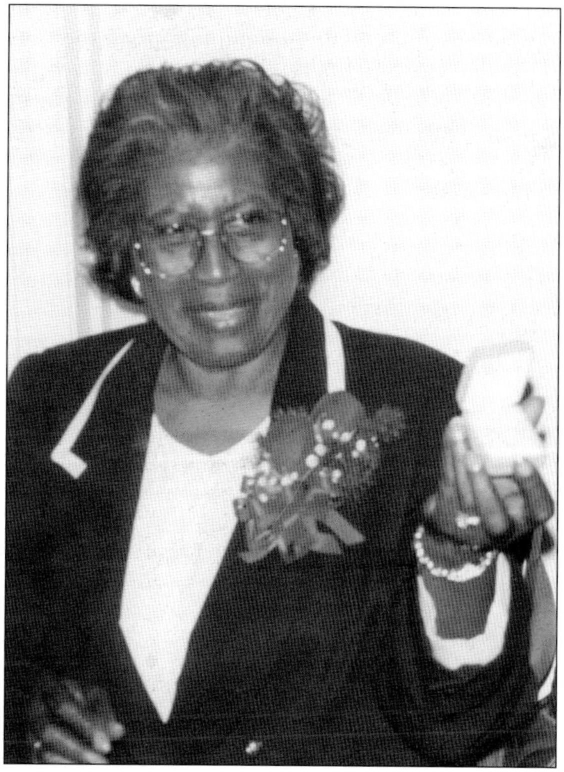

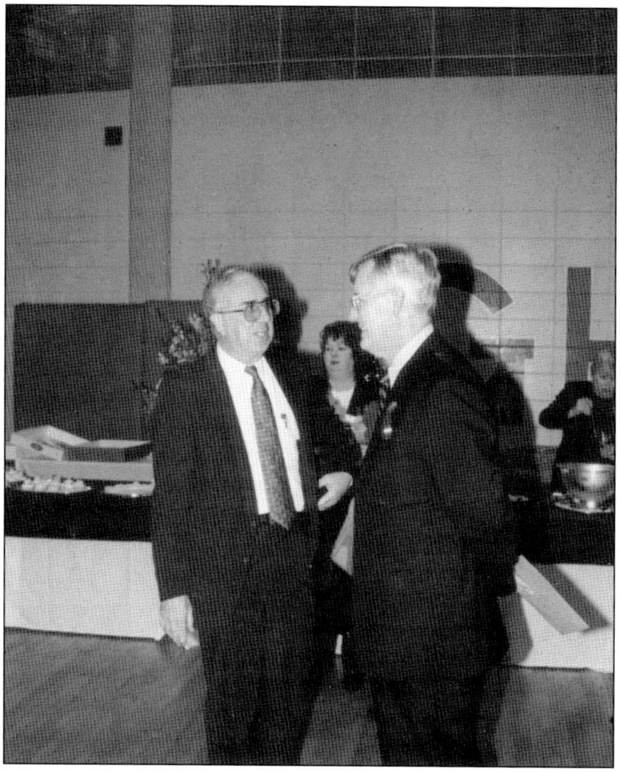

Jerry Cornelius (left) is shown with mayor James Townson (right). Cornelius collected football programs, sports' memorabilia, and 2,375 vintage photographs of Guntersville and Marshall County. The first question for local historians is, "Have you looked in the Cornelius collection?" A youth advocate, Cornelius served on the Recreation Board and enthusiastically supported the Booster Club. (City of Guntersville.)

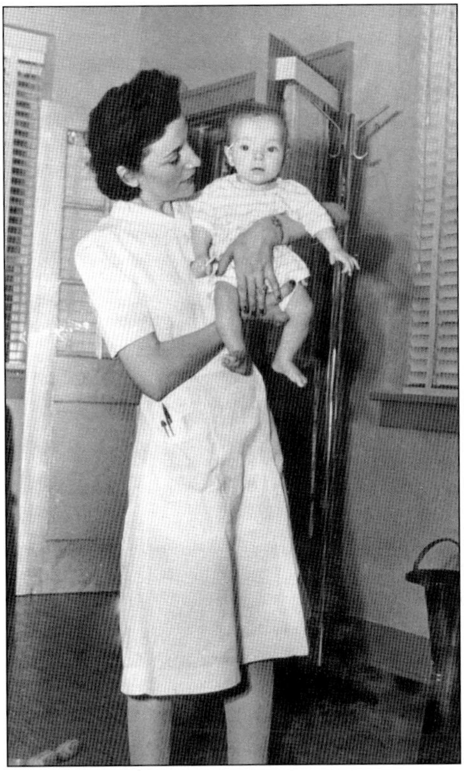

Kathryn Stimecz (pictured holding an unidentified baby), director of nursing at City Hospital, came to Guntersville in 1946 after having been a flight nurse during World War II. She married Tom Conn, loved gardening, and belonged to the St. William Catholic Church. Her sisters, Mary and Elizabeth Stimecz, joined her in working at City Hospital on Ringold Street. All were trained at Hillman School of Nursing in Birmingham. (*Advertiser-Gleam.*)

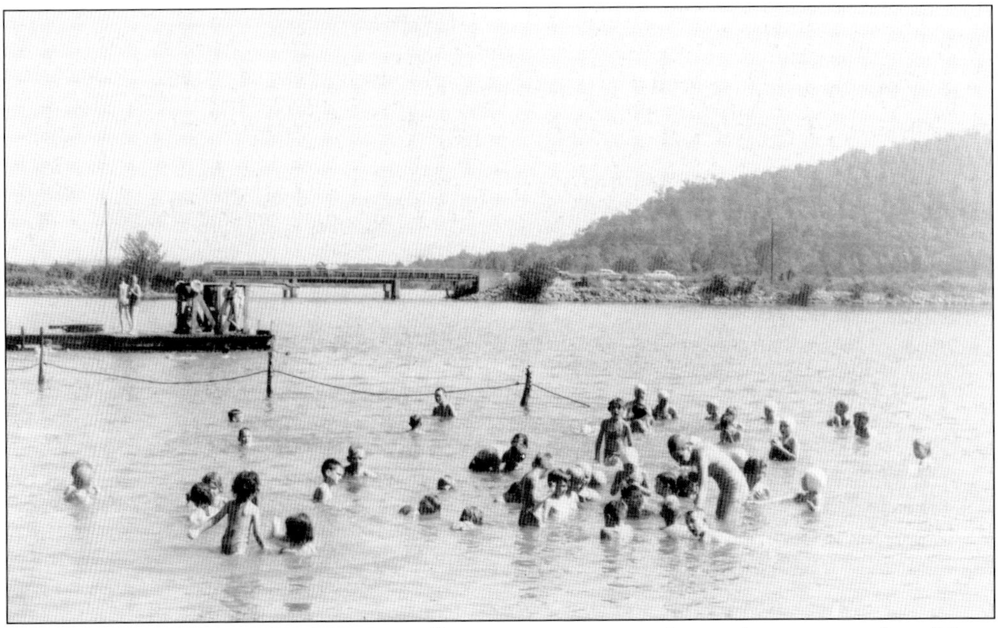

Swimming at the lake offered Guntersville citizens a way to relax on hot summer days. Many youngsters learned to swim through lessons. Others had parents or elder siblings throw them in deep water with some questionable advice—"sink or swim." These days, locals and tourists alike enjoy the beach on Sunset Drive and the one at Lake Guntersville State Park. (Marshall County Archives.)

Hazel Jex is shown ice skating with one of her daughters on Lake Guntersville. She and her husband, Bill, had seven children. Hazel devoted her life to developmentally disabled children. She earned a degree from Brigham Young University. After teaching at Carlisle Park School, she directed the Community Achievement Center. In her fifties, she acquired a master's degree from Alabama A&M University. (Marshall County Archives.)

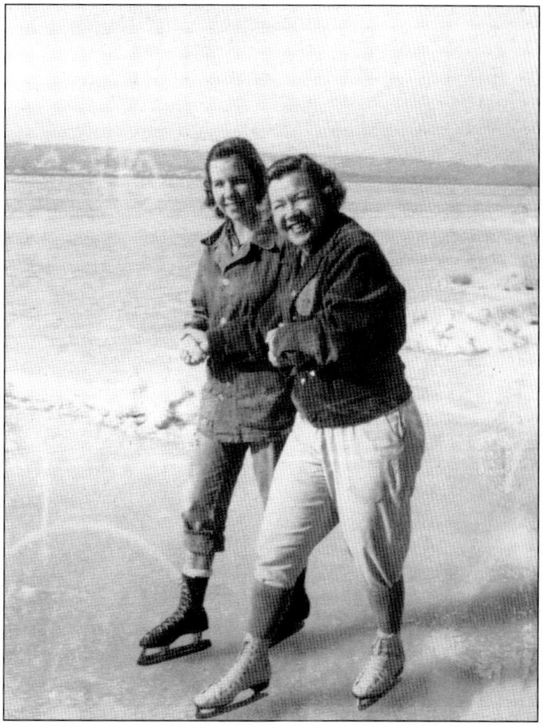

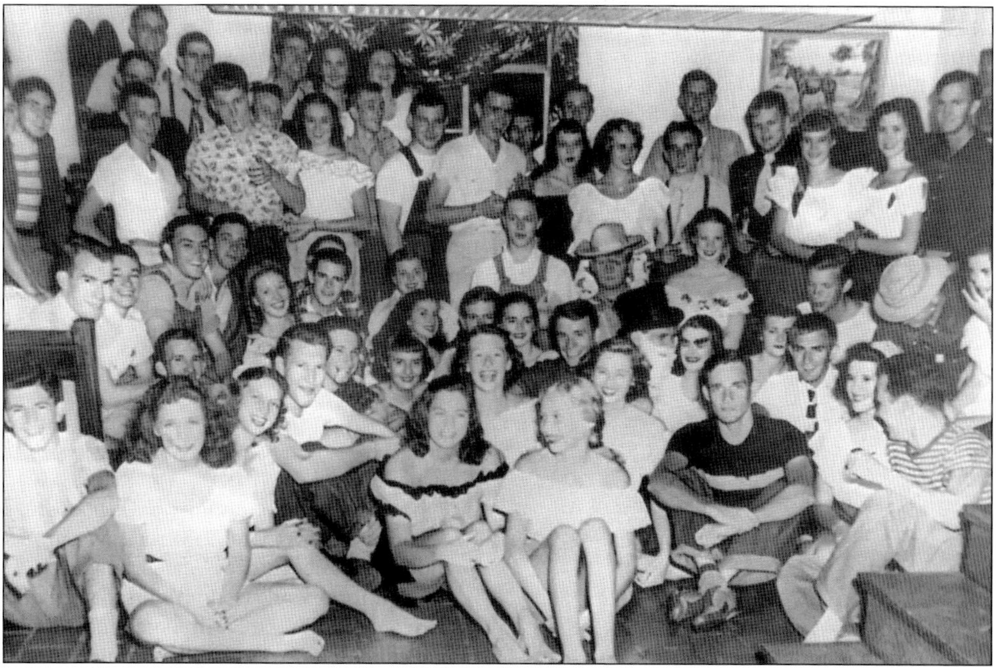

As shown in this photograph, Frances Smith and Dale Woodall entertained about 75 friends prior to the 1948 boat races. The party, billed as "Dogpatch," was held at the home of Della and Minor Woodall Sr. The costume voted best for women was Margaret Brown's Daisy Mae. The male winner was Bill Byrd Jr. for Li'l Abner. In 1948, Brown was chosen as Miss Guntersville Lake. (Marshall County Archives.)

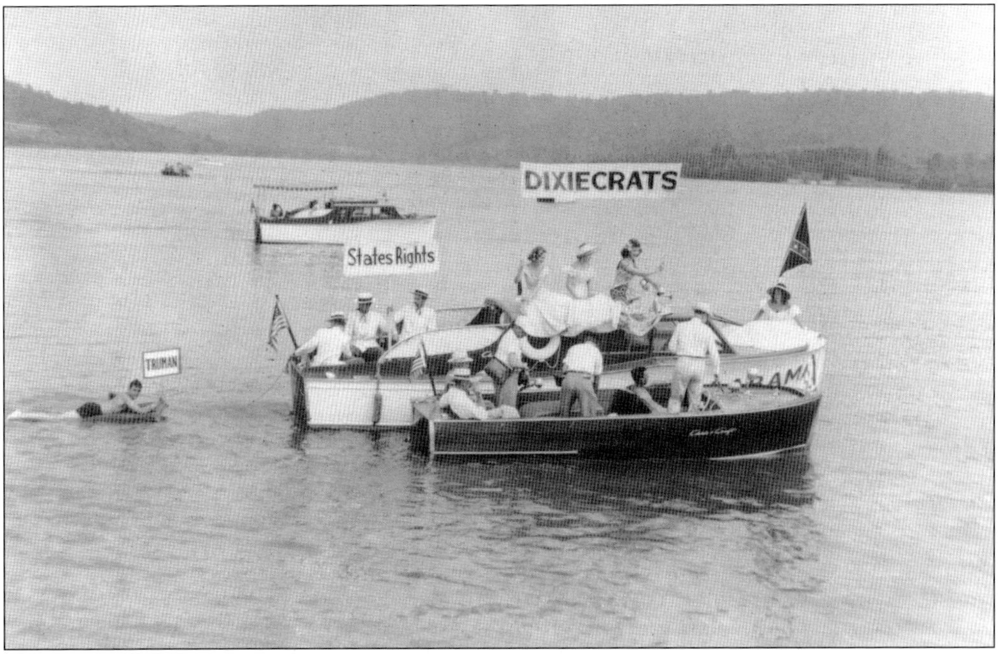

In the 1948 contest for best-decorated boat, Clay Woodall won. He called his entry "The Dixiecrat," and it featured the US and Confederate flags as well as young women in brightly colored antebellum dresses. That year's judges included Joe Starnes (chamber of commerce), John P. Willis (First National Bank), and Walter Newman (city commission). (Guntersville Museum.)

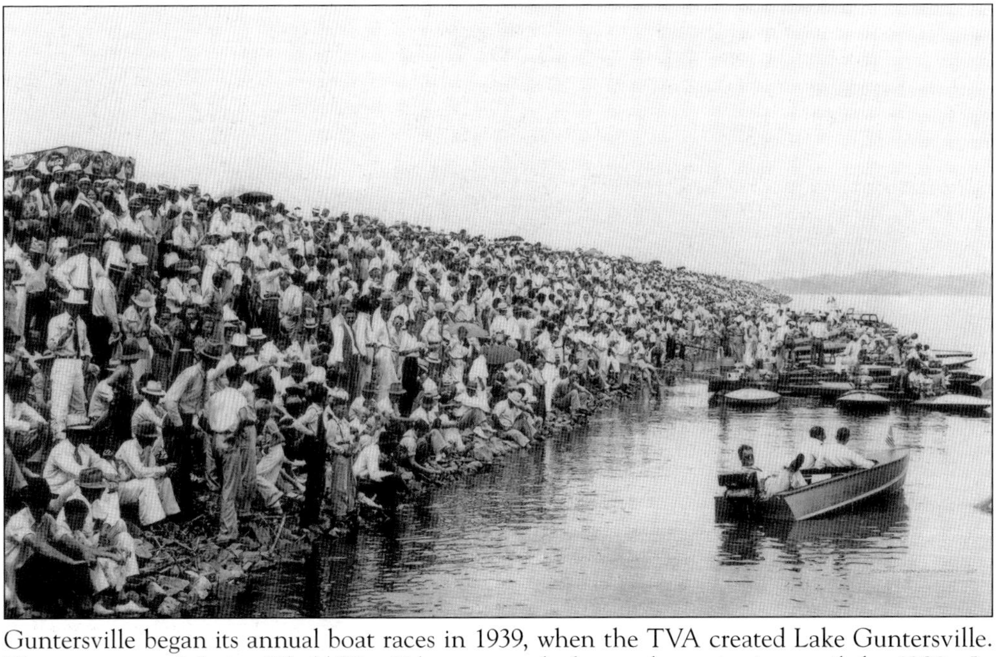

Guntersville began its annual boat races in 1939, when the TVA created Lake Guntersville. The races ceased during World War II but resumed afterward, continuing until the 1980s. In conjunction with the races, local businesses, the Jaycees, and the chamber of commerce sponsored events such as dances, pageants, parties, and concerts. Hydroplane races have recently returned to Guntersville. (Alabama Department of Archives and History.)

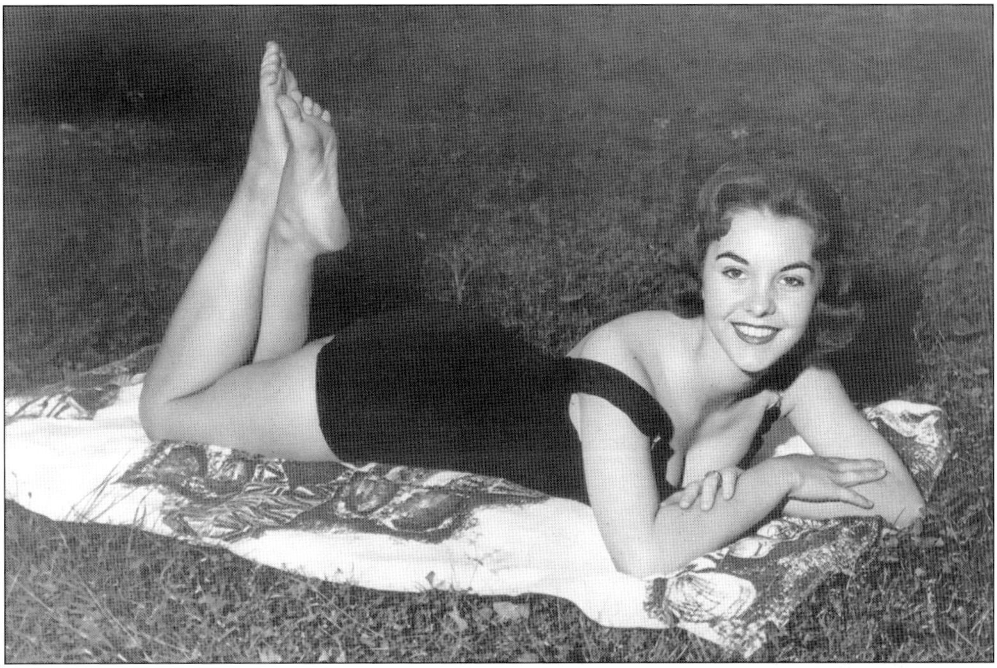

For the 1959 boat races, Gov. John Patterson served as flag master to wave Marion Cooper of Louisville, Kentucky, across the final finish line. Jerolyn Ridgeway (shown) was selected Miss Guntersville Lake with Jackie Hamilton in second, Martha Campbell in third, and Sarah Glenn Barnett in fourth. Kathleen Manning won Little Miss Guntersville Lake. Her runners-up were Dianne Rains and Sharon Drinkard. (Marshall County Archives.)

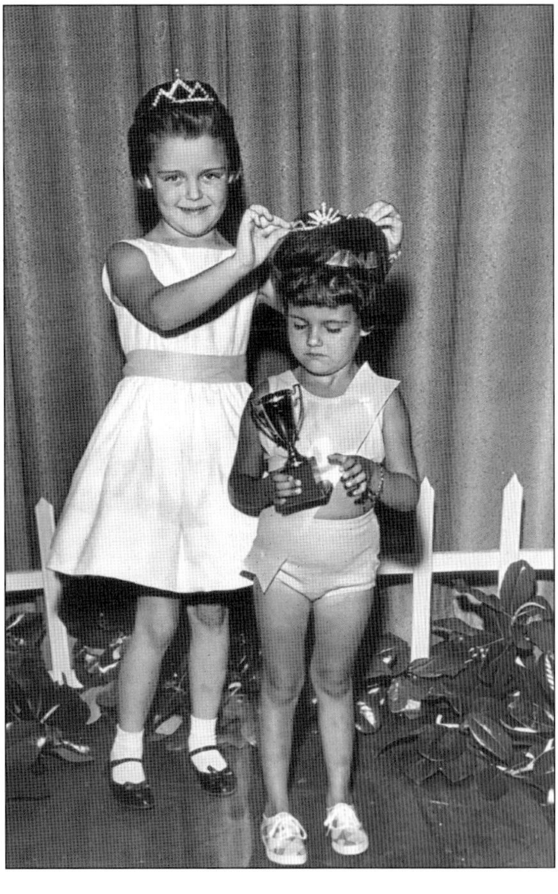

In 1963, Elisa Rainwater (right) became Little Miss Guntersville Lake. She is being crowned by Pam Godfrey, the 1962 winner. Sharon Barnard won second place, and Teresa Jean Hemrick came in third. That year, the Miss Guntersville Lake title went to Linda Vaughn of Anniston. Other winners included Cathy Miller (first alternate), Sandra Hubbard (second alternate), and Manola Harris (third alternate). The contestants voted Chris Akin as Miss Congeniality. (Marshall County Archives.)

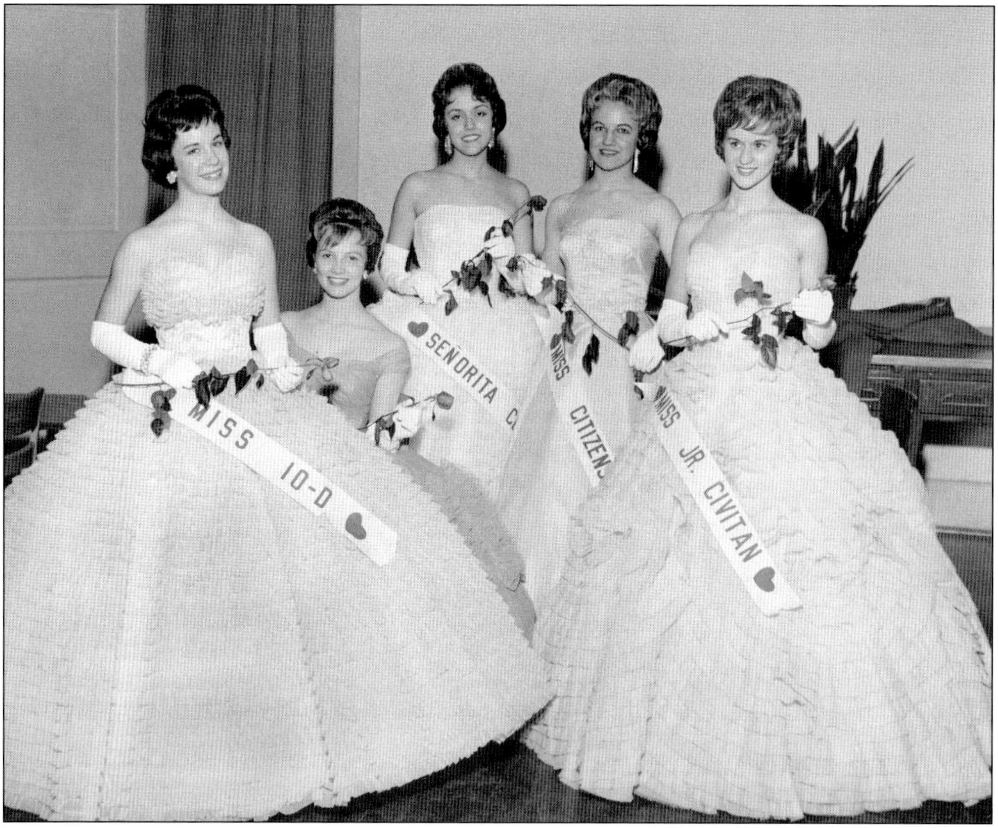

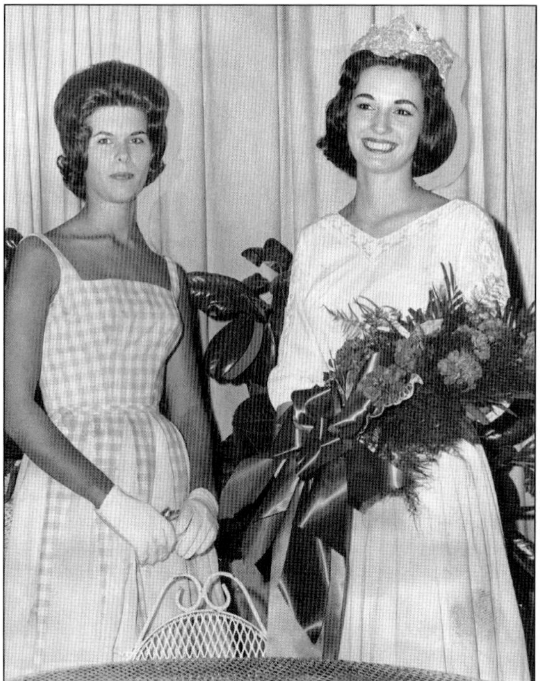

In this 1962 photograph are, from left to right, Candy Wasson (first alternate), Anne Lee, Milla McCord, Sherry Douglas (Miss Sweetheart), and Diane Shields (second alternate). The annual Miss Sweetheart fundraiser included girls from various clubs and homerooms. The theme for 1962 was "Girl of My Dreams," a song sung by band director Maurice Lacey. (Marshall County Archives.)

In 1962, the Marshall County Farm Bureau sponsored its annual Maid of Cotton pageant. The judges selected Rozanne Thrasher (left) of Guntersville as alternate and Jill Laura Tate (right) of Boaz as Maid of Cotton. In the junior division, the winners were Virginia Hudgins of Albertville with Brenda Morrison of Boaz as alternate. (Marshall County Archives.)

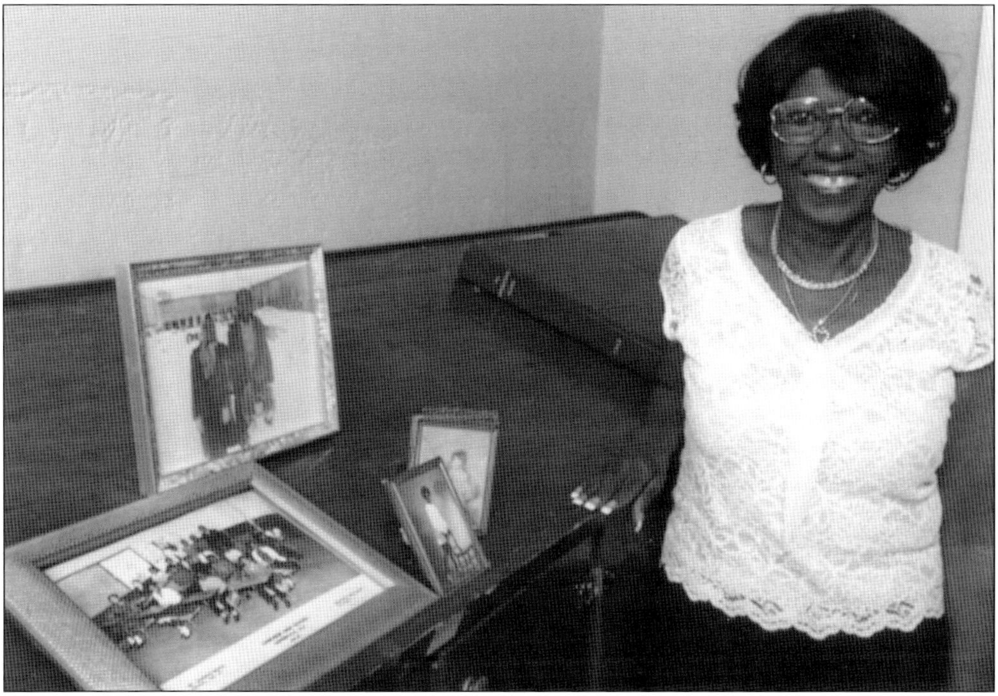

In 1966, Sue Chapman (shown) transferred from Lakeview School to Boaz High School. Chapman, the first Black student at Boaz High, was chosen band sweetheart in her senior year. In a newspaper article, she reflected, "Don't let the situation shape you, but you shape it." After graduating, she worked at Lee Plant, earned a college degree, and became a social worker. She and her husband, Samuel Herron, have three children. (*Advertiser-Gleam.*)

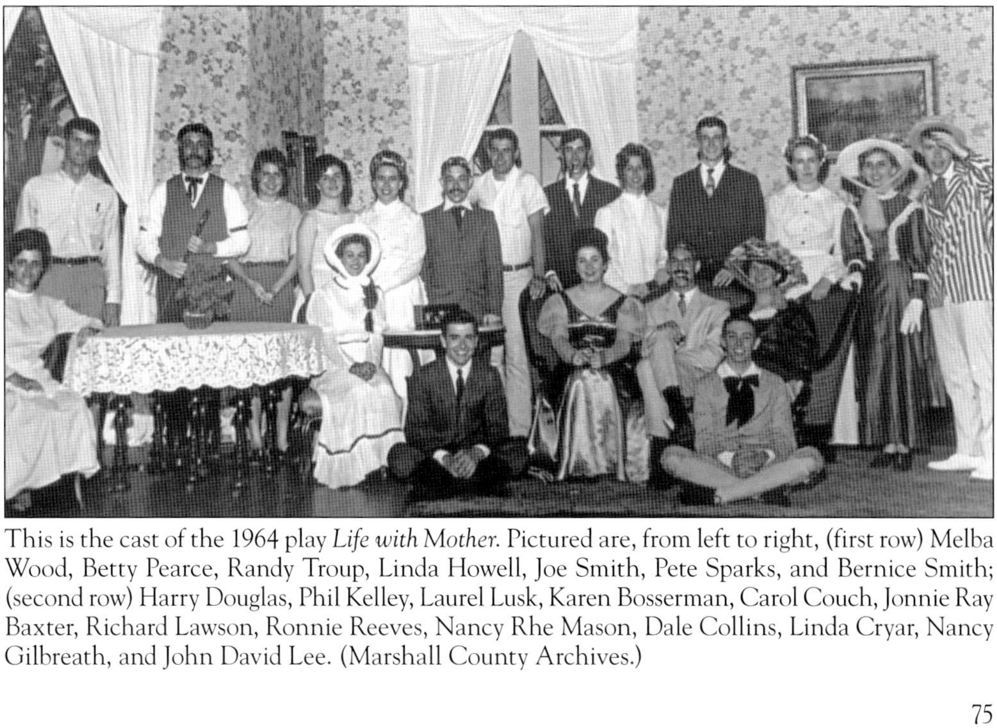

This is the cast of the 1964 play *Life with Mother.* Pictured are, from left to right, (first row) Melba Wood, Betty Pearce, Randy Troup, Linda Howell, Joe Smith, Pete Sparks, and Bernice Smith; (second row) Harry Douglas, Phil Kelley, Laurel Lusk, Karen Bosserman, Carol Couch, Jonnie Ray Baxter, Richard Lawson, Ronnie Reeves, Nancy Rhe Mason, Dale Collins, Linda Cryar, Nancy Gilbreath, and John David Lee. (Marshall County Archives.)

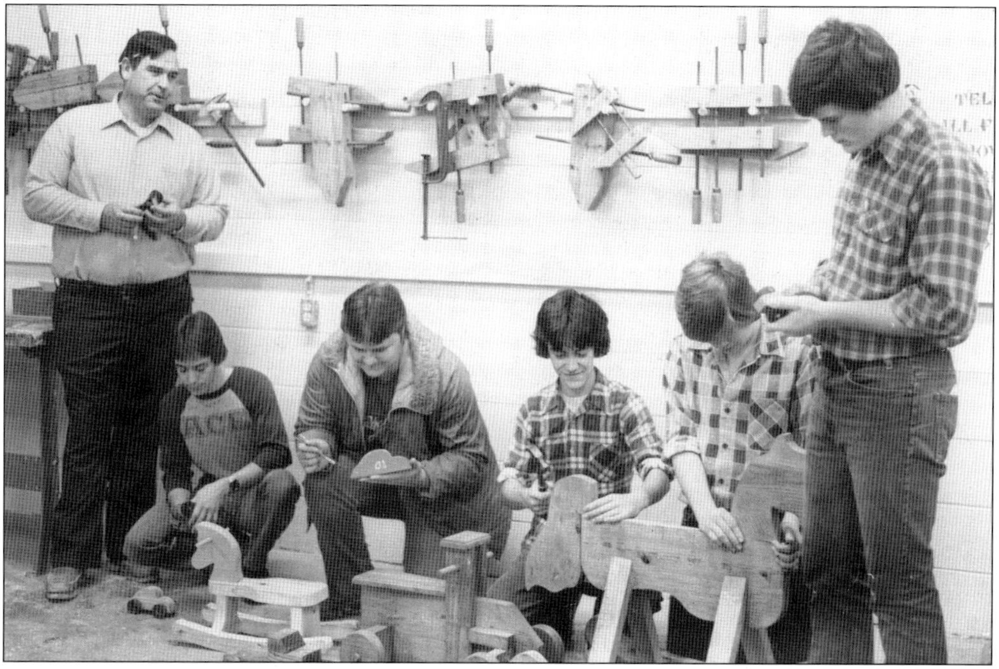

A member of the Marshall County Sports Hall of Fame, Frankie McClendon (left) is shown teaching carpentry at Marshall Technical School. In 1961, McClendon graduated from Marshall County High School, where he lettered from eighth grade. At the University of Alabama, he played on the 1964 national championship team. For "Frankie McClendon Day" in 1965, he, his teammates, and coach Paul Bryant visited Guntersville. McClendon played two years of professional football. (*Advertiser-Gleam.*)

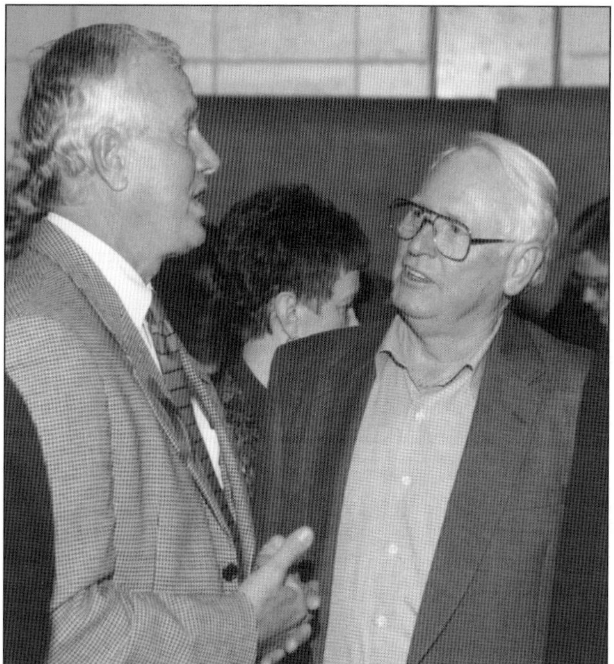

Ray Benefield (right) is shown with Alabama state senator Hinton Mitchem. From 1946 until 1976, Benefield ran Benefield's Jewelry Store. A civic-minded man, he served as a director of the Alabama Jewelers' Association, on the Guntersville Housing Authority, and as a Baptist deacon for more than 40 years. For 45 years, he presided on the sight-saving committee for the Lions Club. Benefield died in 2006. (*Advertiser-Gleam.*)

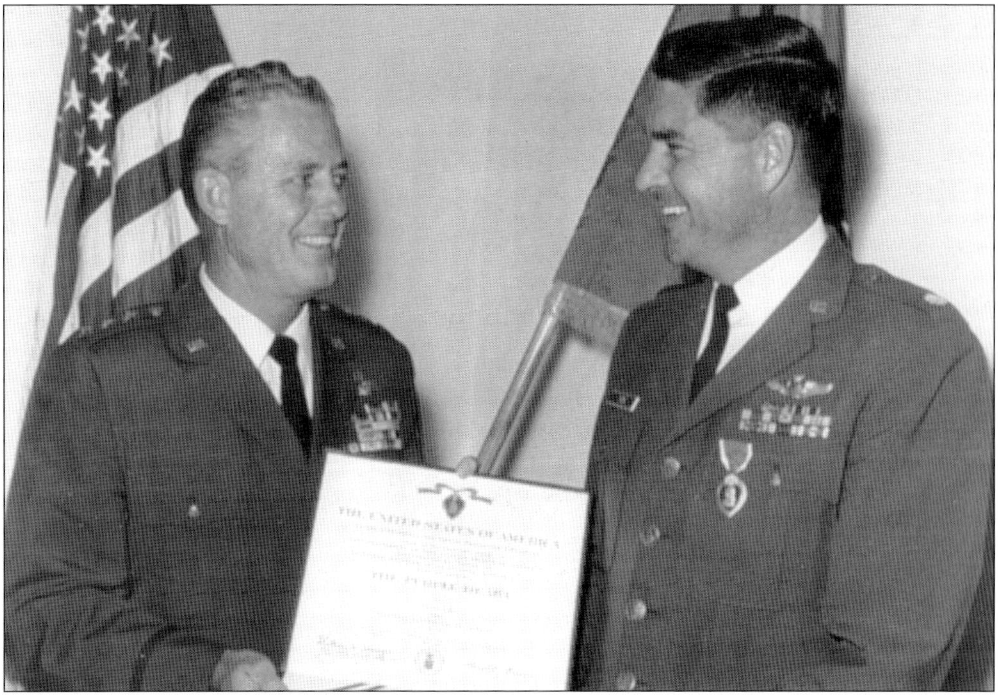

The son of Vernal and Tish Cobb, Kenny Cobb (right) is pictured receiving his Purple Heart certificate. He retired as an Air Force colonel and gained a reputation as Guntersville's "unofficial pilot ambassador." Cobb had his F4 Phantom jet shot down in Vietnam in 1967. He was involved in an operation to steal a Russian prototype jet from Syria in the 1980s and was the inspiration for the Clint Eastwood movie *Firefox*. (*Advertiser-Gleam*.)

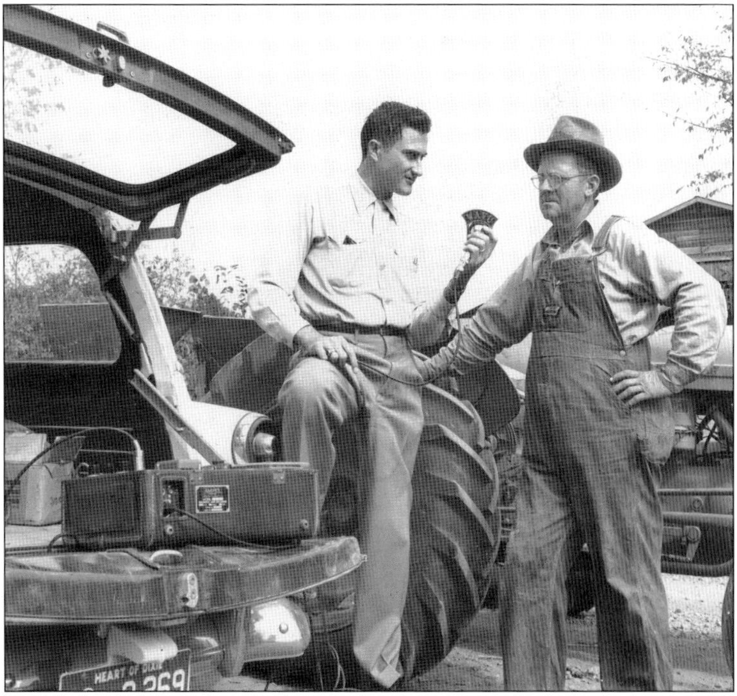

Jesse Culp (1927–2009; left) spoke daily on WAVU, wrote *Jesse Culp's Corner* for 48 years, edited the *Sand Mountain Reporter* for 19 years, and reported for other newspapers, like the *Advertiser-Gleam*. He penned a book called *The Good Ole Days*. As a member of the commission for the US Space and Rocket Center, Culp saw early rocket launches, met historical figures, and once even stepped on Pres. Dwight Eisenhower's foot. (Danny Maltbie.)

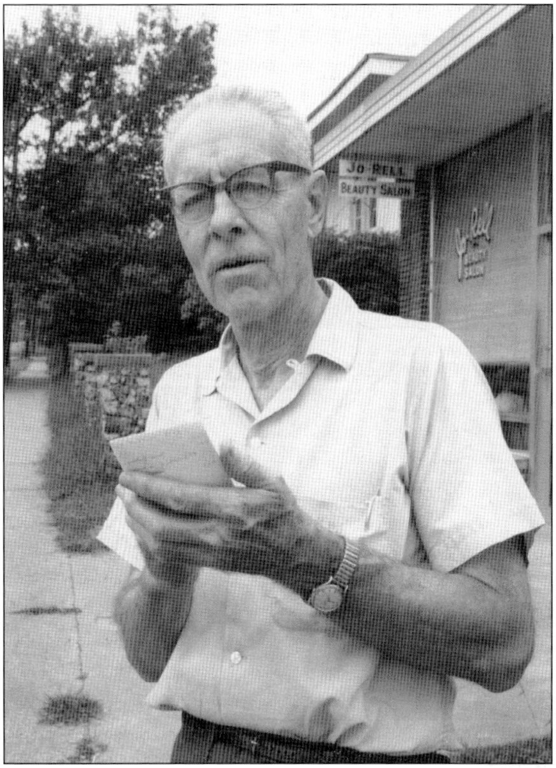

Though he suffered from polio as a child, Porter Harvey (shown), editor/publisher of the *Advertiser-Gleam*, loved adventure and even went bungee jumping at age 90. Harvey's newspaper career covered 68 years. His accolades included serving as president of the Alabama Press Association (1967–1968), being honored as Citizen of the Year (1992), and being inducted into the Alabama Communications Hall of Fame (1998). Harvey made four long-distance boat trips with Lake Theatre owner Bill Harris. (*Advertiser-Gleam*.)

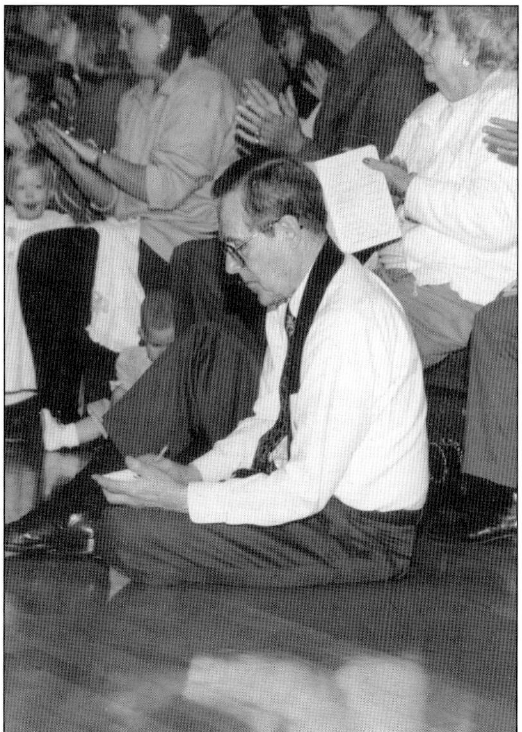

The son of Alice and Porter Harvey, Sam Harvey had printer's ink in his blood. After graduating high school in 1947, he went to the University of Alabama and edited the student newspaper. He reported for the *Dispatch* in Columbus, Ohio, and worked as an assistant editor at the *Louisville Times*. In 1967, Harvey became editor at the *Advertiser-Gleam*, where his father was publisher. Sam Harvey retired in 2014. (City of Guntersville.)

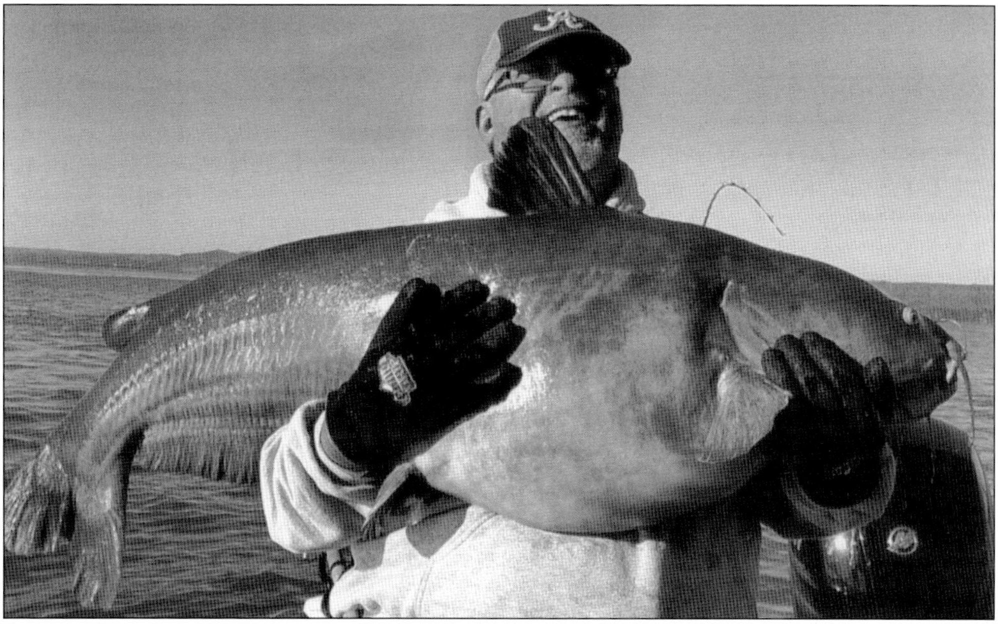

Anthony Campbell rightly bragged about this catch—a 90-pound catfish. After high school, Campbell attended the University of Alabama in Huntsville and reported for the *Advertiser-Gleam*. After graduating college, he joined the *Advertiser-Gleam* staff. A number of his fishing/hunting articles have been published in game magazines. In 2014, Campbell became editor of the *Advertiser-Gleam*. He and his wife, Mary, have two children, Anna and Kyle. (Anthony Campbell.)

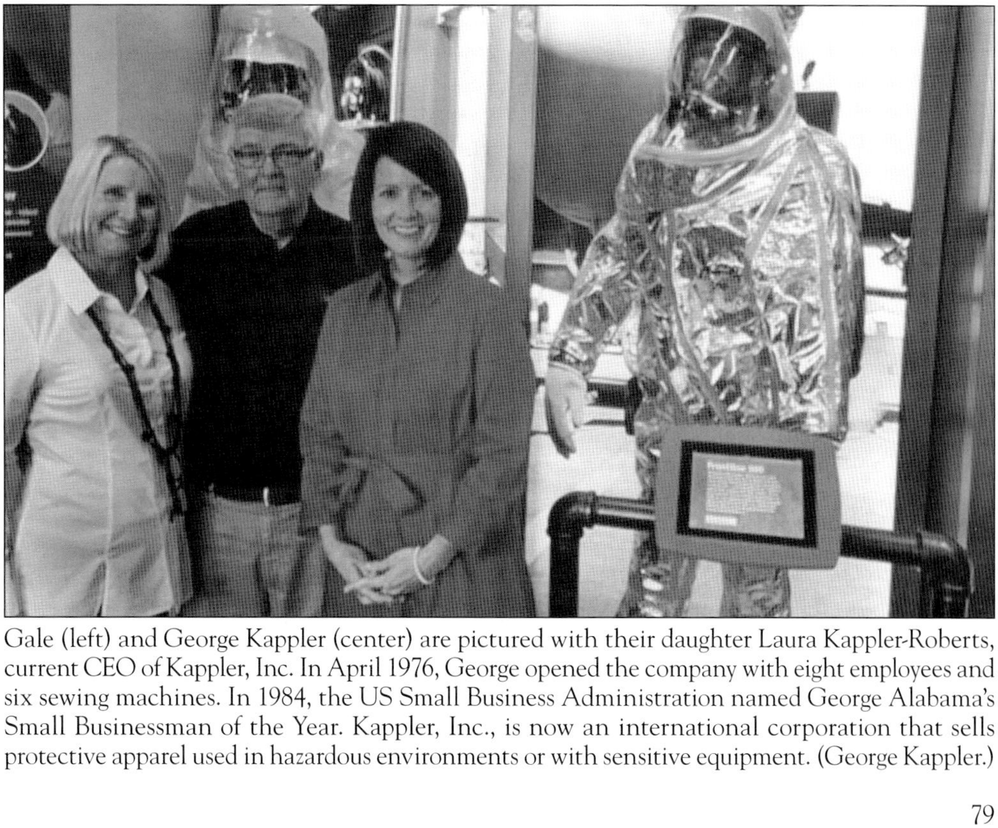

Gale (left) and George Kappler (center) are pictured with their daughter Laura Kappler-Roberts, current CEO of Kappler, Inc. In April 1976, George opened the company with eight employees and six sewing machines. In 1984, the US Small Business Administration named George Alabama's Small Businessman of the Year. Kappler, Inc., is now an international corporation that sells protective apparel used in hazardous environments or with sensitive equipment. (George Kappler.)

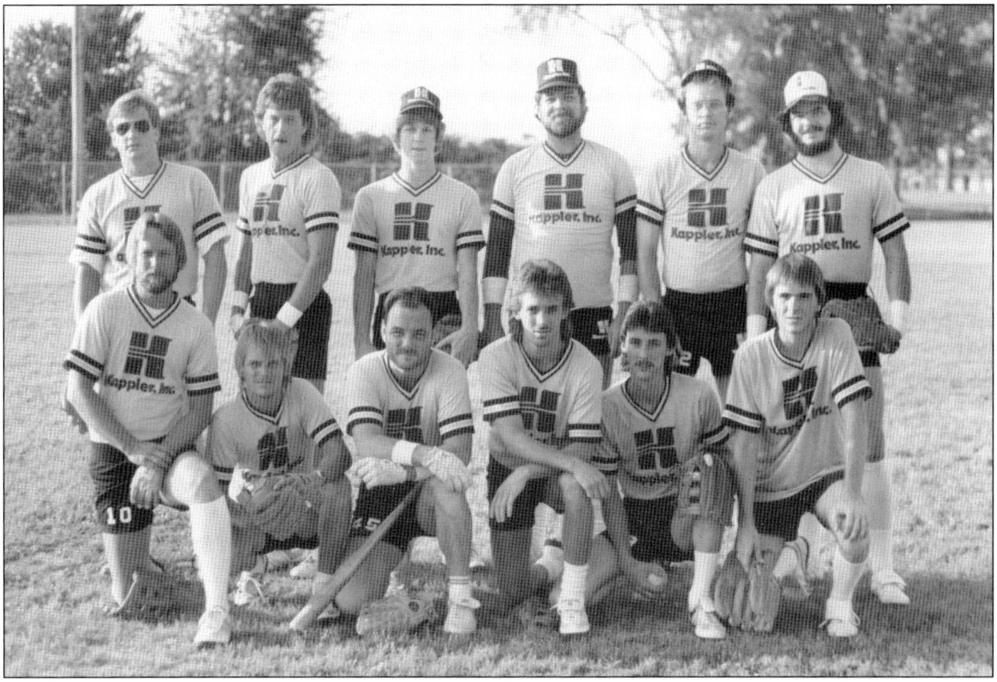

In 1985, this Kappler men's softball team competed in the Guntersville Recreational League. Pictured are, from left to right, (first row) Gary Thomas, Brian Slusher, Steve Chamblee, Phillip Woods, Randy Whitehead, and Bobby Gunter; (second row) Kurt Wilson, Keith Diamond, Phillip Sims, coach Thomas Boozer, Ronnie Clark, and James Hardin. (George Kappler.)

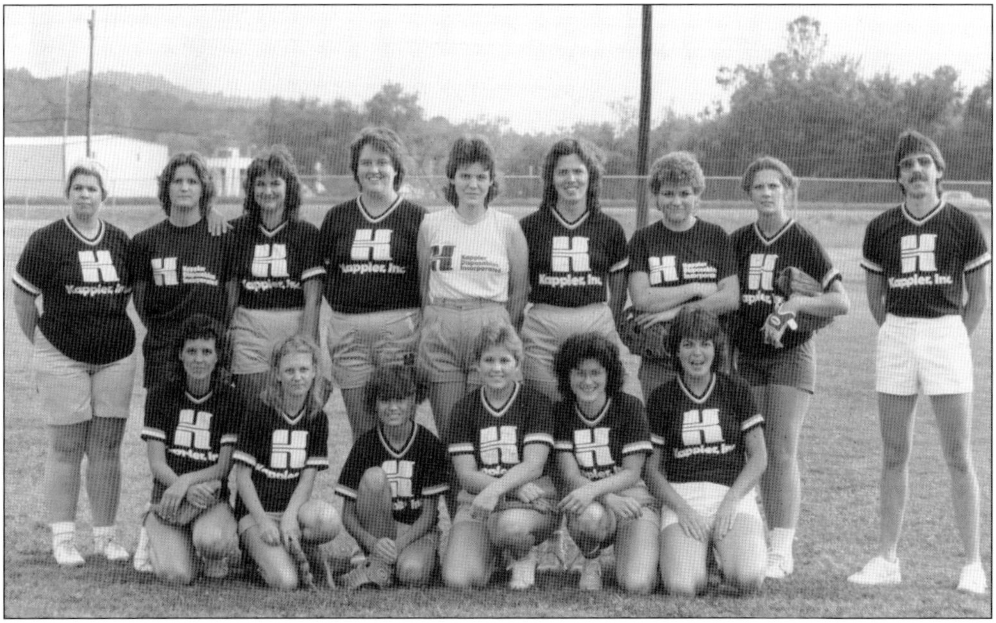

This is the 1985 Kappler women's softball team. Pictured are, from left to right, (first row) Janice Watkins, Nancy Gross, Annette Hubbard, Tina Bowen, Keli Maddox, and Patty O'Dell; (second row) Ruth Sharp, Cindi Steele, Phillis Gaunt, Kathy Duke, Kathy Davidson, Diane West, Kerrie Scott, Connie Stewart, and coach David Maddox. (George Kappler.)

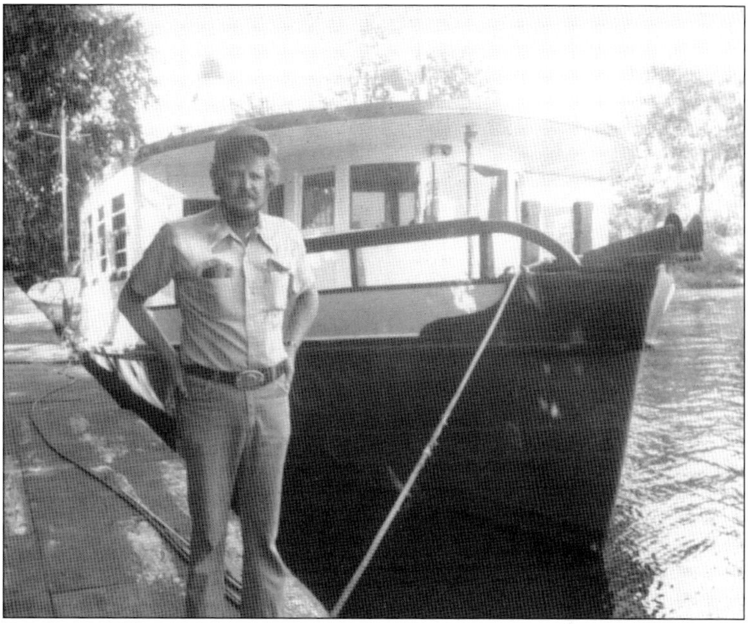

In 1981, near Buck Island, Grady Sauls (shown) bested two other stern-wheelers in an unofficial race of three miles with speeds of 8 to 10 miles per hour. Sauls's *Dixie Darling* won. Pete Grassie's *Princess Margy* came in second, and Gene Fitch's *Claire-E* claimed third. Monitoring the race and its spectators were water patrol officers John Clifton and Tennie McClendon. (*Advertiser-Gleam*.)

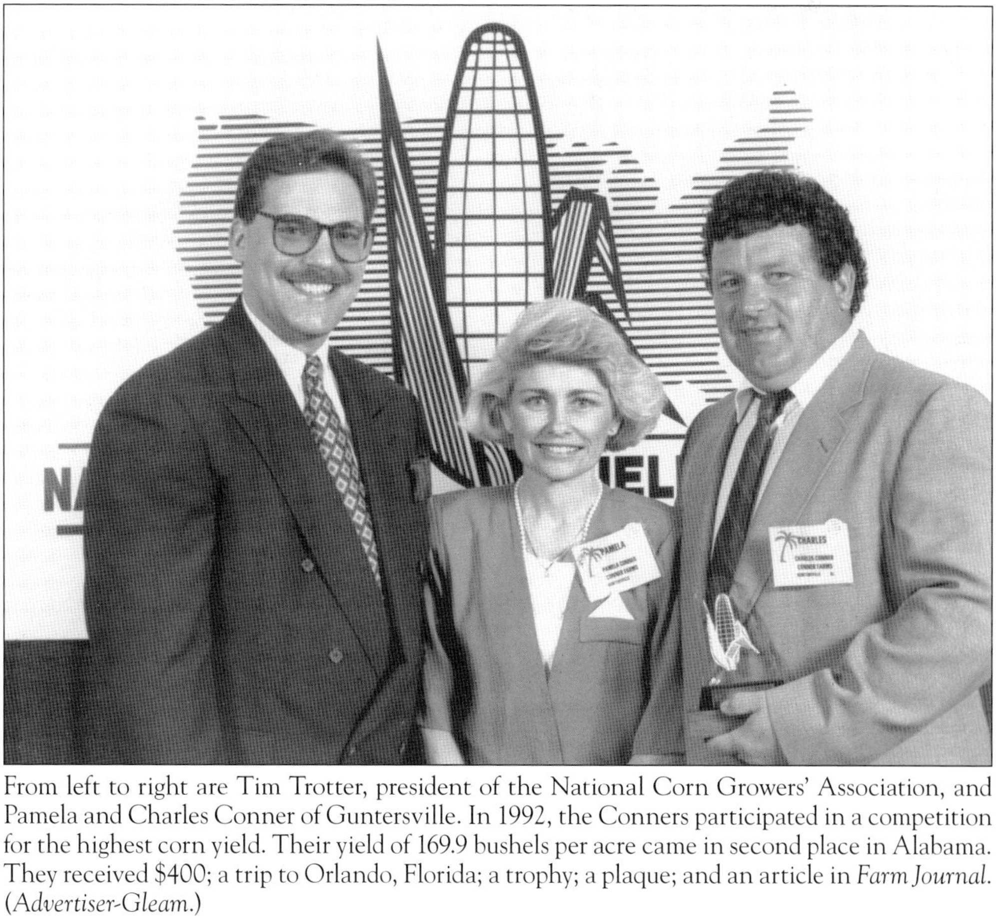

From left to right are Tim Trotter, president of the National Corn Growers' Association, and Pamela and Charles Conner of Guntersville. In 1992, the Conners participated in a competition for the highest corn yield. Their yield of 169.9 bushels per acre came in second place in Alabama. They received $400; a trip to Orlando, Florida; a trophy; a plaque; and an article in *Farm Journal*. (*Advertiser-Gleam*.)

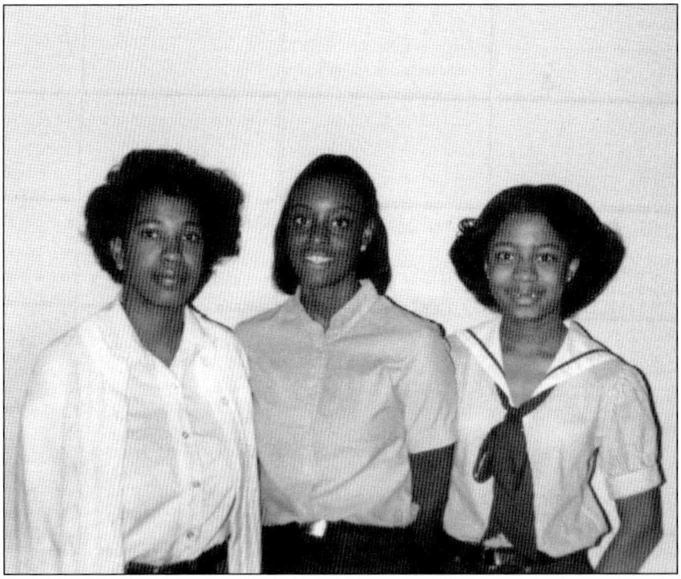

Shown around 1982 are, from left to right, Rita Stewart, Leslie Wherry, and Jacqueline Chandler, office aides at Carlisle Park School. Garnering academic success, these students were listed on the honor rolls. Opened in 1959, the middle school operated for approximately 50 years before being replaced by Guntersville Middle School. Principals included Percy Lee, Curtis Williams Jr., Lawayne Vanzandt, Bobby Irwin, Keith Swisher, and Dale Edwards. (Betty Taylor.)

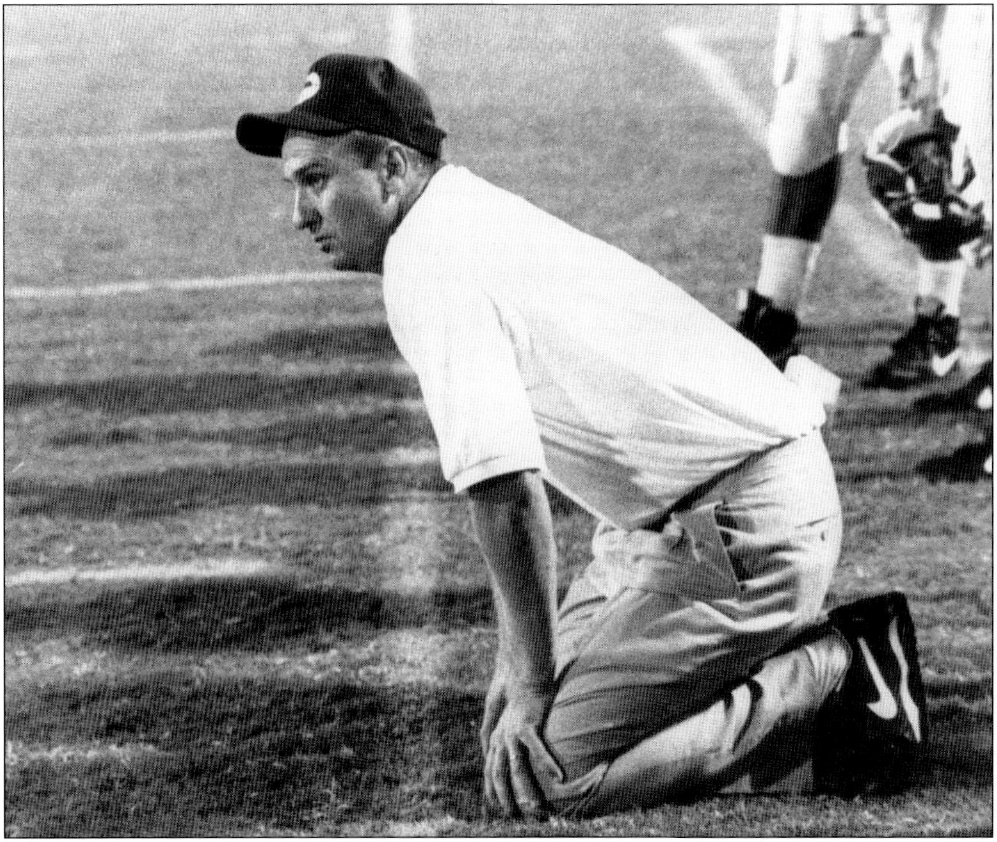

The head football coach at Guntersville High School from 1999 to 2011, Phil Isom (shown) amassed a record of 90 wins versus 38 losses. He led the Wildcats to the 4A State Championship in 2006 and was inducted into the Marshall County Sports Hall of Fame in 2010. To honor his amazing record, the field at Chorba-Lee Stadium was named Phil Isom Field. (*Advertiser-Gleam.*)

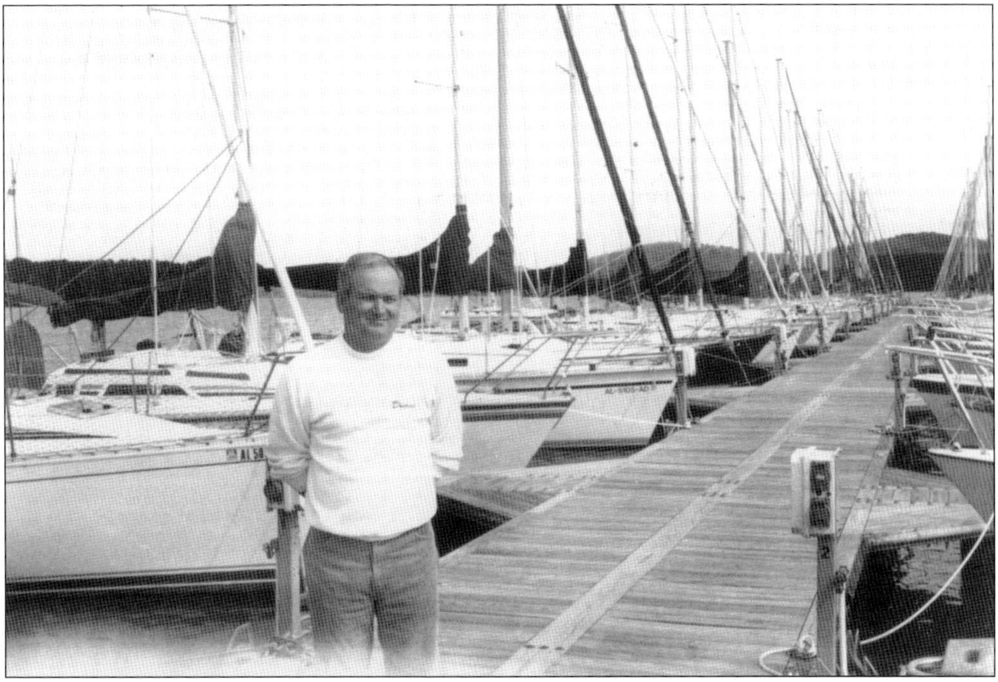

Duane Sammons operated sailboat marinas at Claysville and Warrenton from 1987 to 2007. This image shows Sammons standing on floating docks he designed and built at his Anchorage Sailboat Marina in 1995. To encourage families' participation, he promoted sailing weekends. Sammons fostered environmentally conscientious boaters with pump-out stations and received the TVA's Alabama Clean Marina award. He also worked to control aquatic weeds on Lake Guntersville. (*Advertiser-Gleam.*)

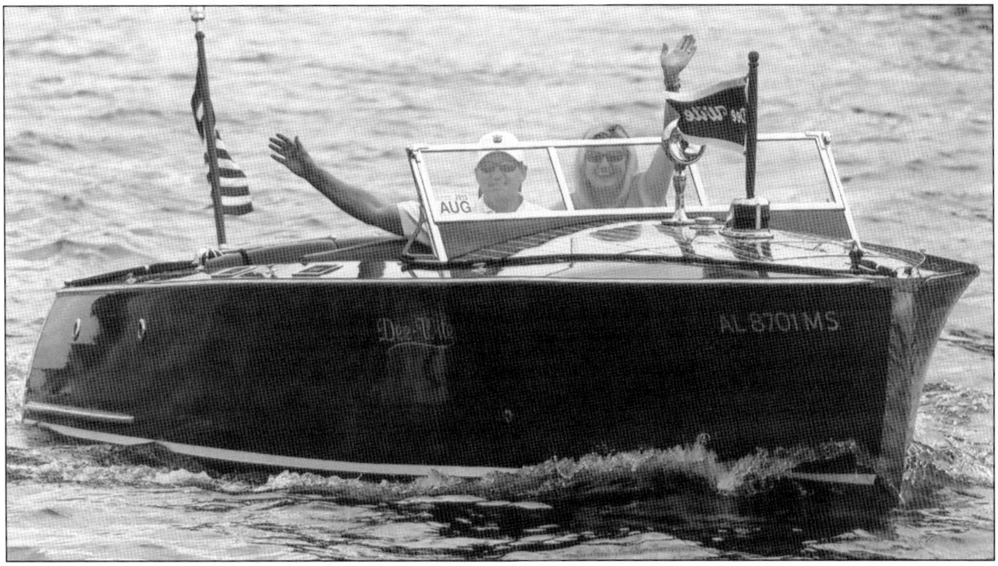

In 2015, Dianna Ratliff (right) competed in the Antique and Classic Boat Show sponsored by the Guntersville Yacht Club. The *Au Revoir* (shown), a 1931 Dee-White restored runabout, garnered Best in Show against 24 other participants. Ratliff is actively involved in the Mountain Valley Arts Council. Michael Kirkpatrick is in the passenger seat. (Bryan Leazenby.)

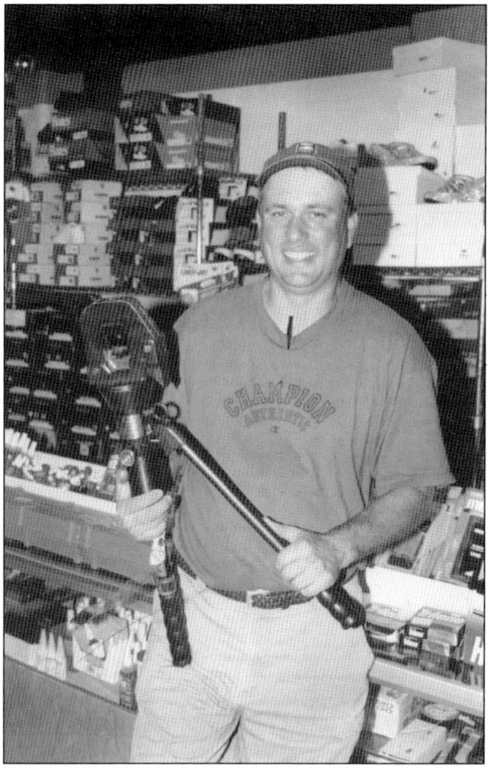

Mike Jones (shown) and his father, Ray, transitioned from the machining business to buying goods at auction and reselling them. Their company, Mike's Merchandise, became a successful franchise. Mike was named Retailer of the Year in 2007 by the Alabama Retail Association for sales in the $1 to $5 million category. His store is a shopper's delight, with everything from household goods and clothes to nuts and bolts. (Mike Jones.)

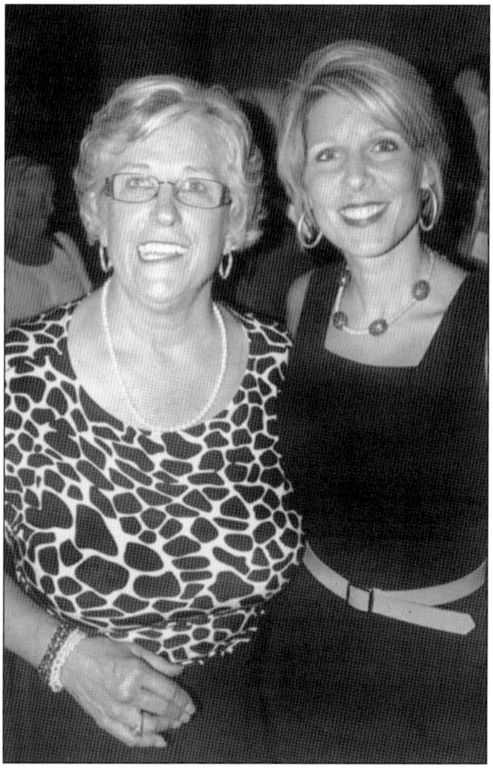

Charlotte Webb (left) is shown with Guntersville mayor Leigh Dollar. Webb and Kathryn Baucom are a mother-daughter duo who own Crawmama's in Guntersville. Originally opened in 1987 as Crawdaddy's Seafood Shoppe, the "bayou style" restaurant has a wide selection on the menu. The delicious fare, coupled with live entertainment, makes Crawmama's the place to be on Thursdays, Fridays, and Saturdays—"depending on SEC football," according to the restaurant's website. (Kathryn Baucom.)

Kenny Moore (shown), son of Matthew and Kathleen Havis Moore, was employed by Guntersville City Schools for 25 years as a custodian at Carlisle Park School and, later, Guntersville High School. Known for his gregarious personality, Moore never met a stranger. With his vast network of associates, he is often greeted with waves and handshakes. (Betty Taylor.)

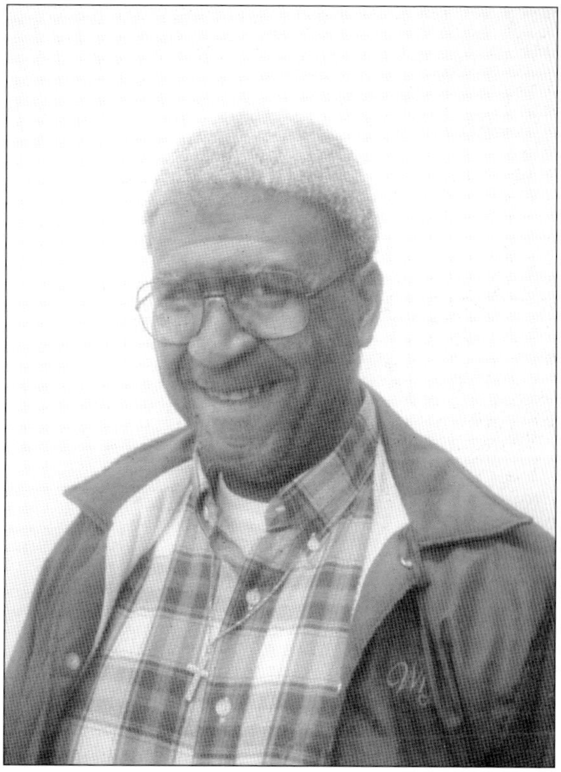

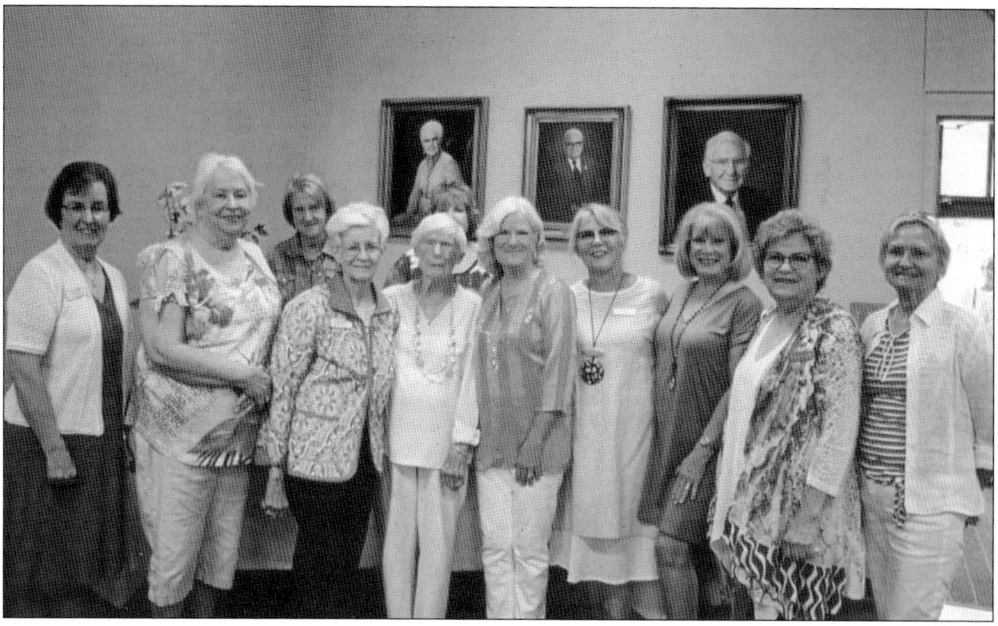

Retired librarian Dot Kennedy (center) was feted with a coffee gathering by the Friends of the Library; it also served as a book signing for her novel *The Playground*. Pictured are, from left to right, (first row) Nancy Wilson, Joyce Kirkpatrick, Jeannie Wallace, Kennedy, Valerie Pailloz, Deborah Belcher, Debbie Newman, Allison Simpson, and Becky Rowe; (second row) Joy Langford and Karen Kimmel. (*Advertiser-Gleam*.)

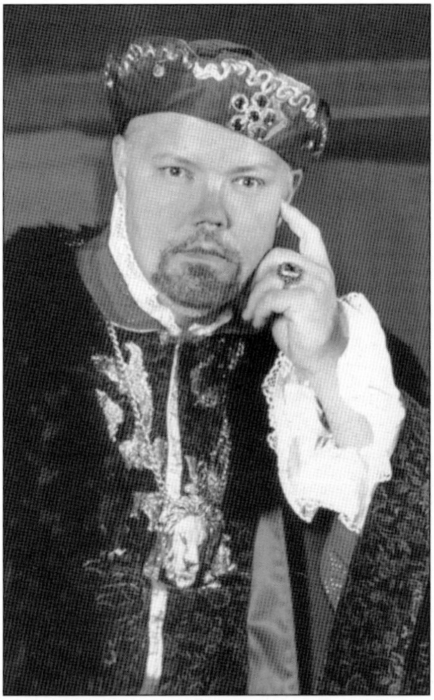

The son of Will and Willie Ruth Brewer, Johnny Brewer (shown) grew up in Guntersville, graduated from Guntersville High School, earned a bachelor's degree at Jacksonville State University, and completed a master's degree at the University of Montevallo. A former band director, he now teaches speech at Snead State Community College. He is an integral part of the Whole Backstage Theatre. (Johnny Brewer.)

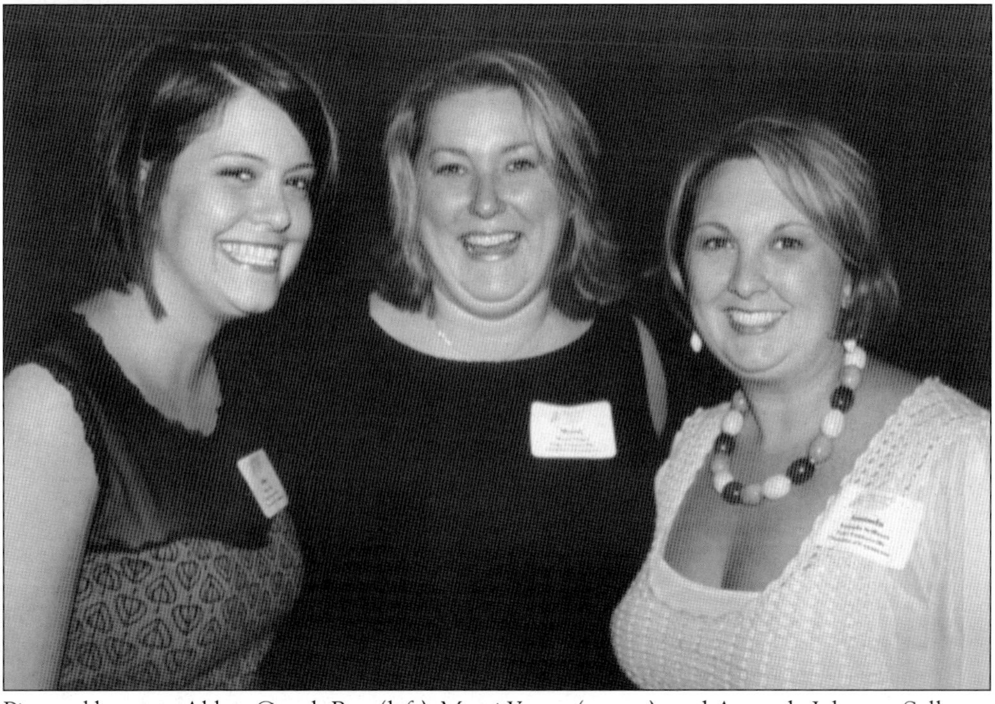

Pictured here are Abbey Couch Ray (left), Morri Yancy (center), and Amanda Johnson Sellnow. Yancy and Sellnow represent the Lake Guntersville Chamber of Commerce as president and director of membership/events, respectively. Comprised of 600 members, the chamber supports events like the Christmas parade, historical walking tours, and hydroplane races. Morri is the daughter of Bill and Barbara Yancy. (Morri Yancy.)

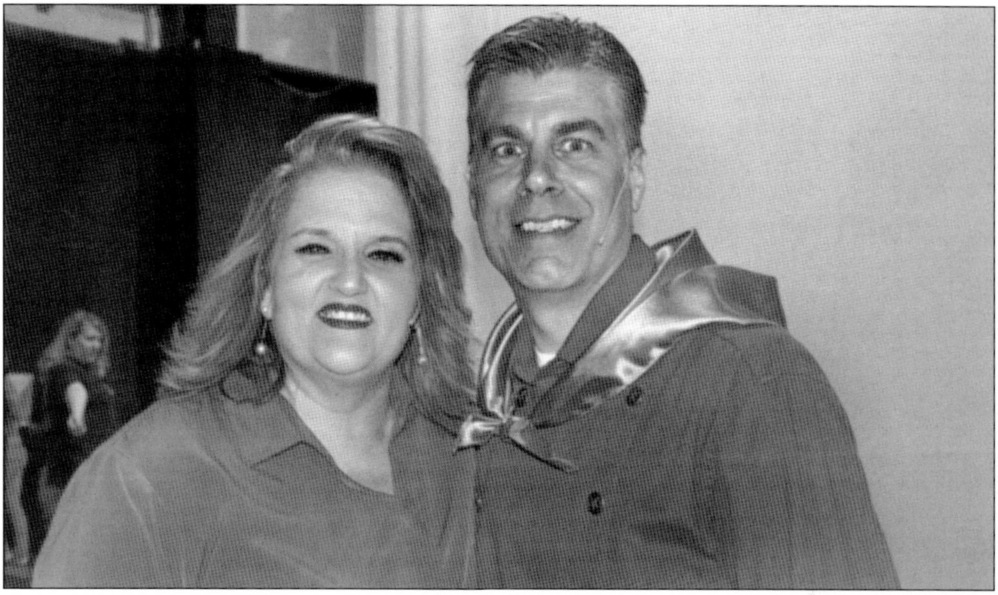

Pictured are Tracy and Steve Downs, who performed as Betty and Will Rogers in the 2019 production of *The Will Rogers Follies* at the Whole Backstage Theatre. Jane Kohl directed and choreographed a large cast. Partnerships for the play included Sonny Lewis and Randy Jones & Associates. Lewis refurbished all the headdresses. During the play, Bruce Brannen performed rope tricks. (Johnny Brewer.)

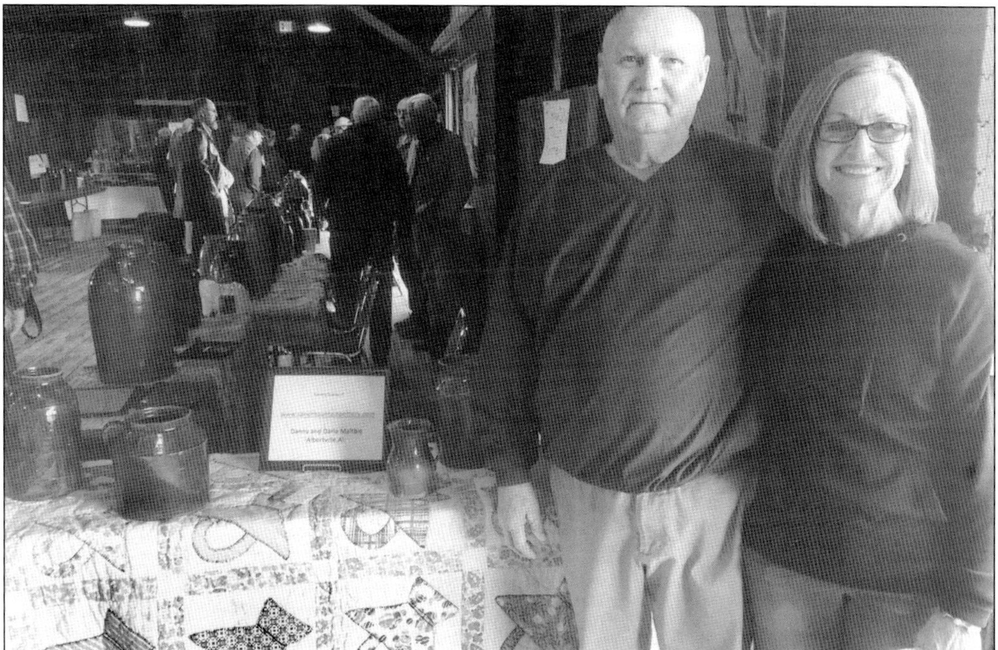

Danny Maltbie is shown with his wife, Darla, at the Albertville Pottery Show. A history buff, Danny studies, collects, trades, and writes about Alabama folk pottery. He has assisted in the filming of pottery documentaries for public television. He is also a volunteer at the Marshall County Archives and serves on the board of the Albertville Museum. (Authors' collection.)

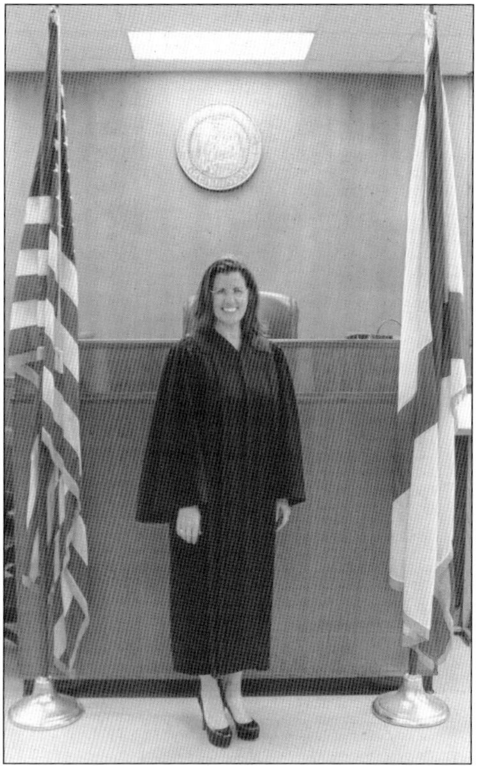

Andrea LeCroy was elected probate judge of Marshall County in 2018. LeCroy is the first woman to hold that position in the county's history. She worked as chief probate clerk for former judge Tim Mitchell. She promotes the Marshall County Guardianship Program to assist "precious people"—elderly or infirm citizens who need help in making decisions. She has been married to Michael LeCroy for almost 30 years. (Authors' collection.)

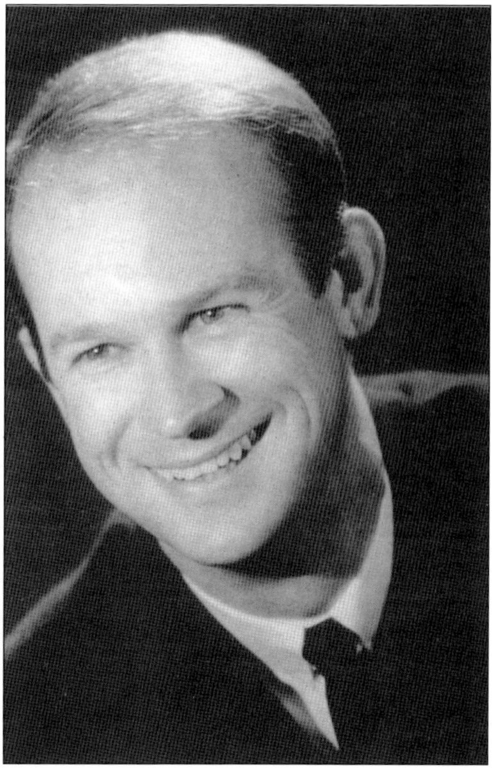

Guntersville native William E. "Sonny" Lewis earned a degree from Auburn University, had a career in fashion design in Los Angeles, and taught at the University of California, Irvine. After retiring, he returned to Guntersville, where he became the benefactor of the museum, historical society, and Whole Backstage Theatre. He spearheaded the development of Errol Allan Park and contributed to the preservation of the Gilbreath House. (Sonny Lewis.)

This postcard is an advertisement for Cathedral Caverns. Developer Jay Gurley called the cave "the greatest show in earth" with the largest entrance. Since it opened in 2000, Cathedral Caverns State Park has hosted thousands of visitors. *Secrets of the Phantom Caverns* (1984) and *Tom and Huck* (1995) were partially filmed at Cathedral Caverns. (Authors' collection.)

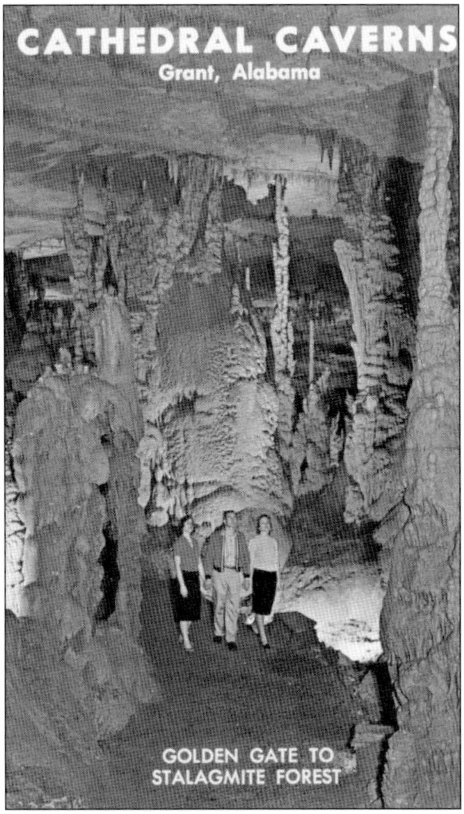

From left to right, Ada Shields, Clifford McGowin, Jay Gurley, and Forrest Shields are shown sitting outside the Lake Shore Motel around 1957. McGowin owned the motel, Gurley owned/operated Cathedral Caverns, and Forrest Shields worked as a contractor at the Woodward & Shields Contracting Company. Forrest Shields had previously managed the Guntersville Grain Company (formerly the Guntersville Ginning Company). (Marshall County Archives.)

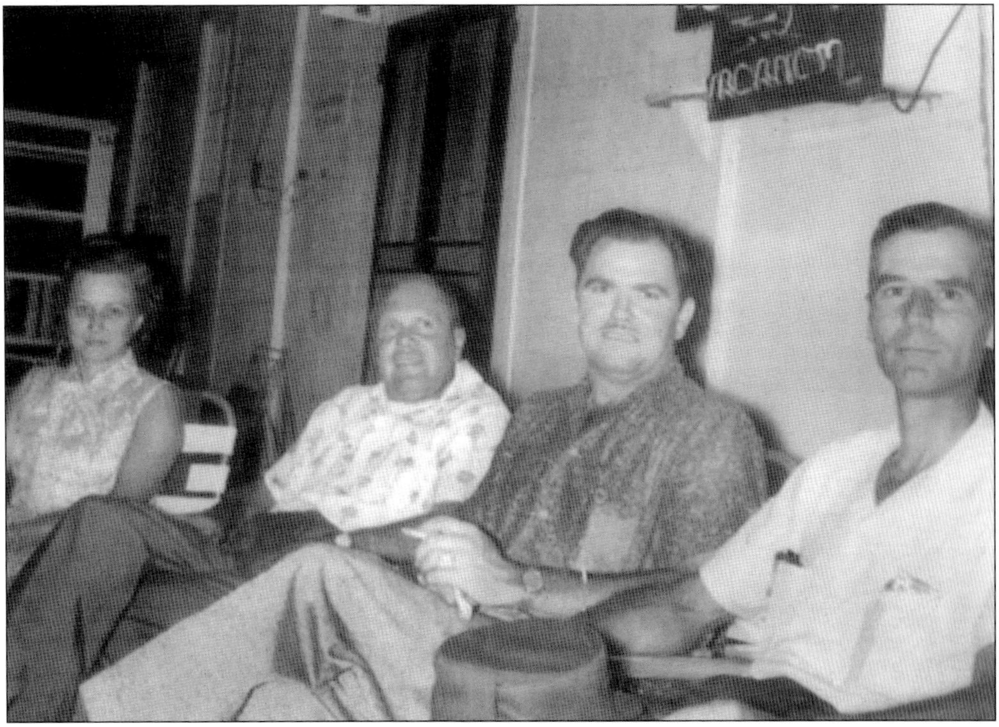

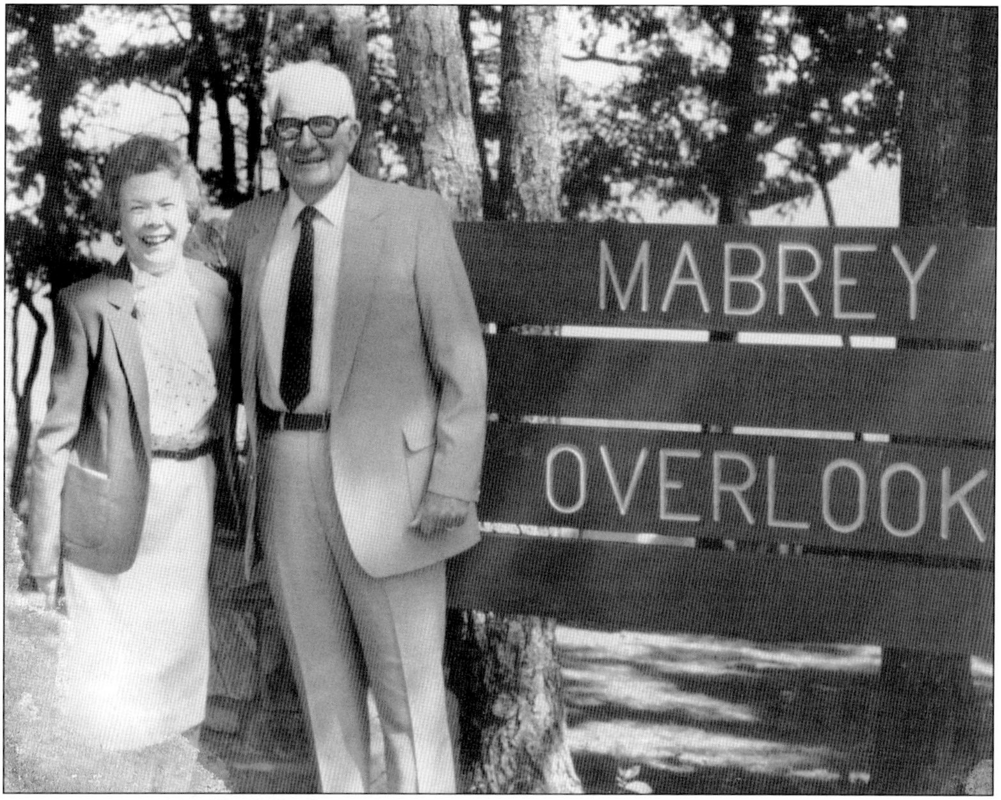

Velpo and Sue Mabrey are shown posing in front of the Mabrey Overlook at Lake Guntersville State Park in 1985. For the dedication, officials untied a knot in the ribbon's middle to keep with the park's policy against cutting trees. Before becoming manager of the park, a position he held from 1970 to 1983, Velpo managed Val Monte Shores resort. (Lake Guntersville State Park.)

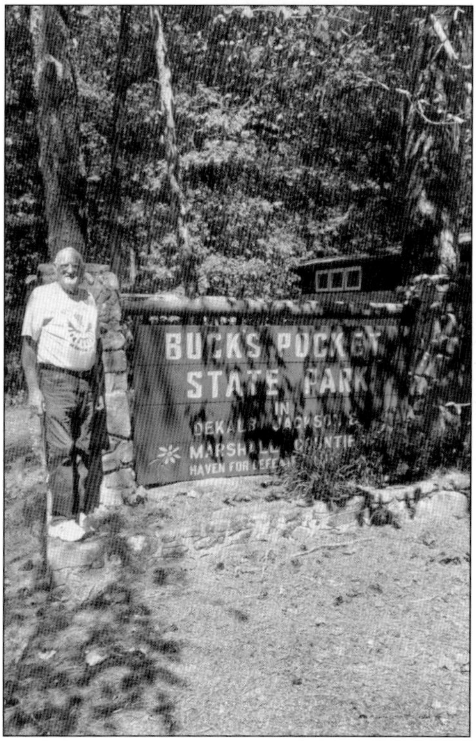

Max Snow, who served in the National Guard and retired from the Alabama Highway Department, is shown posing with the sign at Buck's Pocket State Park. Offering a stunning glimpse of nature, the mountainous retreat provides tranquility and relaxation for day-trippers. Walking trails are located near South Salty Creek at the junction of Dekalb, Jackson, and Marshall Counties. Historically, Buck's Pocket afforded a sanctuary for rejected politicians. (Max Snow.)

Three

Politicians, Celebrities, and Notables

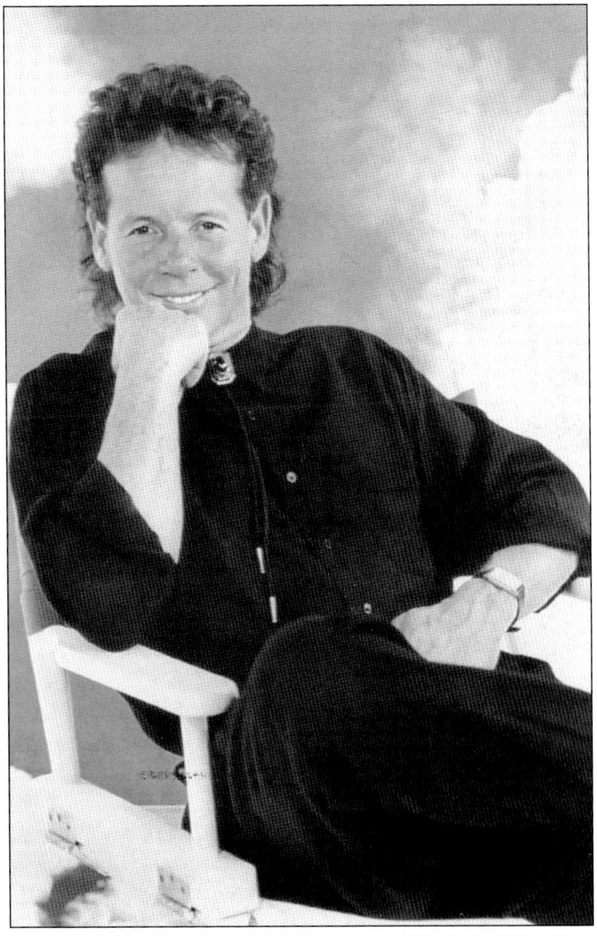

Pictured is singer, musician, and songwriter Pat Upton (1940–2016). With his band Spiral Starecase, he signed with Columbia Records and went to number 12 on the *Billboard* charts in 1969 with "More Today Than Yesterday." The band played concerts with Three Dog Night, Sly and the Family Stone, the Beach Boys, and Creedence Clearwater Revival. After the band separated in 1971, Upton worked as a session musician in Los Angeles and performed as a solo artist. After he was invited to a recording gig with Ricky Nelson, Upton ended up performing with Nelson's band for four years. In 1983, Upton moved to Guntersville and used his business acumen to open the club PJ's Alley. (Jennifer Bearden.)

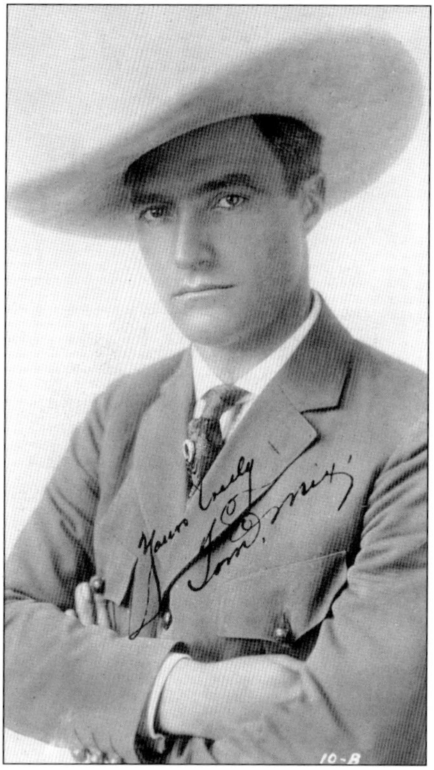

Tom Mix, shown on this postcard, was the first Western film star. On October 1, 1933, Tom Mix's Road Show passed through Guntersville on its way to Anniston. The company included three trucks and a touring car that carried Mix; his wife, Mabel Ward; and their daughter Ruth. One truck carried Tony, Mix's favorite horse. (Authors' collection.)

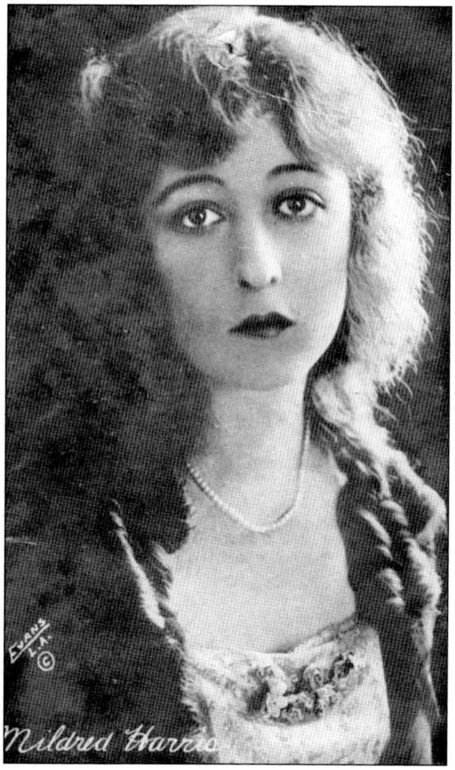

This vintage arcade card features film actress Mildred Harris. In August 1939, she came to Guntersville with the Heffner-Vinson Tent Theater. The first wife of Charlie Chaplin, Harris had been a vaudeville star before segueing into Hollywood. Catapulted to fame, she appeared in 130 movies. In 1960, she received a star on the Hollywood Walk of Fame. (Authors' collection.)

Pictured on this postcard is film star Tim McCoy, who, as part of Tommy Scott's International Folk Singers and Hollywood Hillbilly Stage Show, performed at the Guntersville Town Hall on April 5, 1966. After an impressive career in silent films, McCoy transitioned to talkies before briefly touring with Ringling Bros. Circus. After serving in the military during World War II, he hosted *The Tim McCoy Show.* (Authors' collection.)

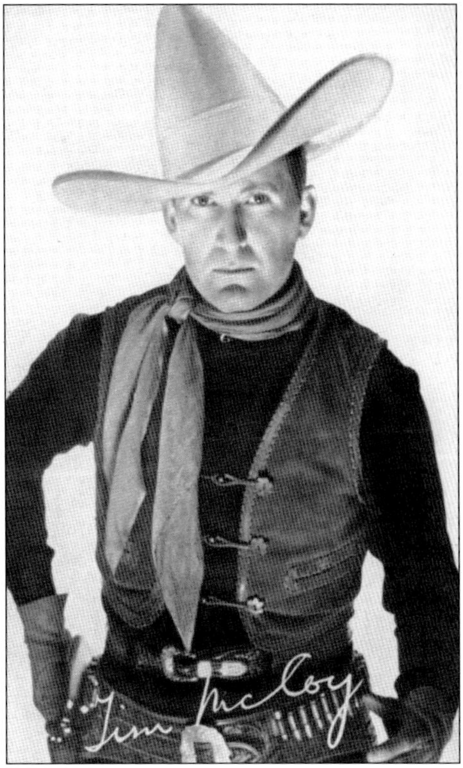

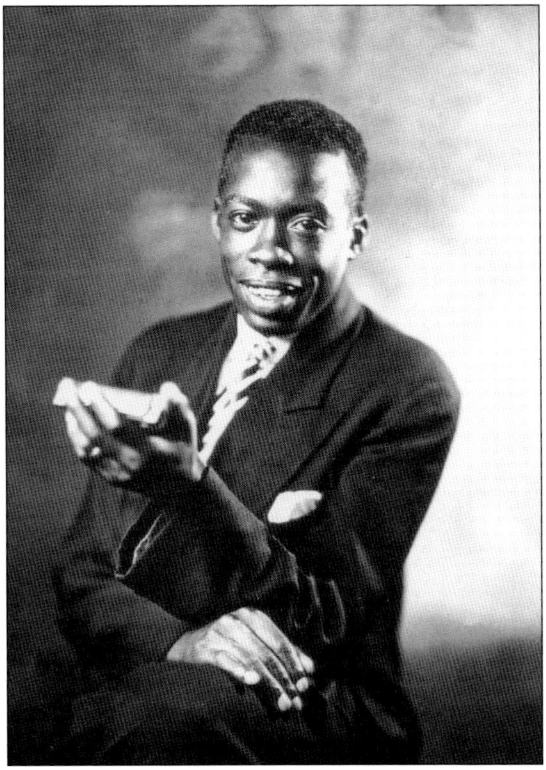

A skilled harmonicist, DeFord Bailey created innovative arrangements like "Fox Chase," performed on WSM's *National Barn Dance*, and became a Grand Ole Opry star. On July 30, 1939, Bailey appeared at Guntersville's Star Theatre with Uncle Dave Macon. Tickets cost 10¢ for children and 25¢ for adults. Bailey was the first Black person inducted into the Country Music Hall of Fame. (Country Music Hall of Fame and Museum.)

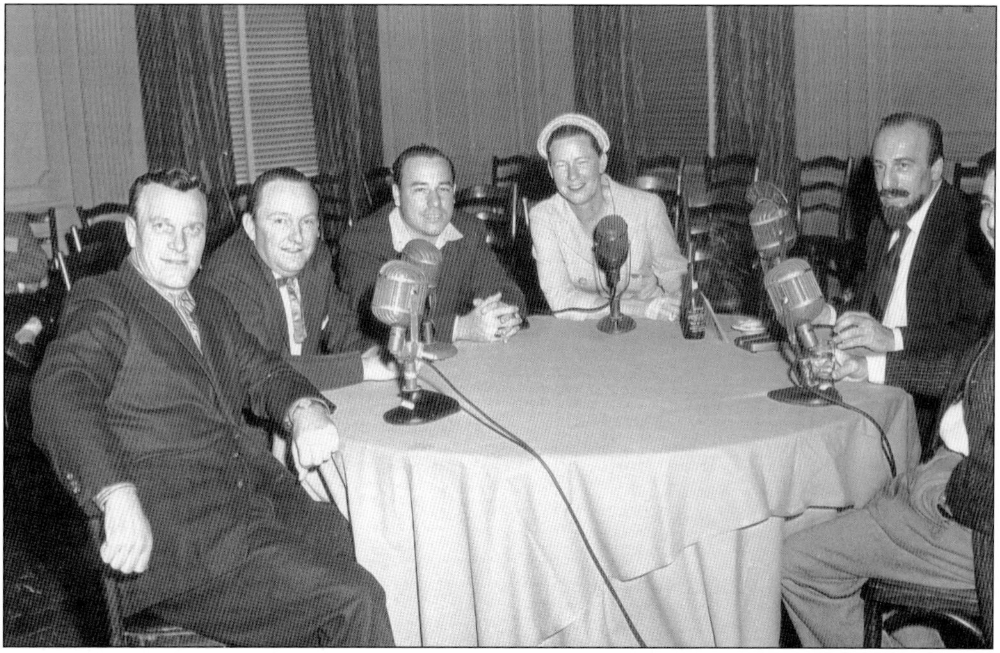

Shown are, from left to right, Eddy Arnold, Lester Flatt, Earl Scruggs, Minnie Pearl, Mitch Miller, and unidentified. Guntersville's 1971 Ladies' Prayer Luncheon had Sarah Ophelia Colley Cannon (Minnie Pearl) as the keynote speaker. In Guntersville, she received a key to the city and donated her gratuity to charity. Cannon's career began in 1936 with a plan to "always keep it kind" during comic routines. (Country Music Hall of Fame and Museum.)

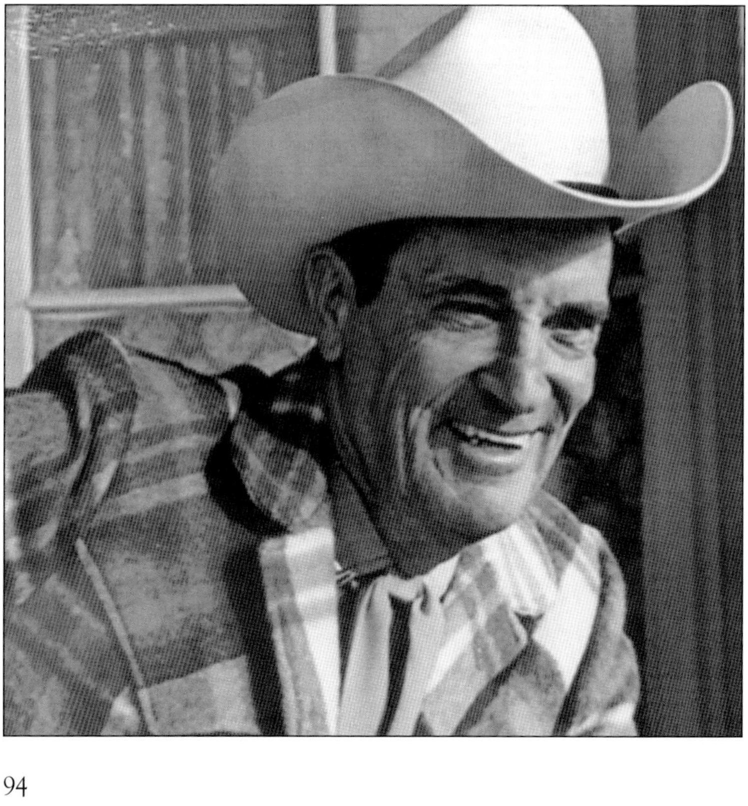

Country singer Ernest Tubb smiles on this vintage postcard. On September 18, 1944, he performed in Guntersville at the City Boat Dock Park. Part of WSM's *Grand Ole Opry* tent show, he was billed alongside Paul Howard and his Arkansas Cotton Pickers, the Poe Sisters, and comedian Rod Brasfield. For admission, adults paid 75¢, while children paid 50¢. (Authors' collection.)

Comic and musician Stringbean (left) and musician/actor Roy Acuff (right) performed at the opening of the Ralston Purina Feed Mill in 1957. Acuff first visited Guntersville on December 30, 1938, two years after appearing on WSM's *Grand Ole Opry.* Singing "Wabash Cannonball," he and his Smoky Mountain Boys wowed audiences. Acuff became the "king" of his genre and was inducted into the Country Music Hall of Fame. (Marshall County Archives.)

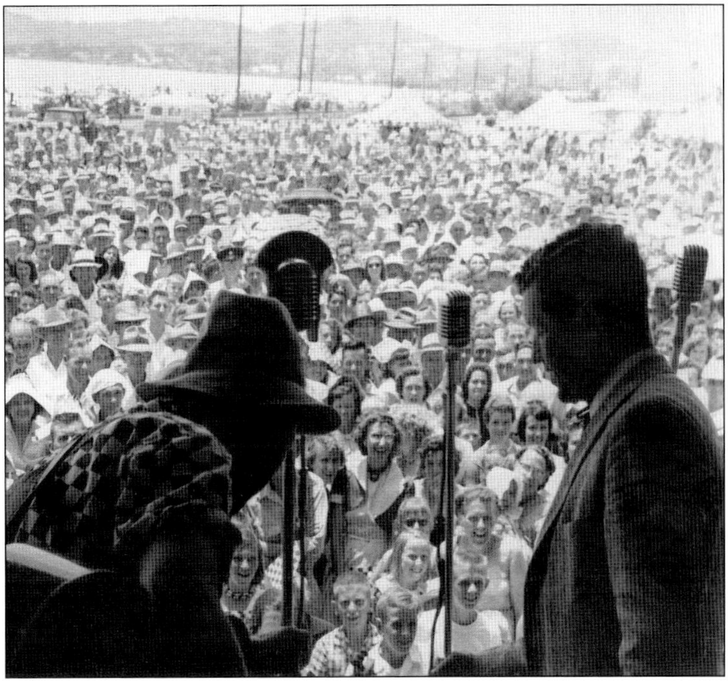

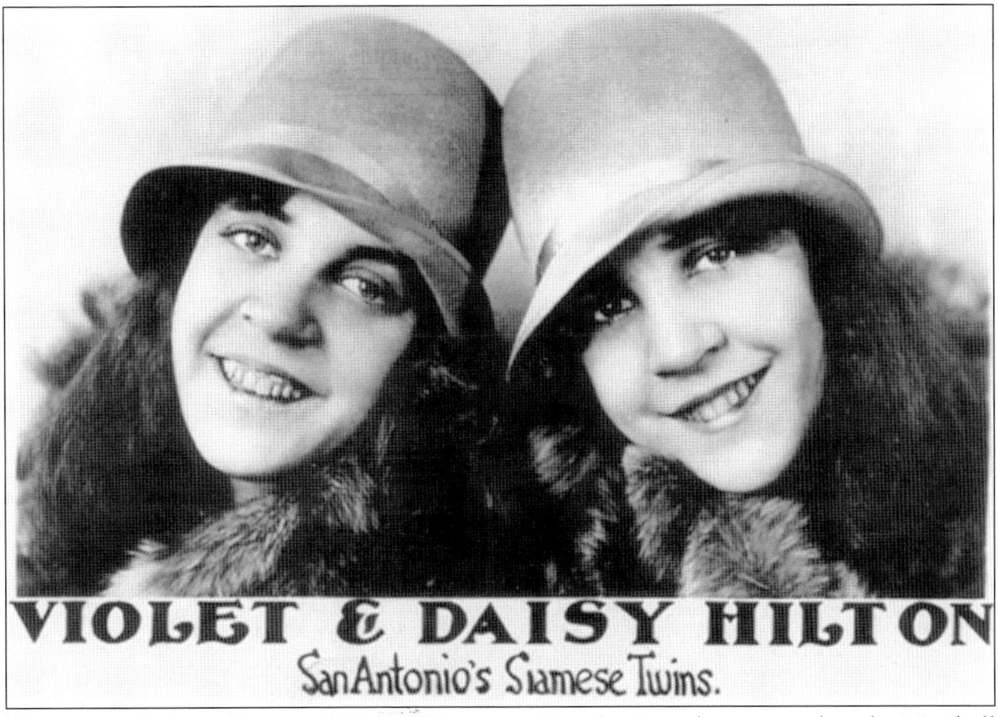

This postcard shows Daisy and Violet Hilton, conjoined twins who appeared at the Marshall Drive-In on November 2 and 3, 1953. The drive-in featured the sisters' movie *Chained for Life* (1952). Local historian Larry Smith remembers the sisters performing on top of the concession stand. Their banter enlivened the mood caused by the film's plot about the possible imprisonment of "Siamese twins" should one of them commit murder. (Authors' collection.)

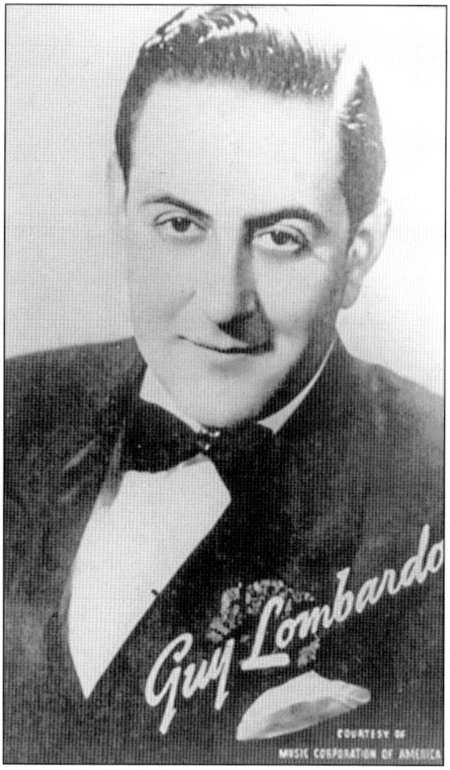

Orchestra leader Guy Lombardo is pictured on this postcard. On June 8, 1955, while on *Arthur Godfrey and His Friends*, Lombardo described Guntersville as "the nation's greatest boat attraction for 1955." In response to his 1958 agreement to perform each season at Val Monte Shores, the resort's boat harbor was named Guy Lombardo Basin. Lombardo came to Guntersville when his boat, *Tempo*, participated in the 1963 boat races. (Authors' collection.)

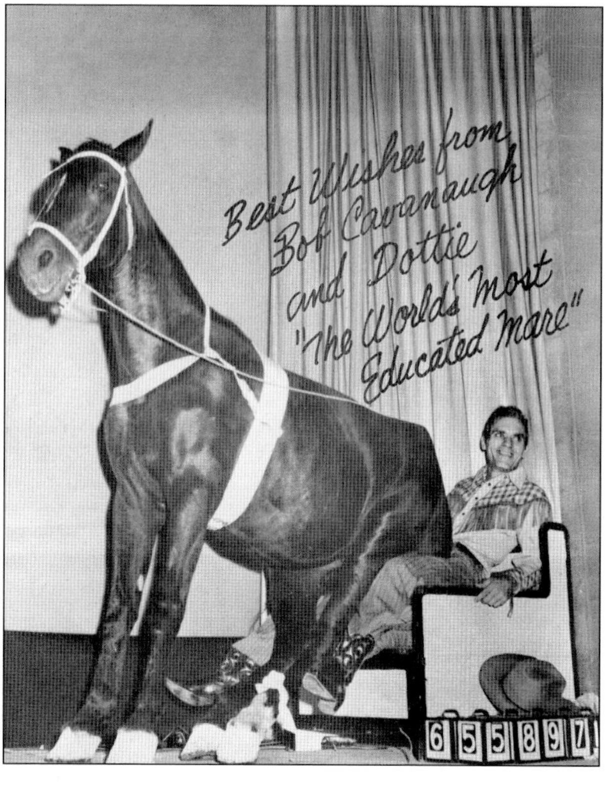

The Marshall Drive-In hosted Dottie, "the world's most educated mare," and her owner Bob Cavanaugh on April 17 and 18, 1957. The promotional material bragged that Dottie knew 600 tricks, while Cavanaugh was billed as a stunt double and radio performer. Their signature trick involved Dottie sitting in Cavanaugh's lap. Cavanaugh reported that Dottie had been awarded nine college degrees. (Authors' collection.)

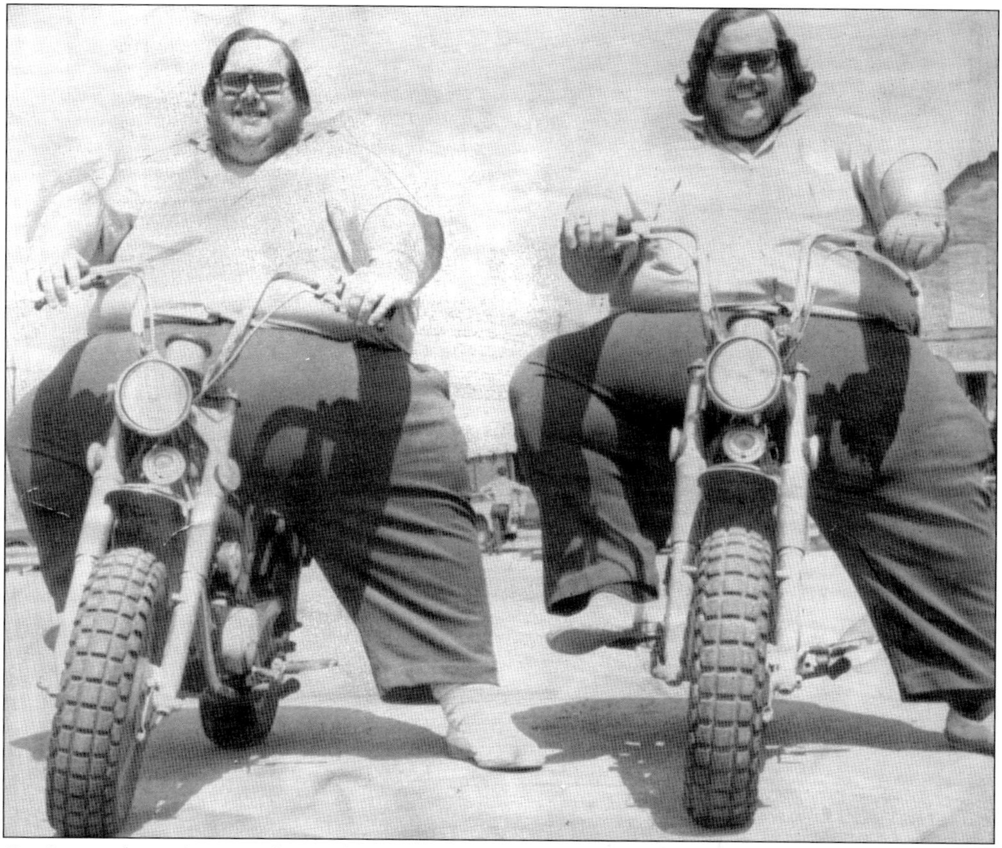

On September 15, 1973, identical twins Benny and Billy McGuire (shown above) wrestled the Blue Demons at the Guntersville Town Hall. Tickets were $2.50, ringside; $2, general admission; and $1 for children under 10. In 1978, the brothers, weighing a combined 1,466 pounds, were declared the "Heaviest Twins" in the *Guinness Book of World Records*. In the picture at right, Cora Combs (right) is shown posing with her daughter Debbie Combs. Appearing in Guntersville on the same night as the McGuire twins, Cora (1923–2015) wrestled Sylvia Hackney. Cora and Debbie often performed as a mother/daughter tag team. Cora continued wrestling until the age of 70, and in 2007, she was inducted into the Professional Wrestling Hall of Fame. (Both, Professional Wrestling Hall of Fame.)

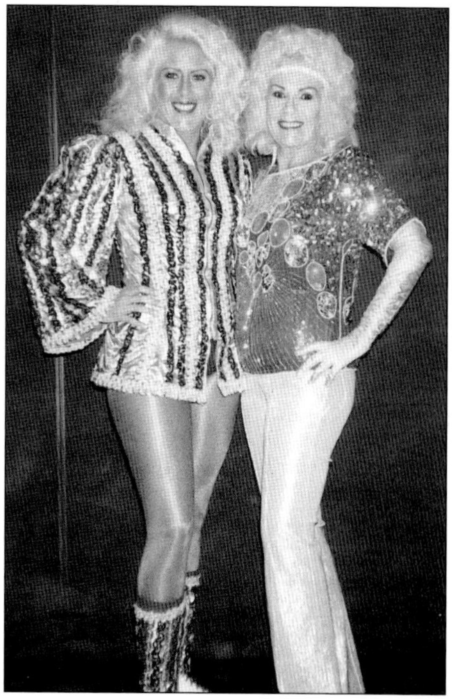

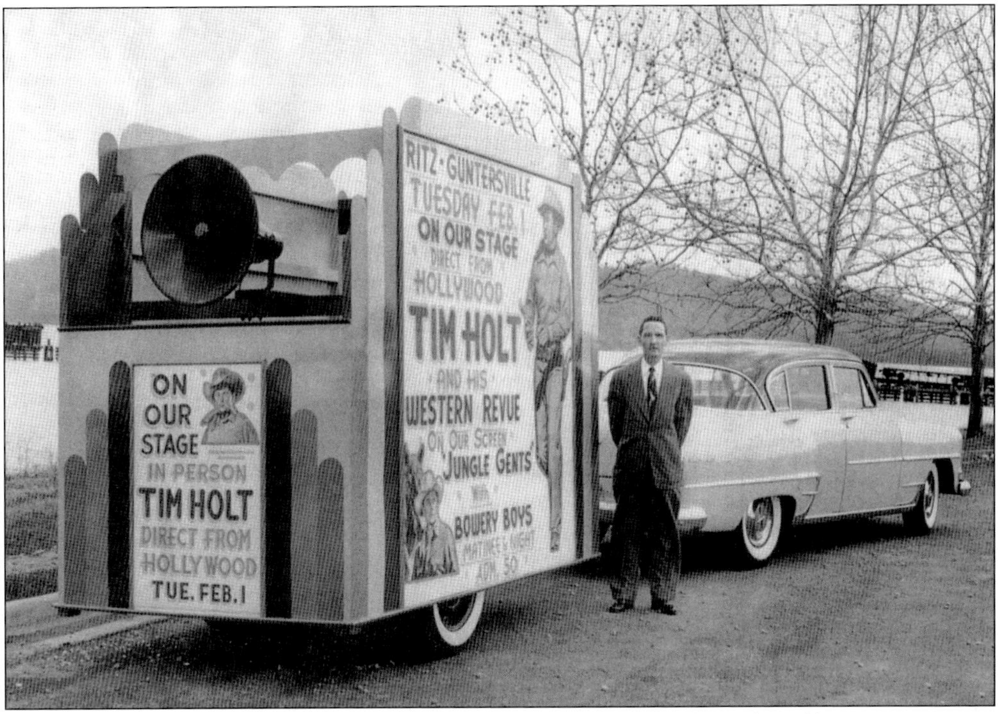

Bill Harris is shown advertising an upcoming appearance by Tim Holt. Holt and his Western revue appeared at Guntersville's Ritz Theatre on February 1, 1955. Known for his horsemanship, Holt appeared in films like *My Darling Clementine* and *The Treasure of the Sierra Madre*. For his service in the Army Air Corps during World War II, he and his crew were awarded the Distinguished Flying Cross. (Nancy Gilbreath Graham.)

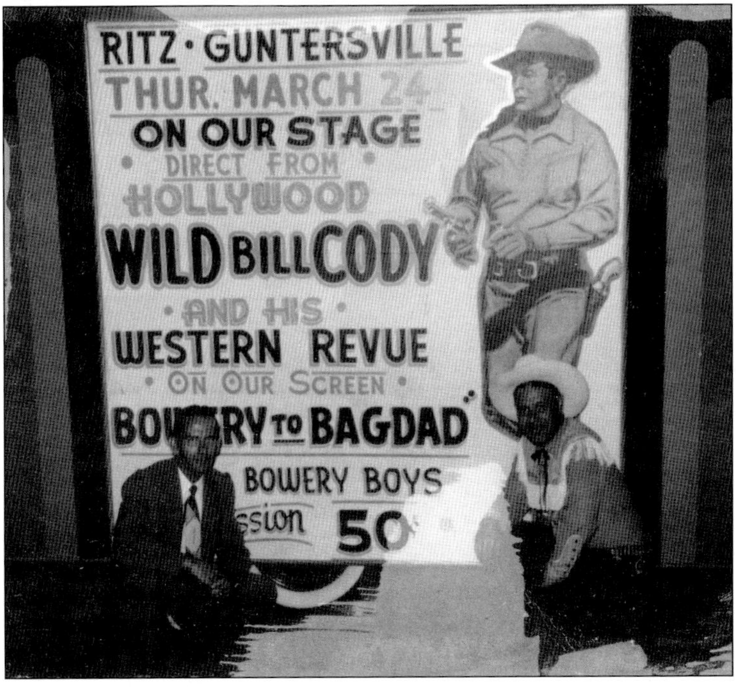

Bill Harris (left) is shown with Wild Bill Cody. On March 24, 1955, Cody and his Western revue appeared at Guntersville's Ritz Theatre. Cody threw knives, while his wife, nicknamed the "Black Whip," wowed the audience with her bullwhip skills. Their daughter Mary Alice, "the world's youngest cow-girl," sang a variety of songs. The Ritz charged 50¢ for general admission. (Marshall County Archives.)

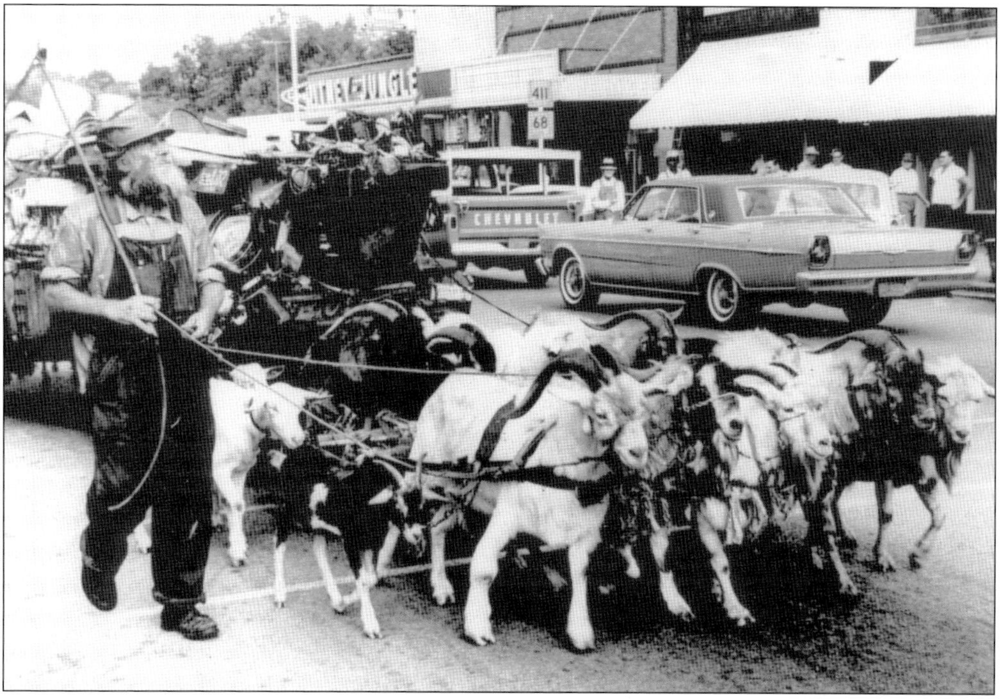

Charles McCartney, known as the "Goatman," trekked nationwide but frequently camped at Guntersville. During Goatman's 1957 visit, Sheriff L.P. Dickson had complaints about the odors at the campground near Jaycee Beach and from boaters whose picnic baskets had been consumed by McCartney's goats. Although he was asked to leave, McCartney often returned. During his 40 years of wandering, he is thought to have traveled an estimated 80,000 miles. (*Advertiser-Gleam.*)

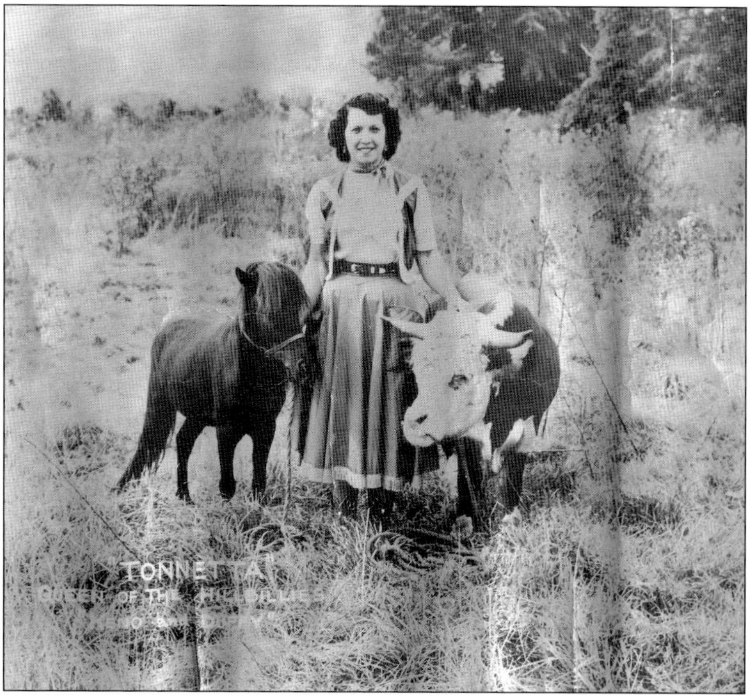

Shown is Tonnetta, "Queen of the Hillbillies," who sang and played the guitar in Chris Church's All-Star Western Rodeo. Advertisements promoted Duffy, a 15-year-old miniature bull; Keno, "last of a tribe of midget wild horses"; and two trick dogs, Queenie and Rags. This image is part of a collection that was owned by the late Bill Harris. (Nancy Gilbreath Graham.)

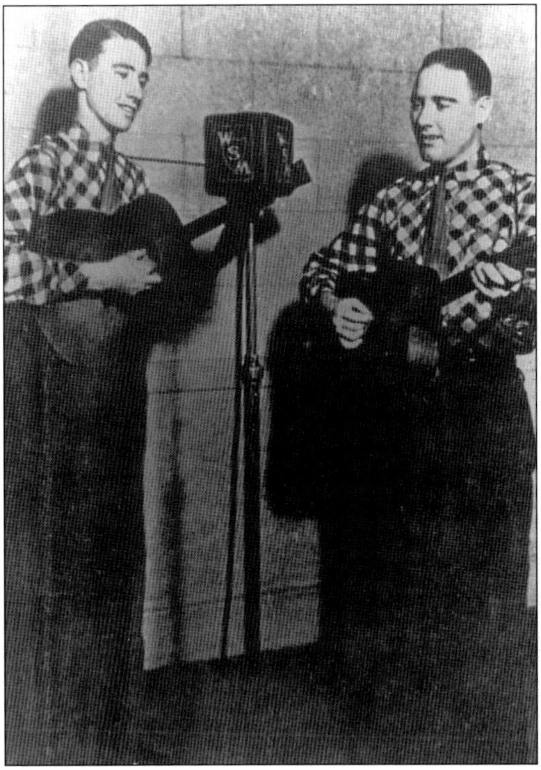

The Delmore Brothers, Rabon (left) and Alton (right), were folk singers, composers, and members of the Grand Ole Opry. Some of their popular songs were "Gonna Lay Down My Old Guitar," "Blue Railroad Train," and "Brown's Ferry Blues." In 2001, the brothers were inducted into the Country Music Hall of Fame. Their Marshall County relatives included the Douglas Gilley family and Lucille Rouse. (Alabama Music Hall of Fame.)

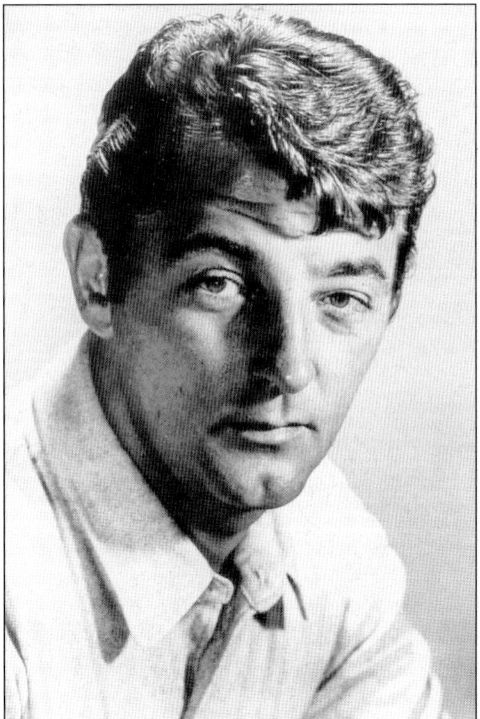

This postcard depicts Hollywood leading man Robert Mitchum (1917–1997). An avid fisherman, he enjoyed vacationing in Guntersville. He always stayed at the Lake Shore Motel, where owners Clifford and Virginia McGowin did their best to keep his presence a secret so as to protect his privacy. Few locals recognized Mitchum dressed in frumpy fishing clothes and a floppy hat. (Authors' collection.)

The son of John and Mary Perkins Starnes, Joe Starnes (left) served in both world wars, taught school, practiced law, and represented Alabama's Fifth Congressional District from 1935 to 1945. While in the House of Representatives, he served on the Dies Committee (also known as the House Un-American Activities Committee) and questioned Fritz Kuhn about the German American Bund. Capitol police had to intervene when Kuhn accused Starnes of lying about the organization's goals. (David Jones.)

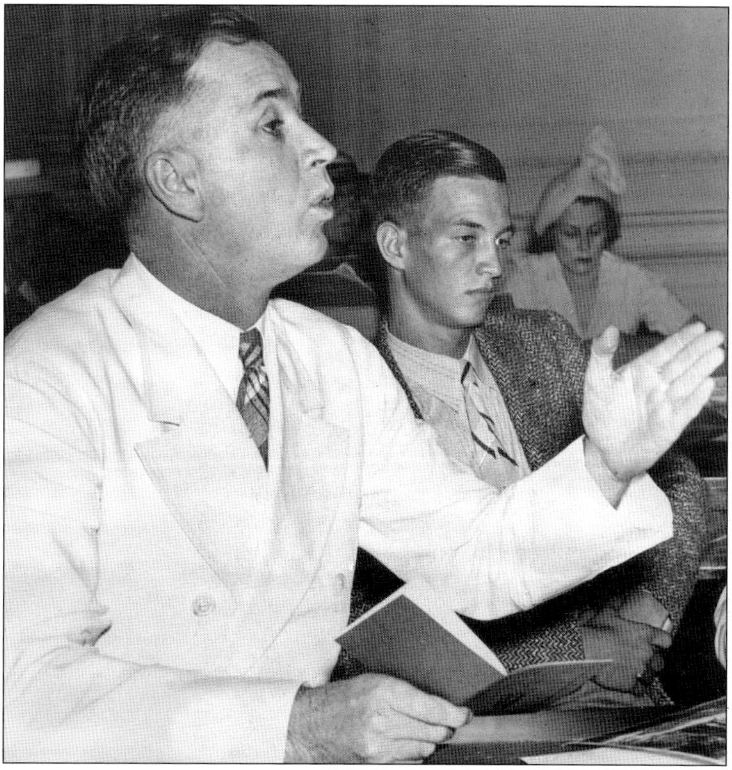

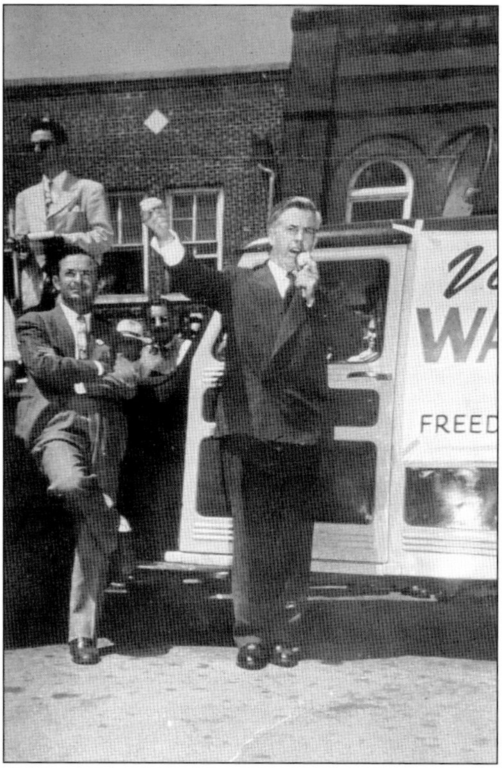

On September 1, 1948, former vice president Henry Wallace visited Guntersville. As the Progressive Party's candidate for president, he had been campaigning across north Alabama. Gathered outside the courthouse, many audience members heckled and shouted things like "Down with Wallace" and "Down with Communism." A few even threatened to pummel him with eggs. Wallace became the second presidential candidate to visit Guntersville; the first was William Jennings Bryan. (Marshall County Archives.)

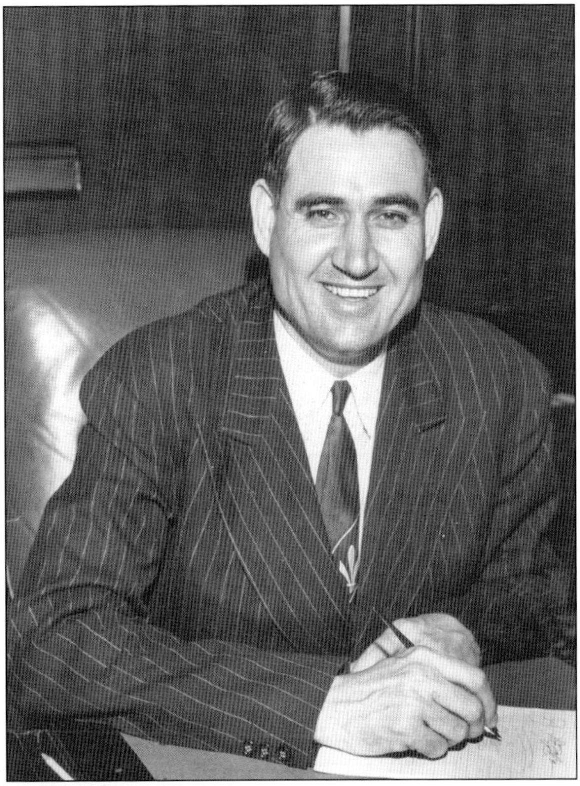

In 1933, James "Big Jim" Folsom (shown) took a job as Marshall County's director of the Civil Works Administration. During his tenure, the Guntersville Armory was constructed. Folsom became the county's Farm Security Administration supervisor. Even after returning to his hometown of Elba and later moving to Cullman, Folsom continued to visit Guntersville. He was elected governor of Alabama in 1947 and again in 1955. (Alabama Department of Archives and History.)

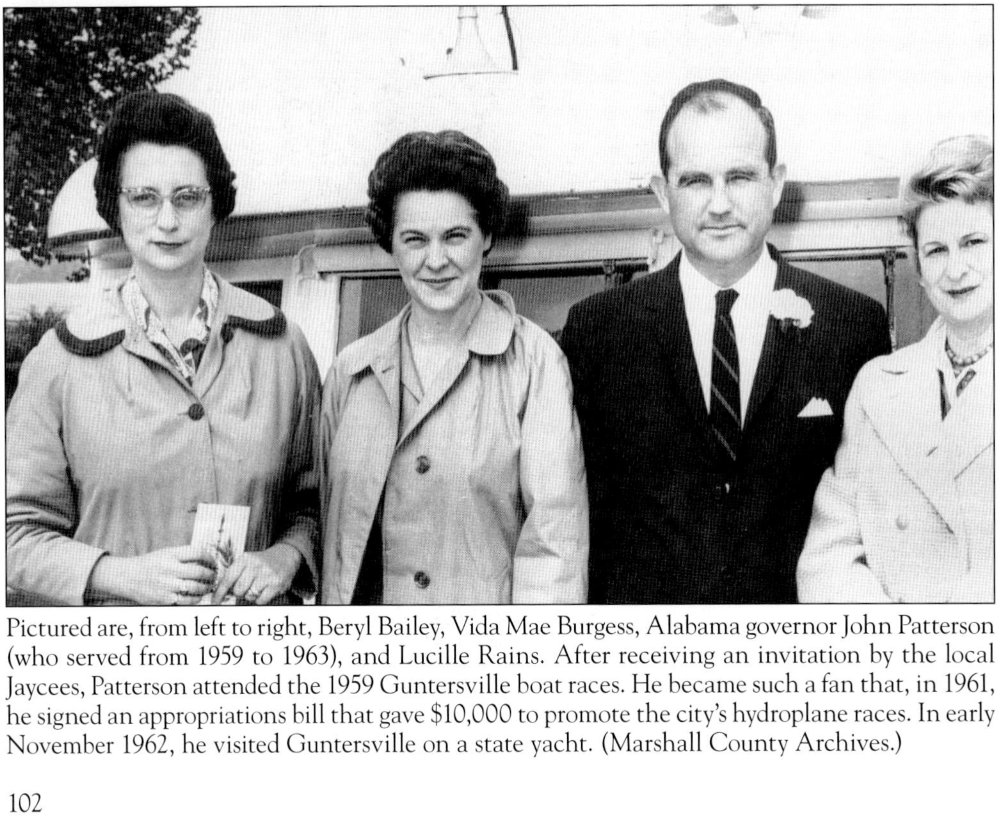

Pictured are, from left to right, Beryl Bailey, Vida Mae Burgess, Alabama governor John Patterson (who served from 1959 to 1963), and Lucille Rains. After receiving an invitation by the local Jaycees, Patterson attended the 1959 Guntersville boat races. He became such a fan that, in 1961, he signed an appropriations bill that gave $10,000 to promote the city's hydroplane races. In early November 1962, he visited Guntersville on a state yacht. (Marshall County Archives.)

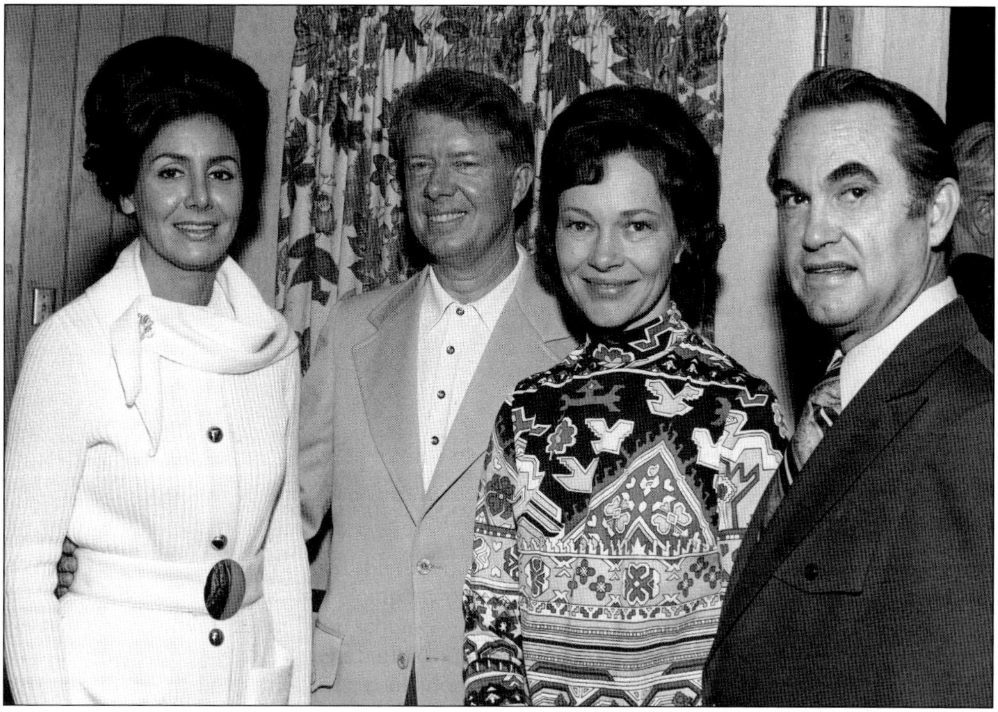

Pictured in this 1971 photograph are, from left to right, Cornelia Wallace, Jimmy Carter, Rosalynn Carter, and George Wallace. Jimmy Carter was the last Democratic presidential candidate to receive the majority vote in Marshall County. George Wallace, best known for his 1963 inauguration speech in which he advocated "segregation forever," served as governor of Alabama from 1963 to 1967, 1971 to 1979, and 1983 to 1987. (Alabama Department of Archives and History.)

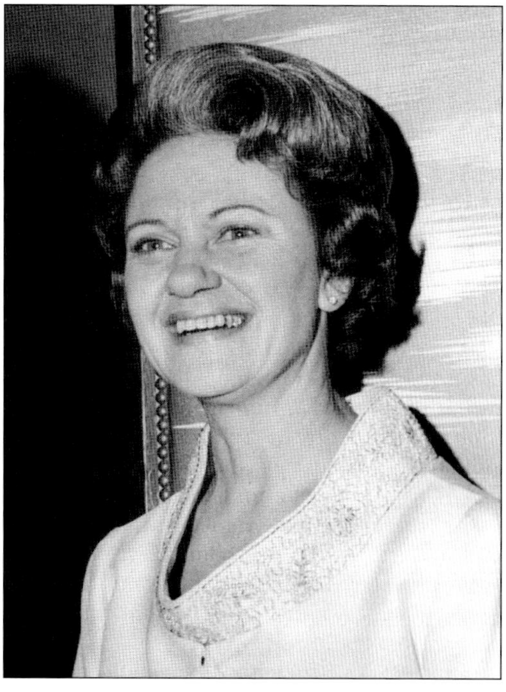

Lurleen Wallace (pictured), first wife of George Wallace, became governor in her own right when she won the 1966 election. She served from January 1967 until her death from cancer in 1968. After her death, Guntersville City Council dubbed a roughly mile-long bypass bordering the lake the Lurleen B. Wallace Memorial Drive. The dedication of the bypass took place on September 17, 1968. (Alabama Department of Archives and History.)

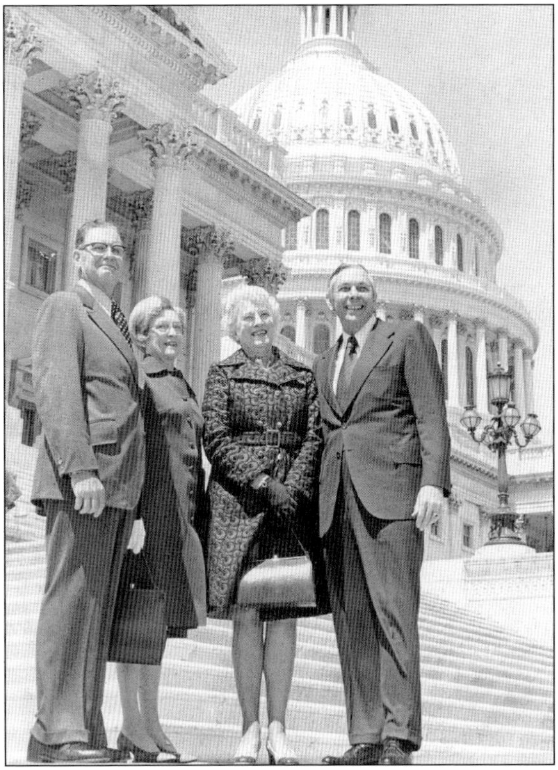

In this 1973 photograph are, from left to right, John and Taska Tyson of the Kate Duncan Smith DAR School, Guntersville historian Katherine Duncan, and US congressman Tom Bevill. Duncan served as regent of the Heroes of King's Mountain Chapter of the Daughters of the American Revolution. The delegation from Marshall County attended the Continental Congress at Washington, DC. (Marshall County Archives.)

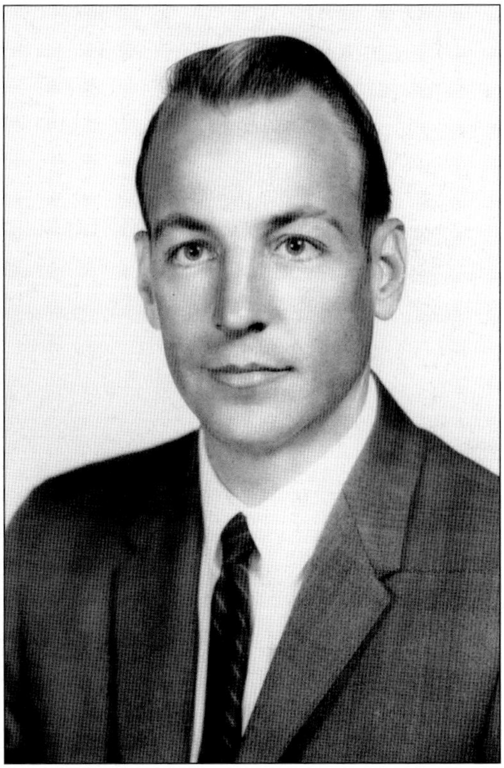

Pictured here is Albert Brewer. After several terms in the Alabama House of Representatives and serving as its speaker, Brewer became lieutenant governor under Lurleen Wallace and governor upon her death. As governor, he expanded Little Mountain State Park, now Lake Guntersville State Park. In 1970, Brewer unsuccessfully ran for governor against George Wallace. (Alabama Department of Archives and History.)

Shown here around 1963, Rev. J. Hodge Alves Jr. was a Guntersville native and Episcopal minister. Educated at Sewanee and Virginia Theological Seminary, his ministry took him to parishes in Alabama, Texas, Virginia, and Arkansas. He had the pleasure of baptizing 1,500 individuals and marrying 500 couples. At Little Rock, he and other ministers preached nonviolence during turbulent demonstrations over integration. (Hodge Alves III.)

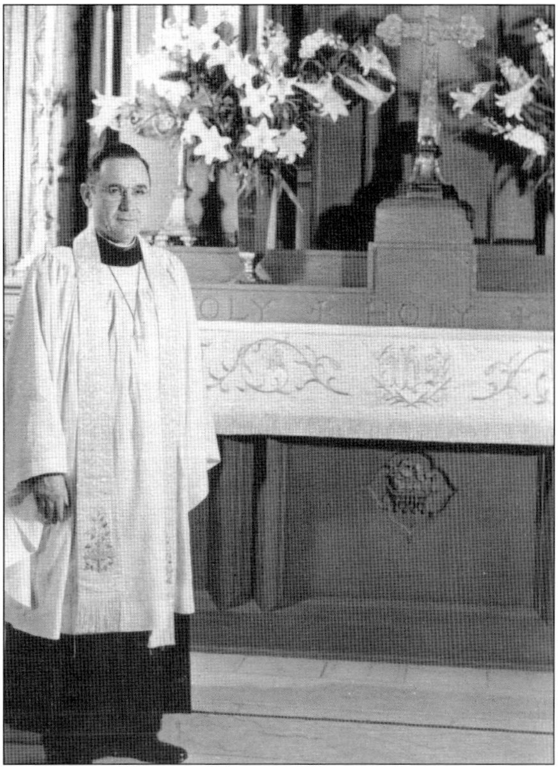

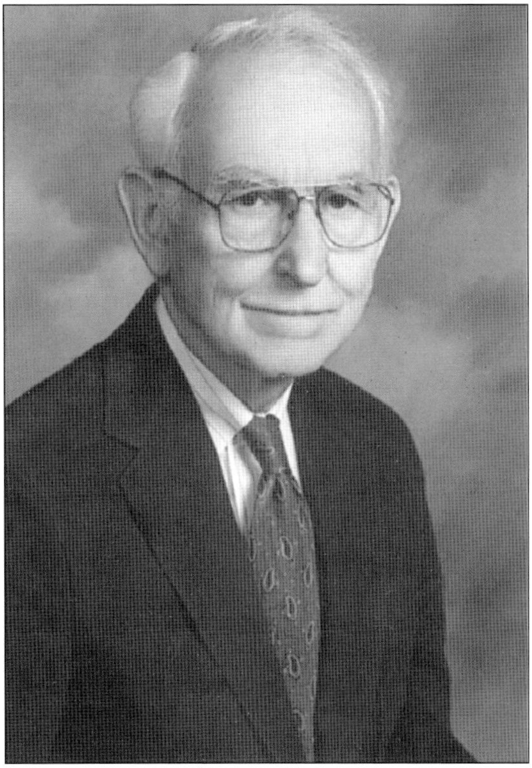

Dr. Samuel Rexford Kennamer (1921–2013), son of Judge Charles and Birdie Kennamer, attended the University of Alabama and Jefferson Medical School. He practiced medicine in Beverly Hills, contributed to cardiac research, and wrote numerous articles. His patients included stars like Rock Hudson, Gary Cooper, Jack Benny, Frank Sinatra, and Elizabeth Taylor. Kennamer appeared in photographs with Taylor after the death of her husband, Mike Todd. (Seaborn Kennamer.)

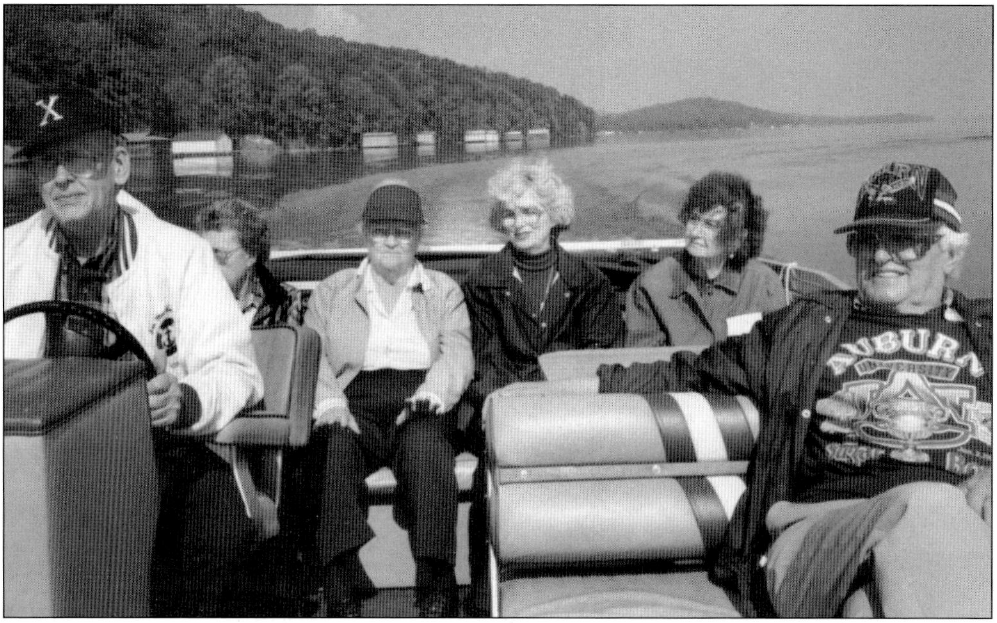

Dr. Frances Roberts (second from left, second row) boated with the DeYoung family at Guntersville. In 1956, Roberts became the first woman to earn a doctorate in history from the University of Alabama. She helped develop the University of Alabama in Huntsville and chaired its department of history until 1970. Roberts edited the *Huntsville Historical Review* and served as president of the Alabama Historical Association. (Salmon Library, University of Alabama in Huntsville.)

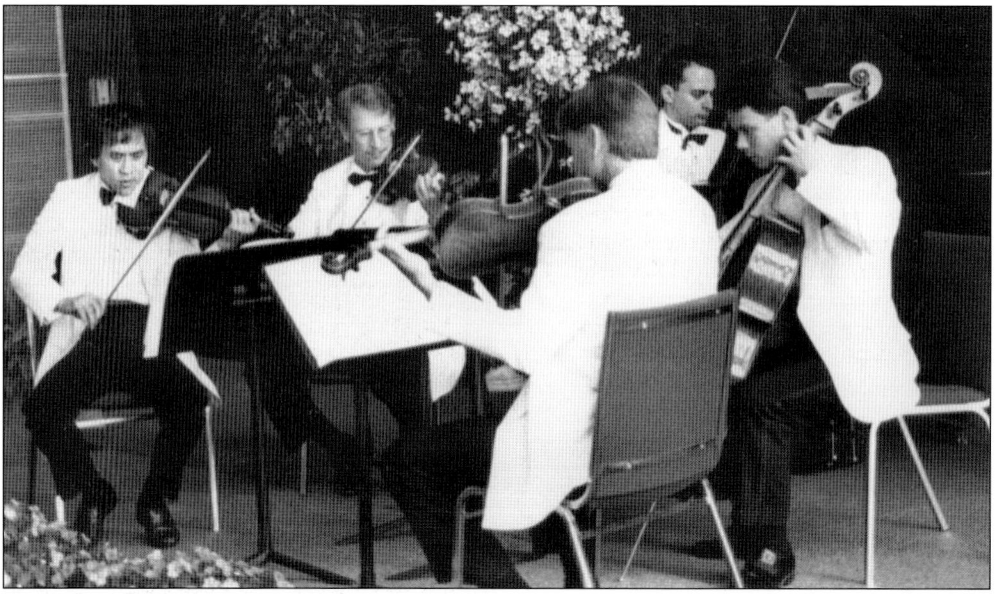

From 1972 to 1982, Pamela and Livingston Gearhart, professors and musicians, operated Youth Makes Music String Workshops. Pamela offered private lessons in violin, viola, bass, and cello, while Livingston served as composer-arranger-consultant. Each camp year ended with a concert. The project morphed into the annual Gerhart Chamber Music Festival for professional musicians. The festival was named for Pamela's father, Russell Gerhart, who served as the conductor of the Huntsville Symphony Orchestra. (*Advertiser-Gleam*.)

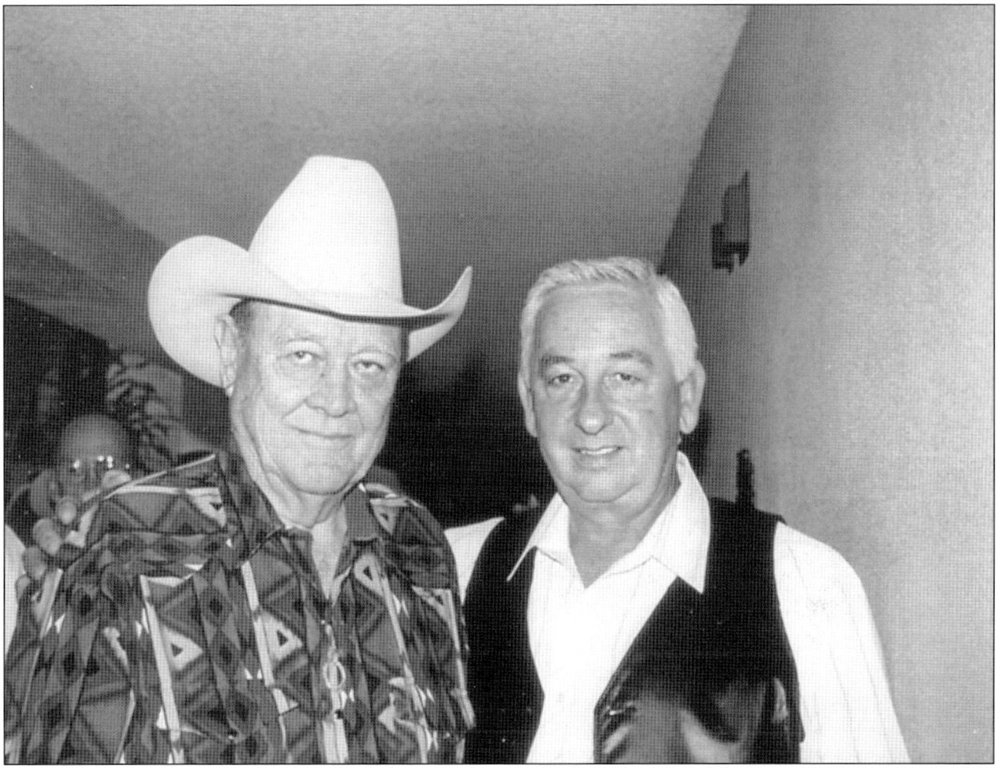

Guntersville native David Kennamer (right) has met myriad celebrities, including Ben Johnson (1918–1996). Johnson began his cinematic career as a stuntman and knew how to sit in a saddle after years performing in rodeos. While he was best known for westerns like *Rio Grande* (1950) and *Chisum* (1970), his role in *The Last Picture Show* (1971) earned him an Academy Award for Best Supporting Actor. (David Kennamer.)

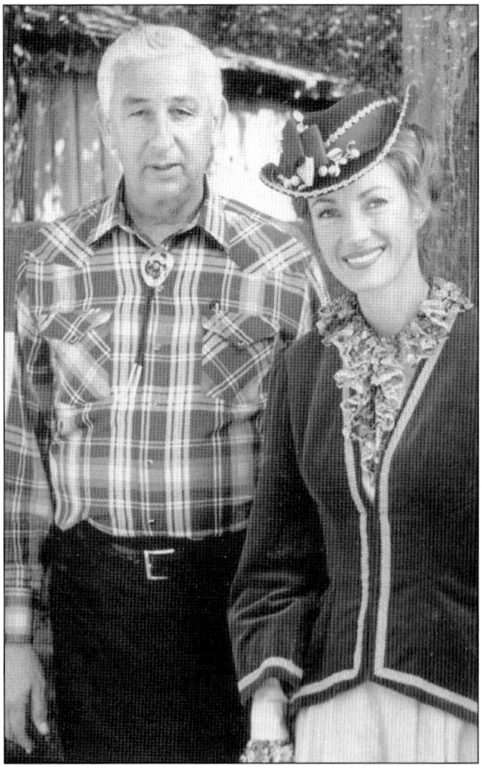

On one trip to Paramount Ranch, David (left) and Ann Kennamer had the pleasure of meeting British actress Jane Seymour (right) on the set of *Dr. Quinn, Medicine Woman*. They also took photographs of the young stars who played her adopted children: Chad Allen, Erika Flores, and Shawn Toovey. While on the set, Ann even posed for a photograph in the trough in front of Hank's saloon. (David Kennamer.)

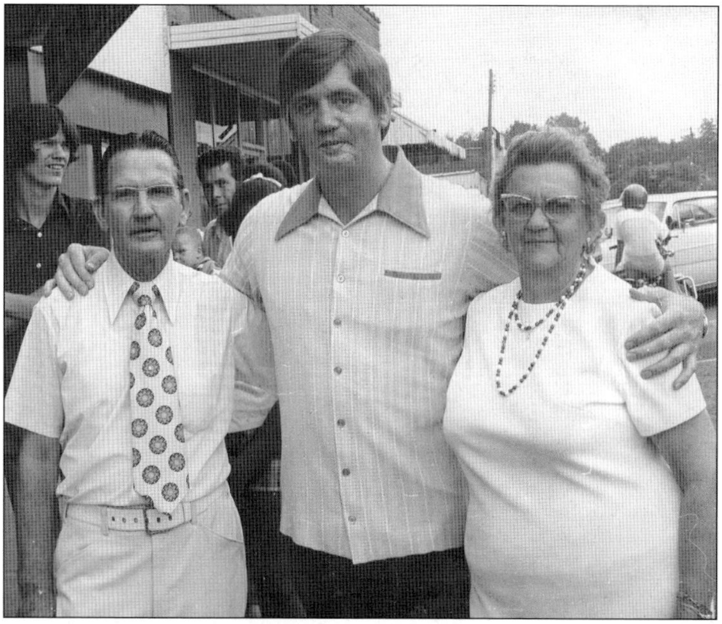

In this July 1973 photograph, Buford Pusser (center) is shown with Bill and Dora Harris. Locals flocked to the Lake Theatre to see the former sheriff of McNairy County, Tennessee. The movie *Walking Tall*, which focused on Pusser's dealings with bootleggers, had a long run at the theater. While in Guntersville, Pusser received keys to four cities. The line to meet him was so long that he shook hands for four hours. (*Advertiser-Gleam*.)

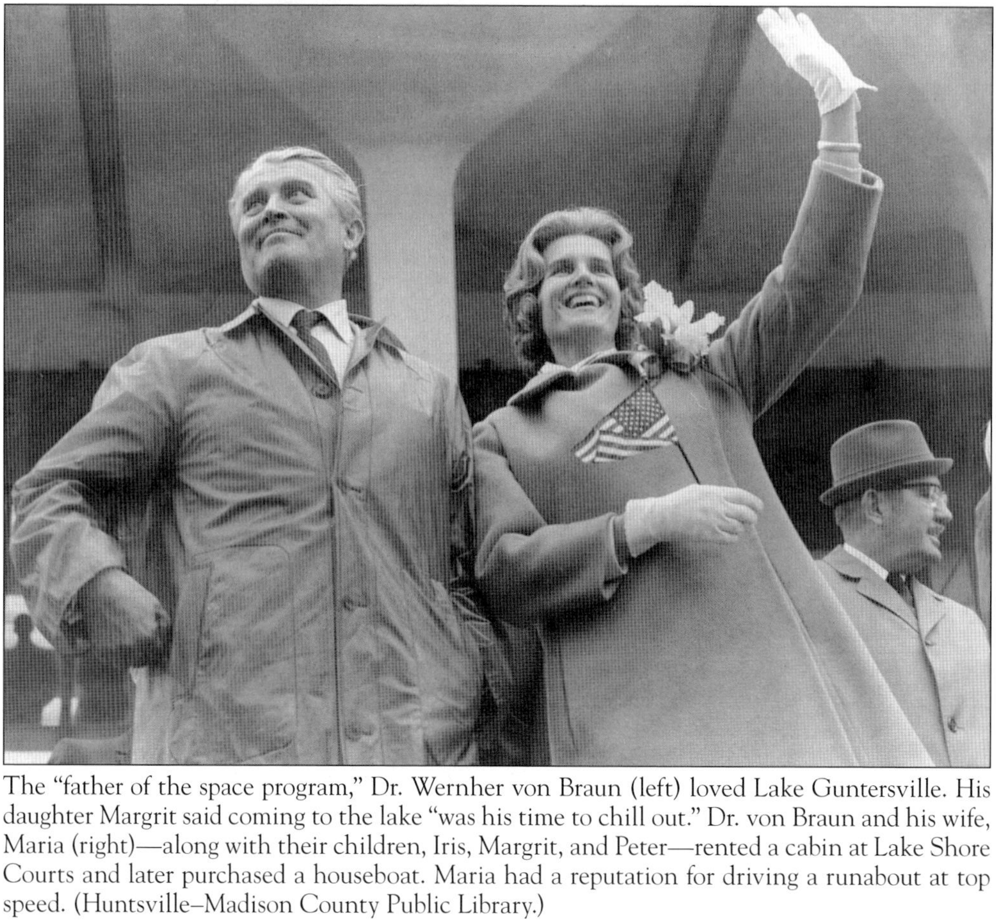

The "father of the space program," Dr. Wernher von Braun (left) loved Lake Guntersville. His daughter Margrit said coming to the lake "was his time to chill out." Dr. von Braun and his wife, Maria (right)—along with their children, Iris, Margrit, and Peter—rented a cabin at Lake Shore Courts and later purchased a houseboat. Maria had a reputation for driving a runabout at top speed. (Huntsville–Madison County Public Library.)

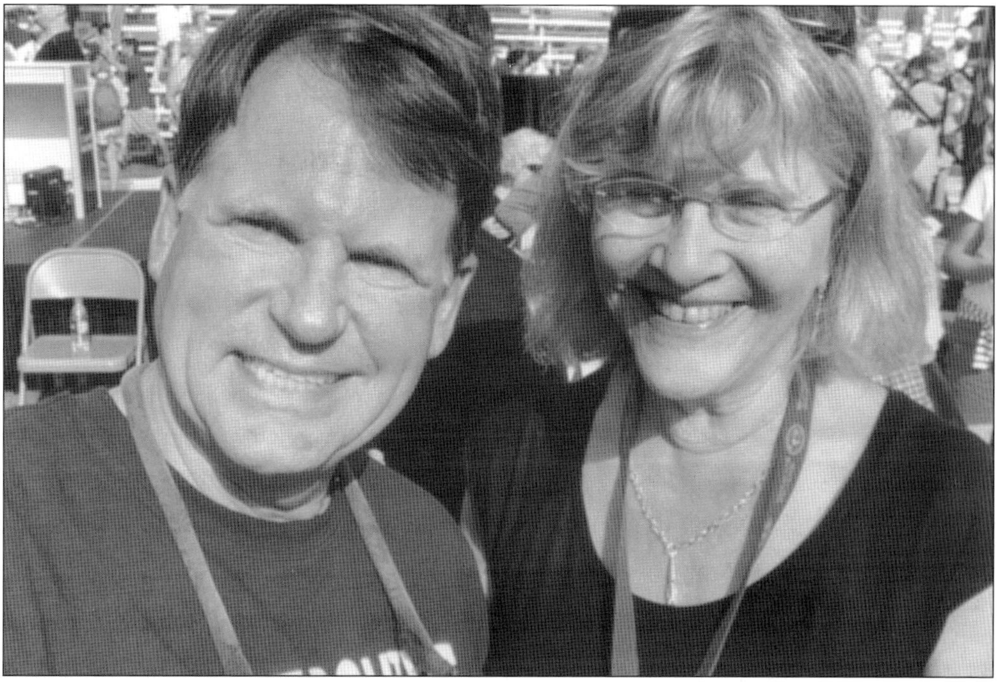

Margrit von Braun (right) is shown with Michael Kirkpatrick on a visit to Huntsville in 2019 for the 50th anniversary of the Apollo 11 mission. Asked about Guntersville, Margrit reminisced about the Chris-Craft named *Orion*, a houseboat she and her siblings called *Surfside 6*, and a speedboat named *A-OK*, a term used by astronaut Alan Shepard. Her ties to Guntersville include contact with childhood friend Liz Kyle Riehl. (*Advertiser-Gleam.*)

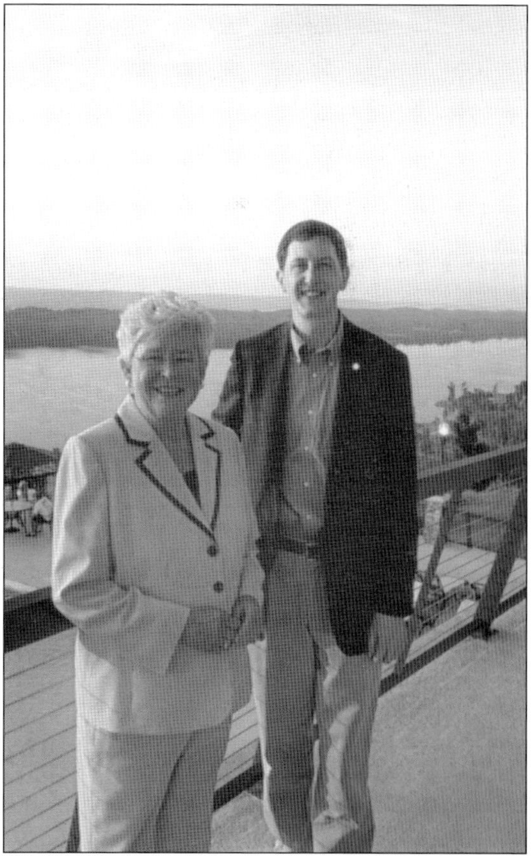

Alabama governor Kay Ivey and state senator Clay Scofield are shown at Lake Guntersville State Park. As lieutenant governor, Ivey assumed office and became the state's second woman to serve as governor after Gov. Robert Bentley resigned in 2017. The following year, she was elected to the position. Scofield has represented District 9 since 2010. (Lake Guntersville State Park.)

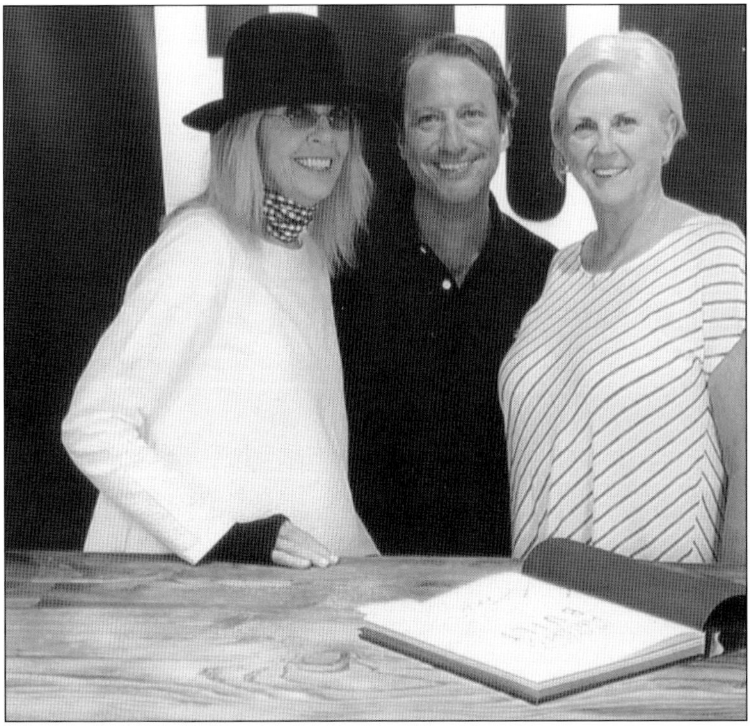

Pictured here are Diane Keaton (left), Jacob Bright (center), and Jacob's mother, Janet Bright. The Brights met the film icon at a 2018 book signing in Atlanta. A 1991 graduate of Arab High School, Jacob earned a psychology degree from Samford University. In 1998, he opened Fine Things, a gift and registry shop in Arab. In his spare time, Jacob enjoys socializing, boating, and traveling. (Jacob Bright.)

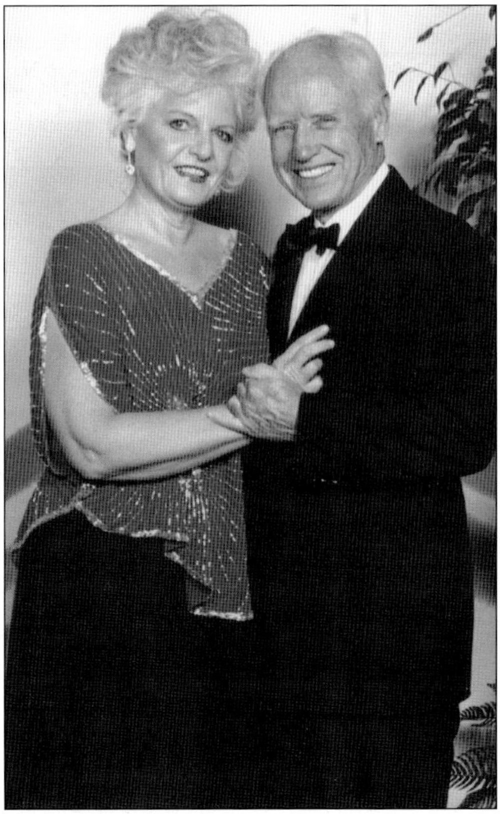

Author William Bradford Huie (right) married Guntersville resident Martha Hunt Robertson in 1977. The two met when she wrote to him after seeing an interview on television. He called her, and the two began dating. After his death, Martha, an art teacher, promoted his legacy. In 2002, she persuaded Herbert Appleman to premiere *Wave Me Goodbye*, an adaptation of *The Americanization of Emily*, at the Whole Backstage Theatre. (Mary Ben Heflin.)

Taken in Tuscaloosa, this photograph shows, from left to right, Mary Ben (Robertson) Heflin, Martha Robertson Huie, William Bradford Huie, and Jamie (Robertson) Lendrum. Huie graduated from the University of Alabama in 1930. In 1998, he was inducted into the Hall of Fame at the College of Communications and Information Sciences. In 2010, Tuscaloosa and the University of Alabama commemorated his 100th birthday. (Mary Ben Heflin.)

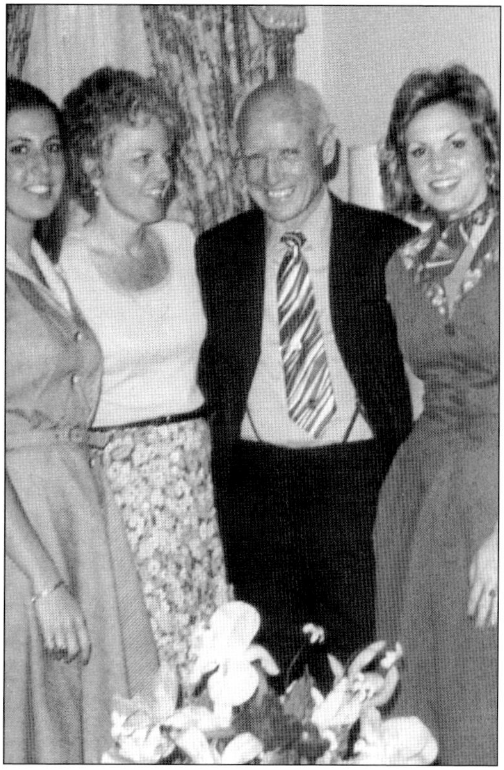

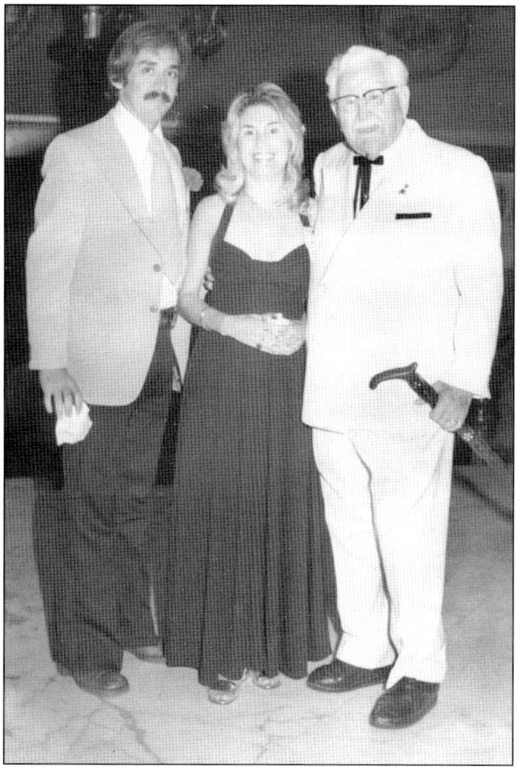

Larue (left) and Jane (right) Kohl are shown posing with Col. Harland Sanders of Kentucky Fried Chicken (KFC) fame. Larue's father, Jack, acquired a KFC franchise for Guntersville in 1974. Two years later, Larue and Jane joined the business and attended KFC University. Jane opened Guntersville's Academy of Performing Arts in 1977. She has been called the "dean" of Guntersville's businesswomen. Larue died in 2019. (Jane Kohl.)

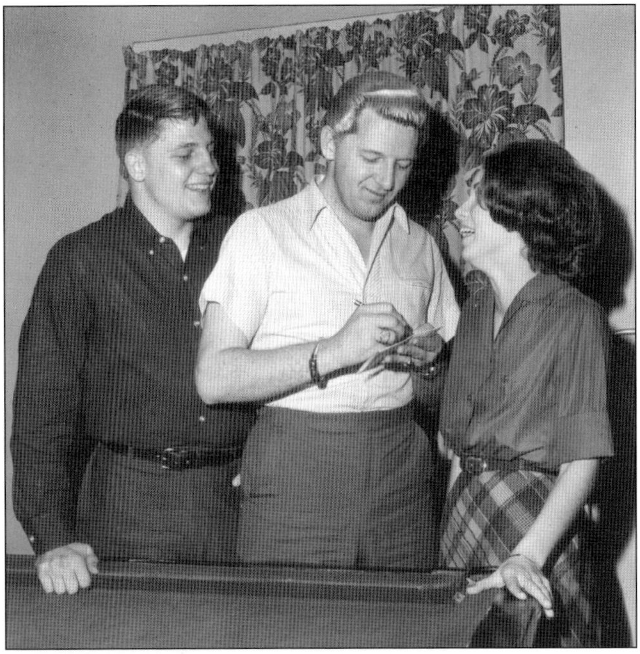

Singer Jerry Lee Lewis (center) is shown with two unidentified fans. Myles Leach of WGSV helped Bill Harris secure an appearance by the "Great Balls of Fire" performer. On April 13, 1960, Lewis appeared at Guntersville's Lake Theatre and played with such vigor that the loaned piano was damaged. (Alabama Department of Archives and History; donated by Alabama Media Group; photograph by Hamilton, *Birmingham News.*)

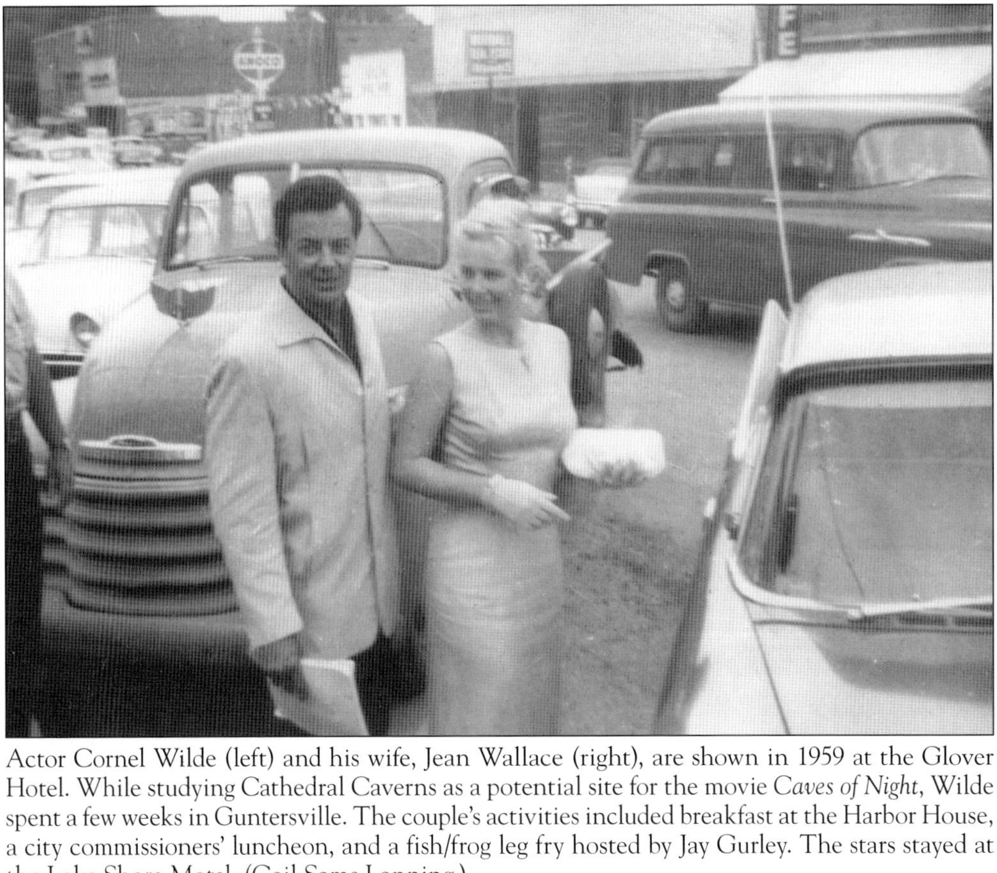

Actor Cornel Wilde (left) and his wife, Jean Wallace (right), are shown in 1959 at the Glover Hotel. While studying Cathedral Caverns as a potential site for the movie *Caves of Night*, Wilde spent a few weeks in Guntersville. The couple's activities included breakfast at the Harbor House, a city commissioners' luncheon, and a fish/frog leg fry hosted by Jay Gurley. The stars stayed at the Lake Shore Motel. (Gail Sams Lanning.)

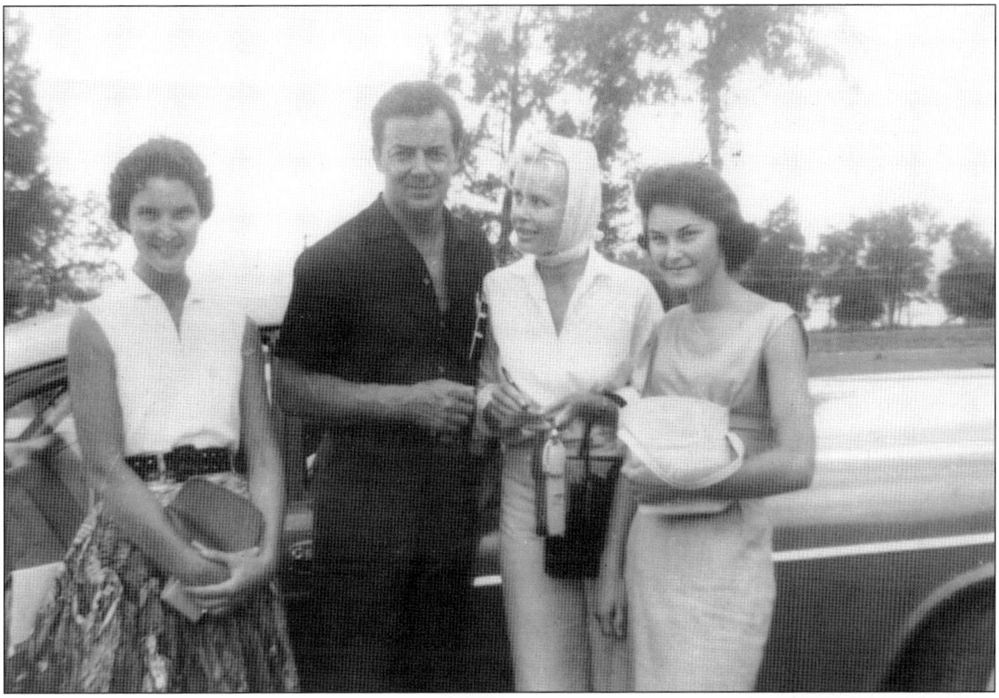

Shown are, from left to right, Gail Sams, Cornel Wilde, Jean Wallace, and Barbara Smith. When Sams approached the couple outside the Glover Hotel, she asked if she might have her photograph taken with the celebrities. According to Sams, Wilde initially declined but agreed after his wife intervened. Gail and her husband, Gary Lanning, live in Wichita, Kansas, and have two daughters, Pamela and Linda. (Gail Sams Lanning.)

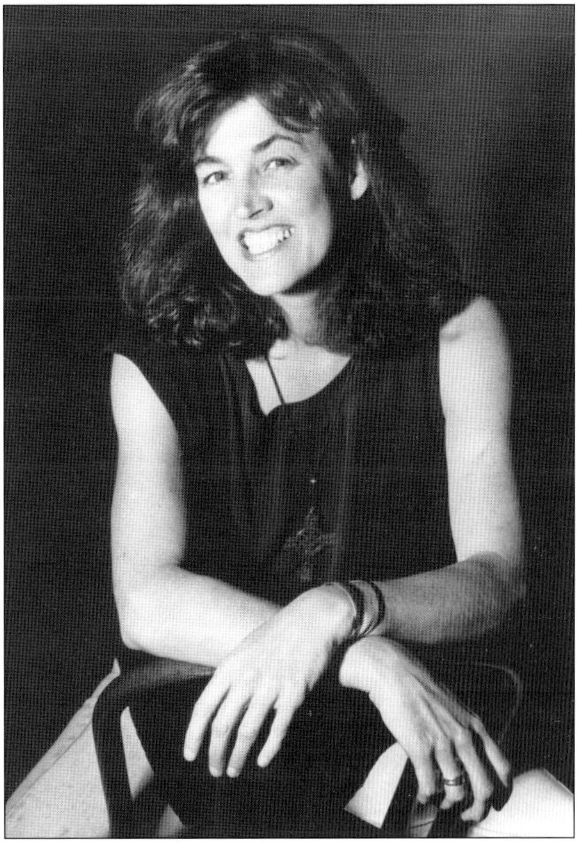

Janet McLaughlin (shown) grew up in Guntersville and began singing at the local Teen Club. She has toured with the Indigo Girls, and her songs have been recorded by artists like Loretta Lynn. Affiliated with the Nashville Songwriters' Association, McLaughlin writes, performs, conducts camps, and judges. In 1985, she and the band Headline, which included Damon Johnson, opened for Ricky Nelson at PJ's Alley in Guntersville. (*Advertiser-Gleam.*)

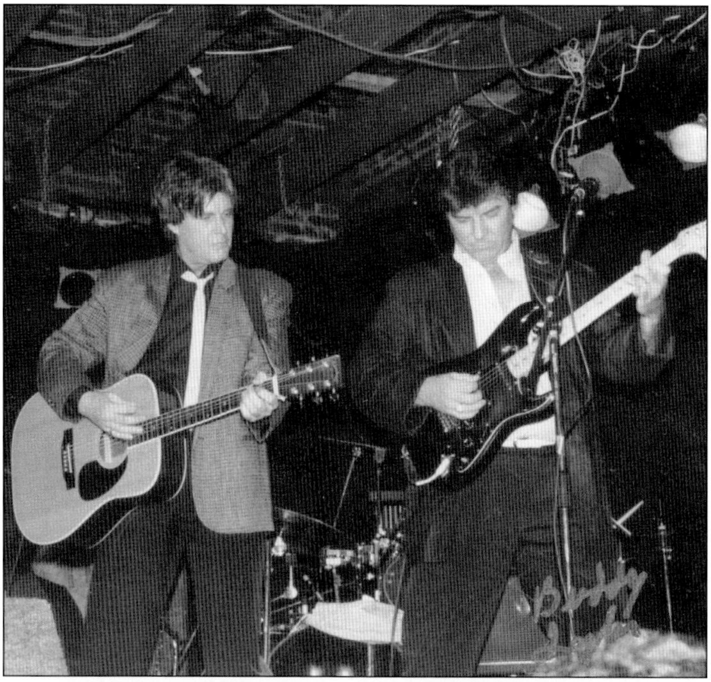

Ricky Nelson (left) is shown with guitarist Bobby Neal of Stone Canyon Band in a December 1985 performance at PJ's Alley in Guntersville. Nelson, his girlfriend Helen Blair, and his band enjoyed this visit, which was a nice stopover before their scheduled New Year's Eve performance in Dallas, Texas. Nelson entertained the Guntersville crowd with his treasured favorites "Bye Bye Love," "Poor Little Fool," "Travelin' Man," and "Hello, Mary Lou." (Buddy Taylor.)

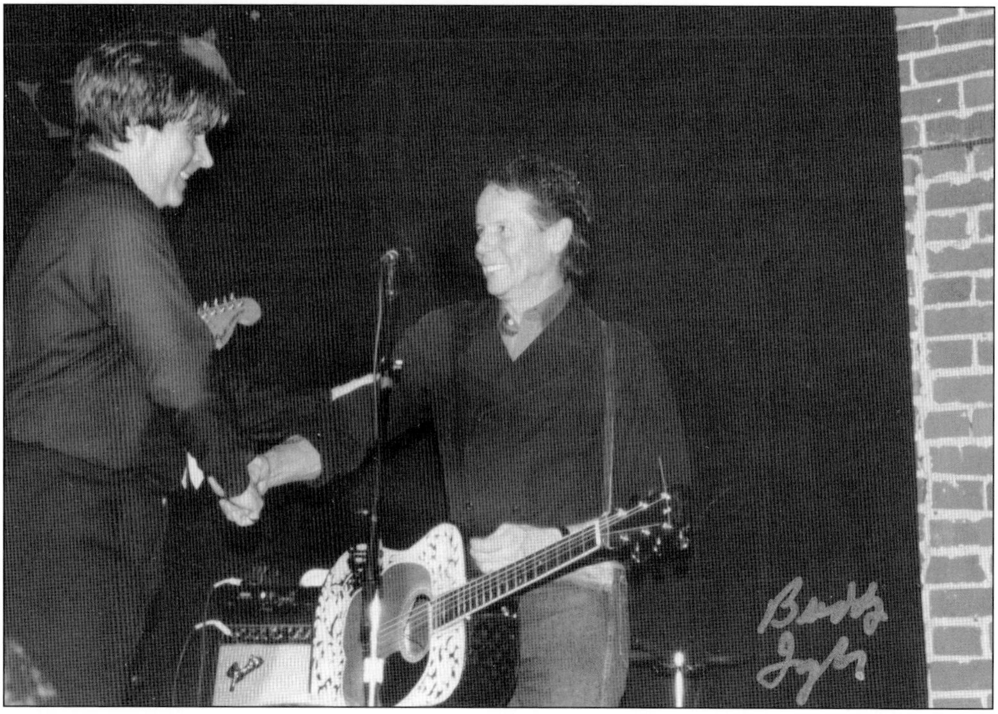

Songwriter and businessman Pat Upton (right) invited Ricky Nelson (left) and the Stone Canyon Band to perform at PJ's Alley on December 29 and 30, 1985. Nelson enjoyed visiting old friends Upton and Jeff Cook of the band Alabama. Upton declined Nelson's invitation to accompany him to Texas. Nelson died in a plane crash on December 31, making Guntersville the last place he ever performed. (Buddy Taylor.)

Pat Upton and the Downtown Horns played classic rock, Motown, and R&B music. In the center is Upton (vocals and guitar). Surrounding Upton are, from left to right, Mark Thompson (guitar), Allen Breland (bass guitar), Curtis Burttram (sax, keyboards, and vocal), Stacy Goss (trumpet and flute), Mike Bruce (drums), and Scott Berry (trumpet and keyboards). The group played for Jimmy Carter's 75th birthday celebration. (*Advertiser-Gleam*.)

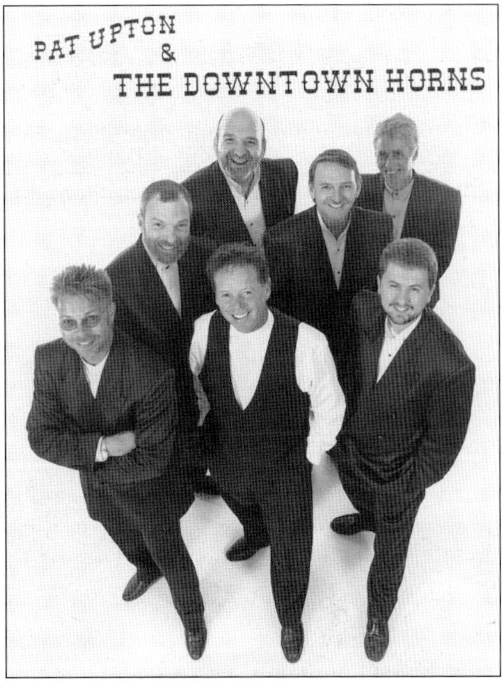

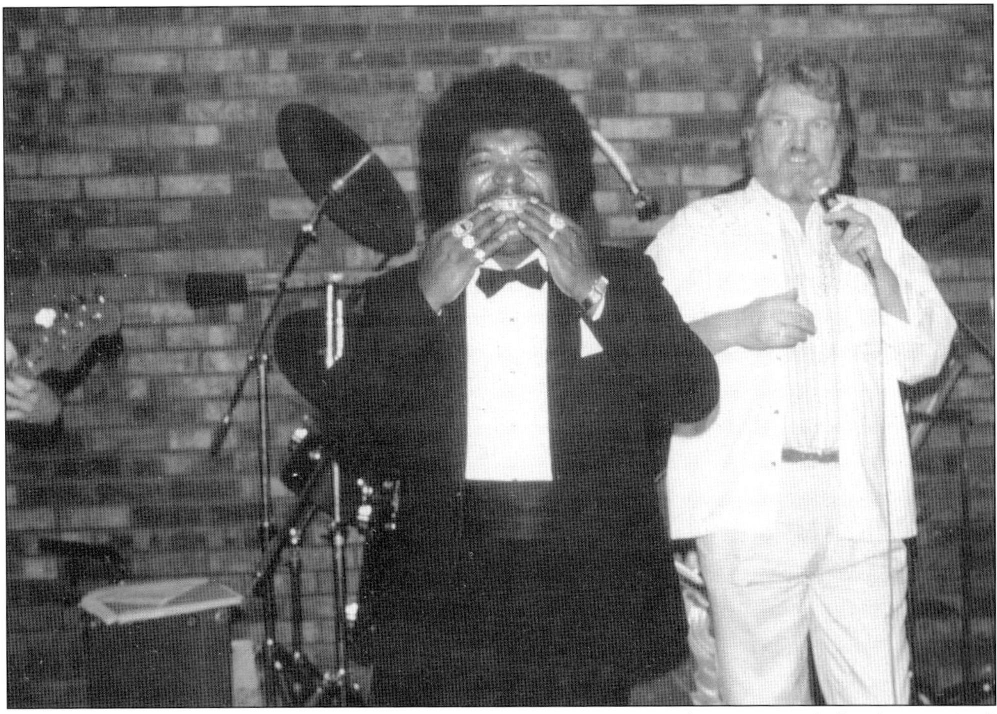

On April 18 and 19, 1986, Guntersville locals got quite a treat when Percy Sledge (1941–2015) sang at the Class of '57, a club opposite Guntersville High School. Sledge entertained the house with his signature song, "When a Man Loves a Woman." Originally from Leighton, Alabama, Sledge was inducted into the Alabama Music Hall of Fame in 1993. In 2005, he was inducted into the Rock & Roll Hall of Fame. (Buddy Taylor.)

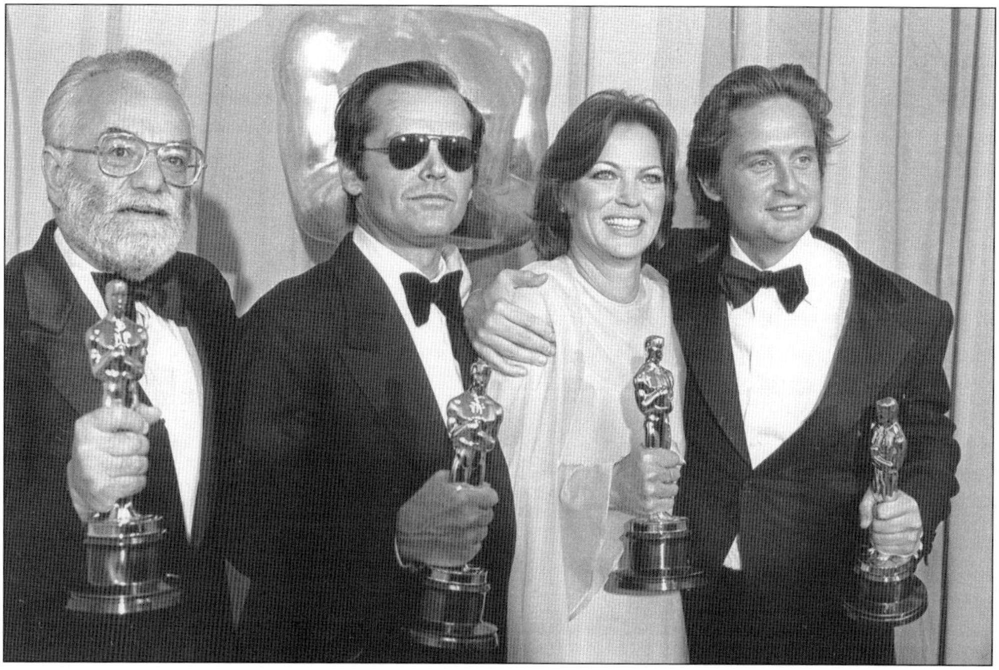

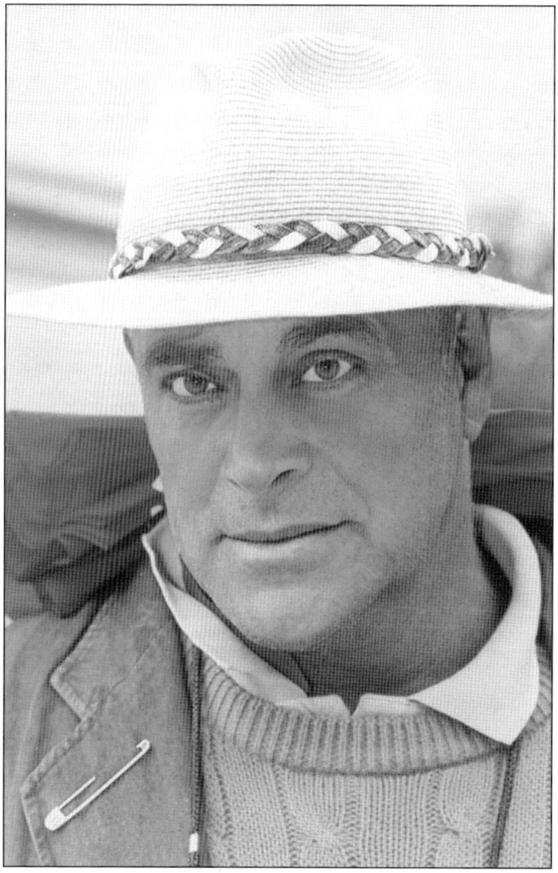

Pictured in this photograph taken at the 1976 Academy Awards are, from left to right, Saul Zaentz, Jack Nicholson, Louise Fletcher, and Michael Douglas. Fletcher won Best Actress for her role as Nurse Ratched in *One Flew Over the Cuckoo's Nest*. In Guntersville, Fletcher visited her grandfather and step-grandmother, Rev. J.D. and Mary Mason Fletcher, as well as the Woodall families. (Library Special Collections, University of California, Los Angeles.)

In 2015, the Mountain Valley Arts Council sponsored Nall Hollis's exhibition. The son of Mary and Joe Hollis, Nall grew up in Arab, graduated from the University of Alabama, and studied at the École des Beaux-Arts in Paris. He was later mentored by Salvador Dalí. In 2007, Hollis was awarded the Governor's Award as Most Distinguished Artist. He also received the Alabama Image Award from his alma mater. (Nall Hollis.)

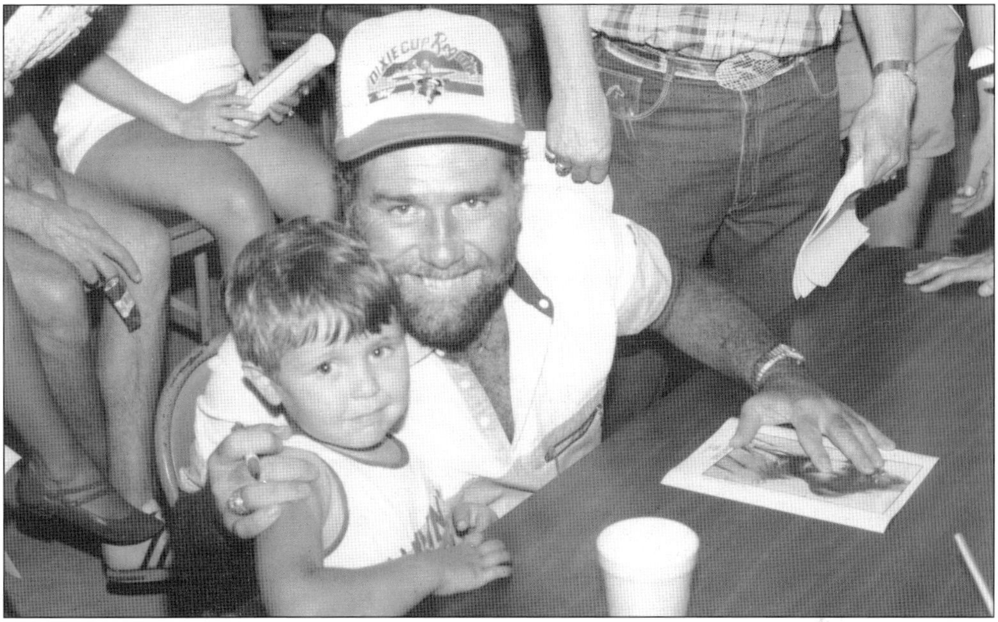

Johnny Lee, shown with an unidentified child, pronounced Marshall County "the most beautiful place." In 1987, promoters offered a Johnny Lee Picnic on McDonald's Farm at Claysville. Although the entertainers included Lee, Loretta Lynn, and Charlie Daniels, attendance and revenue did not live up to expectations. Lee wanted to foster economic development in Guntersville by building Johnny Lee's Show Palace but was denied a license to sell alcohol. (*Advertiser-Gleam.*)

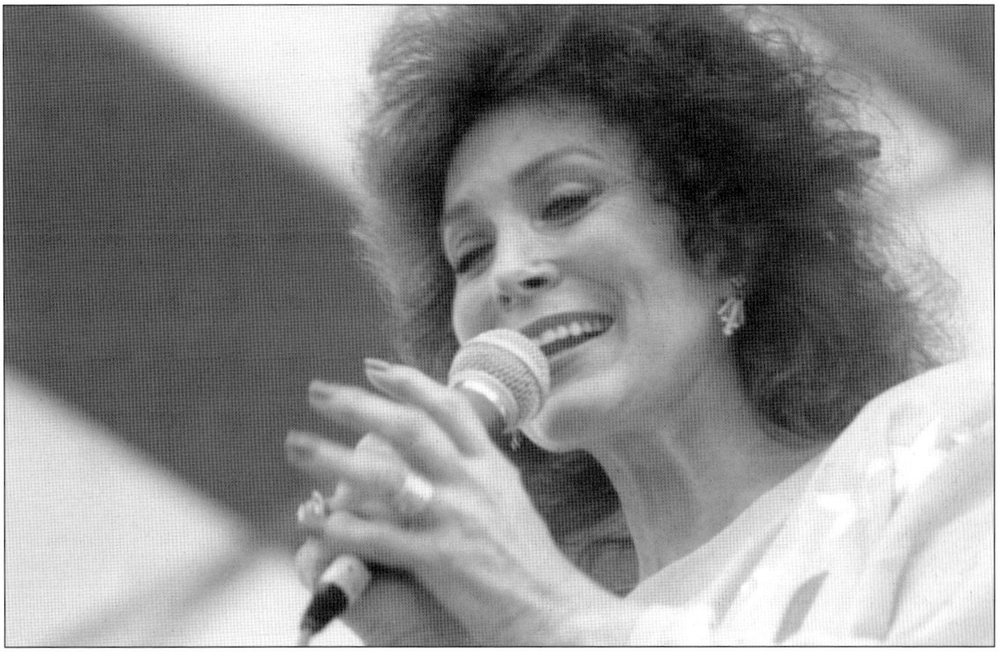

Loretta Lynn is shown at the Johnny Lee Picnic in 1987. Lynn and John Allan Coe exhibited true professionalism by performing longer sets after other performers opted out because of financial concerns. Lee told the crowd, "Loretta Lynn, out of the goodness of her heart, did the best for all you guys." He added, "David Allan Coe has been here all three days, bless his heart." (Buddy Taylor.)

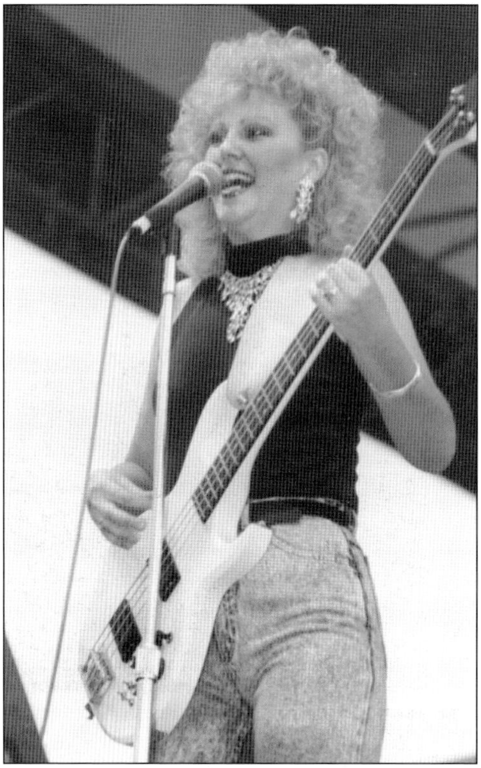

Shelley West is shown performing at the Johnny Lee Picnic in 1987. Although the event was expected to draw 100,000 people, the actual numbers fell far below this threshold. Low ticket sales meant that many artists performed knowing they might not be paid: Bill Monroe, Alton Thrasher, David Frizell, Highway 101, Keith Whitley, and Johnny Lee. (Buddy Taylor.)

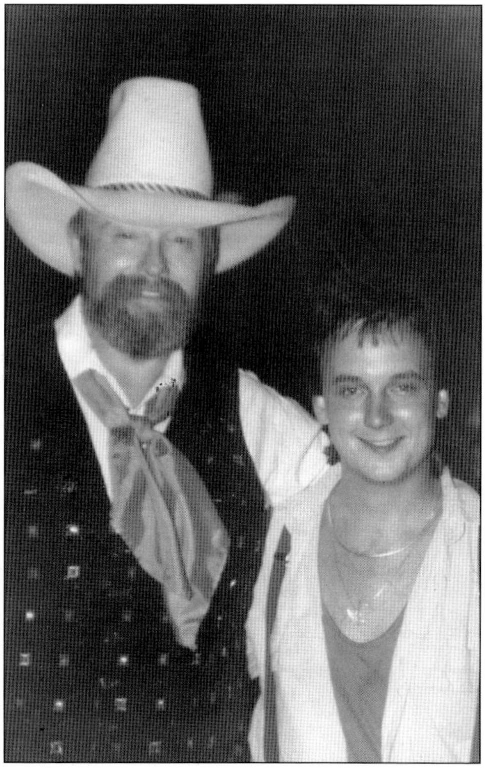

Charlie Daniels (left), best known for "The Devil Went Down to Georgia," is shown with fiddle player Tim Watson at the Johnny Lee Picnic in 1987. Daniels and Watson enthralled the audience with their virtuoso fiddling. Other stars in attendance that evening included Exile, the Hank Williams Drifting Cowboys, John Schneider, and Leon Everette. (Buddy Taylor.)

Marie Osmond (shown) performed at the Johnny Lee Picnic in 1987. Osmond, one of the few fortunate stars at the event, had received payment up front. Represented by the William Morris Agency, Osmond, John Schneider, and Exile were among the performers who did not suffer a financial loss. Osmond's hits include "Paper Roses," "Who's Counting," and "There Is No Stopping My Heart." (Buddy Taylor.)

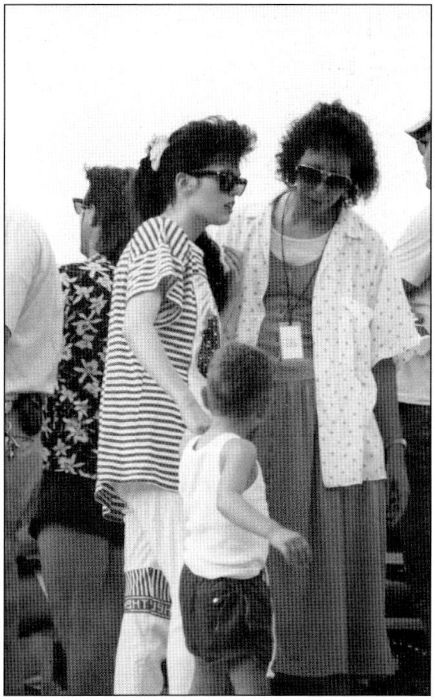

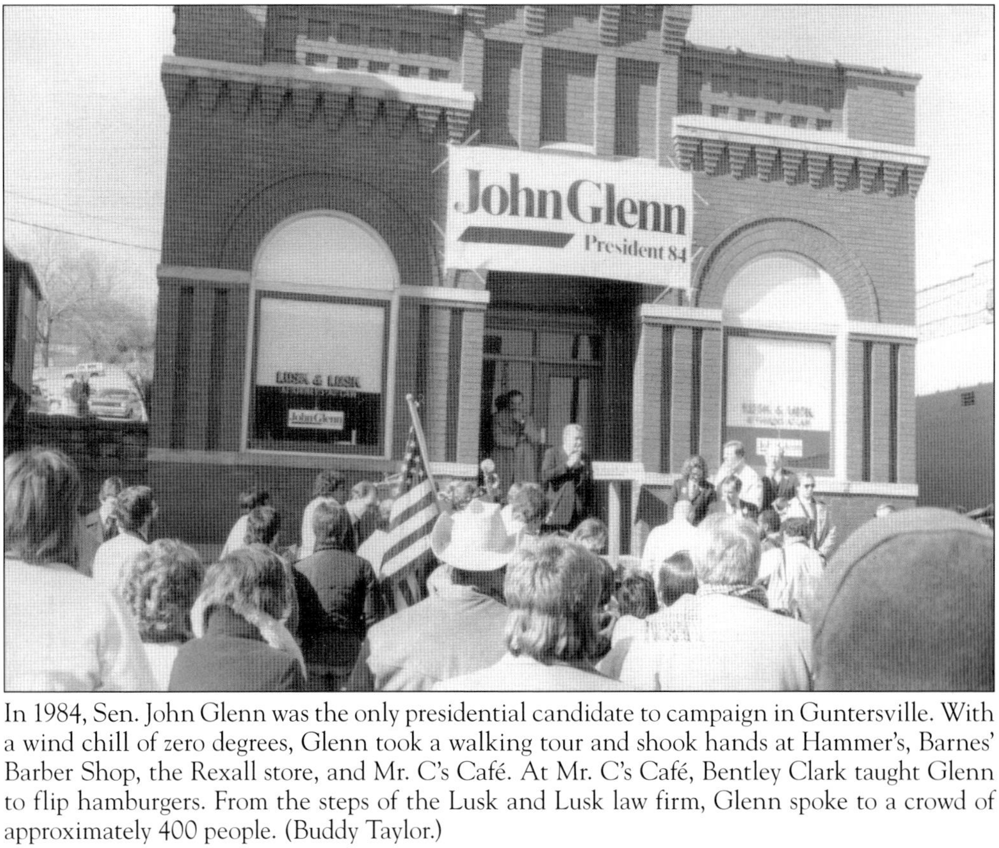

In 1984, Sen. John Glenn was the only presidential candidate to campaign in Guntersville. With a wind chill of zero degrees, Glenn took a walking tour and shook hands at Hammer's, Barnes' Barber Shop, the Rexall store, and Mr. C's Café. At Mr. C's Café, Bentley Clark taught Glenn to flip hamburgers. From the steps of the Lusk and Lusk law firm, Glenn spoke to a crowd of approximately 400 people. (Buddy Taylor.)

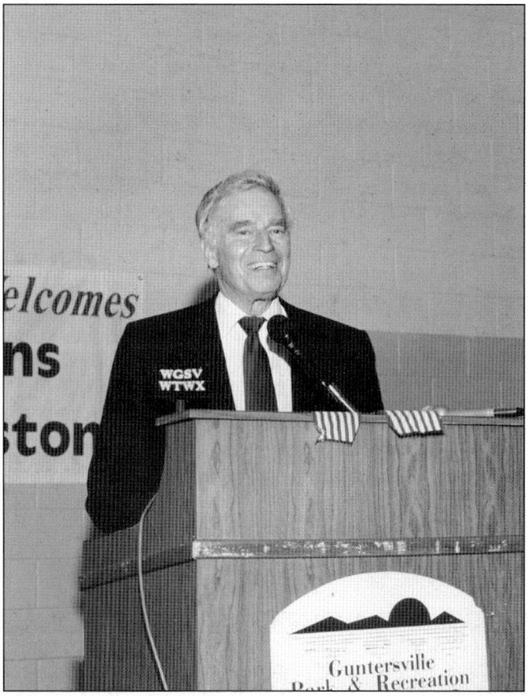

In November 1996, movie star Charlton Heston (shown) toured with Jeff Sessions during Sessions' Senate campaign. At the Guntersville Recreation Center, Billy Cannon, chair of the Marshall County Commission, introduced Heston and Sessions. Speaking to a crowd of approximately 300 people, Heston commented on family values and provided tidbits about his film career. Learning to drive a chariot with four horses was one of his most challenging experiences. (Buddy Taylor.)

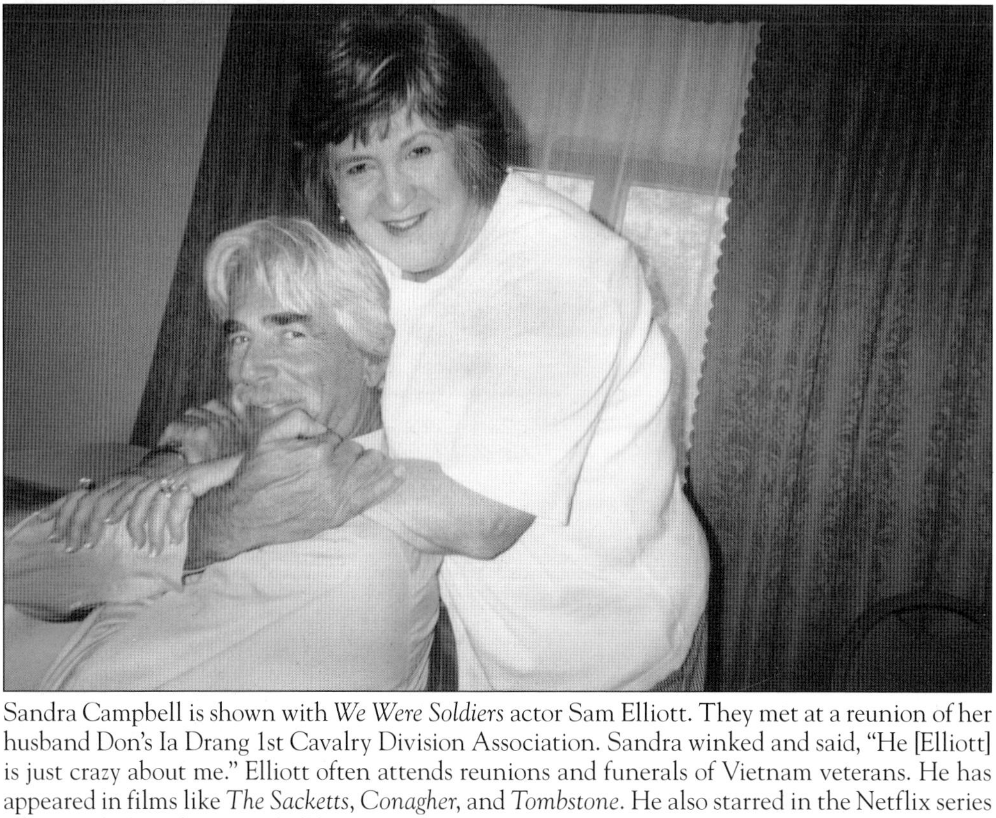

Sandra Campbell is shown with *We Were Soldiers* actor Sam Elliott. They met at a reunion of her husband Don's Ia Drang 1st Cavalry Division Association. Sandra winked and said, "He [Elliott] is just crazy about me." Elliott often attends reunions and funerals of Vietnam veterans. He has appeared in films like *The Sacketts*, *Conagher*, and *Tombstone*. He also starred in the Netflix series *The Ranch*. (Sandra Campbell.)

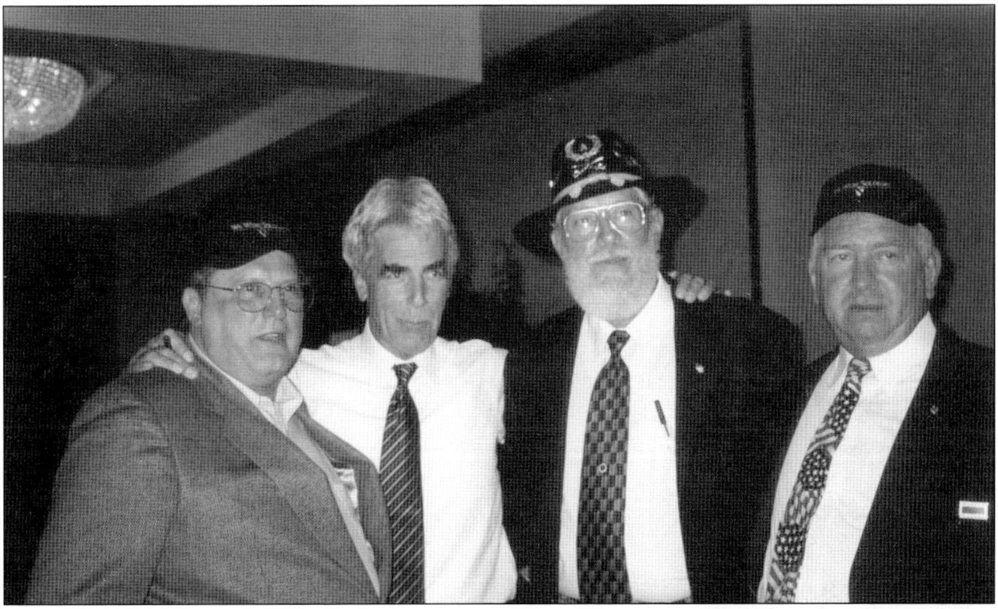

In 2002, at Fort Benning, Georgia, the movie *We Were Soldiers* premiered with many survivors of the 1965 Battle of Ia Drang Valley in attendance. This undated photograph shows members of the 1st Cavalry Division (Airmobile) with Sam Elliott. Pictured are, from left to right, Charles Dashner (Maryland), Elliott, James Comer (North Carolina), and Don Campbell (Guntersville, Alabama). Campbell wrote a book called *The Missing Horsemen: A Memoir of Vietnam*. (Sandra Campbell.)

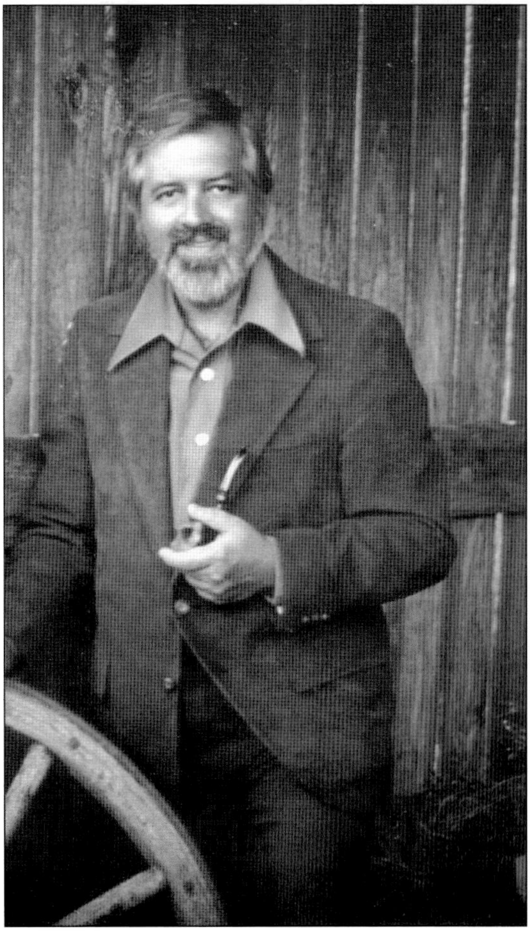

Photographer Leon Kennamer (1930–2000) of Leon's Studio became internationally known for techniques like "subtractive lighting." Recognized with a multitude of awards, Kennamer conducted seminars and wrote extensively about photography. He is remembered for generously giving his time to the Guntersville community, especially assisting with the yearbooks of Marshall County High School and, later, Guntersville High School. (Milla Kennamer.)

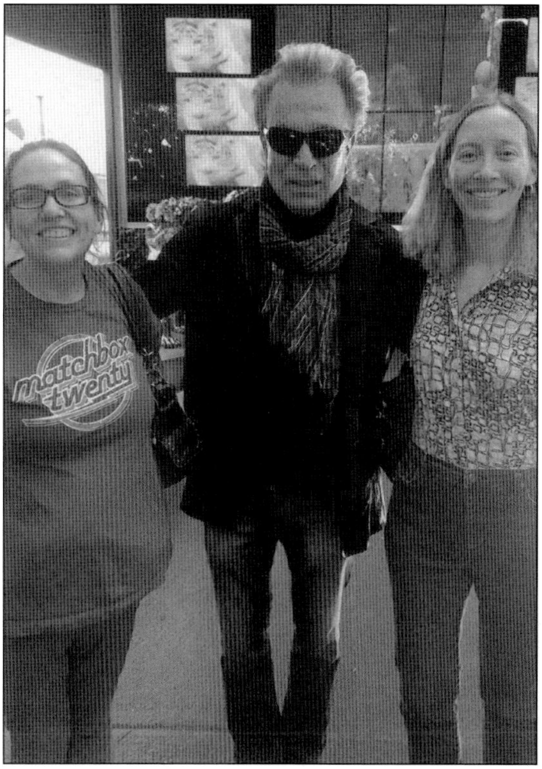

In November 2018, a girls' trip to Las Vegas to see the Backstreet Boys resulted in an unexpected celebrity sighting. While touring Siegfried & Roy's Secret Garden and Dolphin Habitat, Joni Townsend (left) and Whitney Snow (right) spotted none other than Siegfried Fischbacher. Come to find out he often stops by the animal sanctuary to visit the tigers and lions. (Authors' collection.)

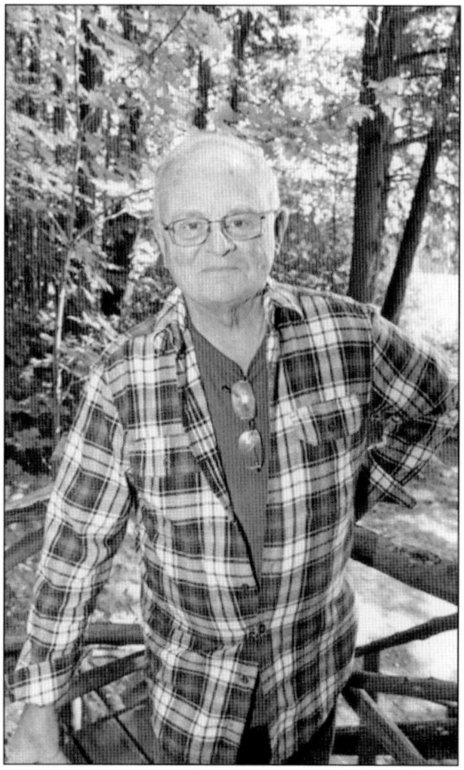

Gary Burghoff (shown), famous for his role as Walter "Radar" O'Reilly on the television show *M*A*S*H*, visited Guntersville in 2007 to promote a recreational vehicle (RV) park for Rod and Blake Spicer. Burghoff, an aficionado of RV living, was friendly, compassionate, and generous with interviews during his stay. A free reception at the La Strada restaurant included an opportunity to meet Burghoff and get an autograph. (Stacie Joy.)

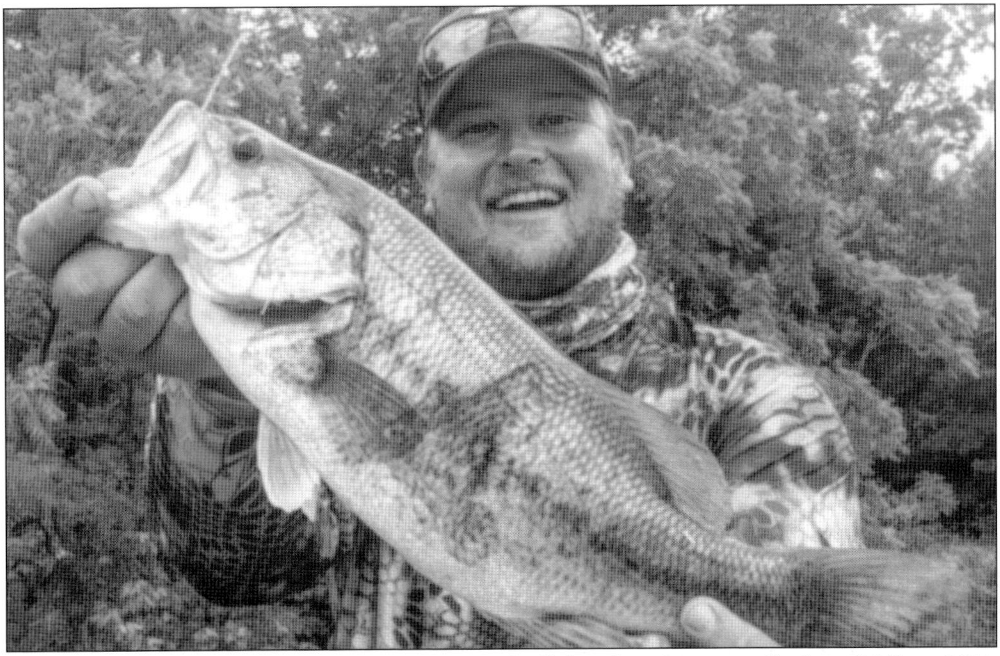

The son of Gary Burghoff, Miles "Sonar" Burghoff, lived in Guntersville from 2012 to 2014. The lake's plethora of bass provided quite a lure for Miles, a professional fisherman. Raised in California, Miles knew from a young age that he wanted to pursue fishing rather than acting. Though he currently resides in Tennessee, Miles fondly remembers Guntersville. (Miles Burghoff.)

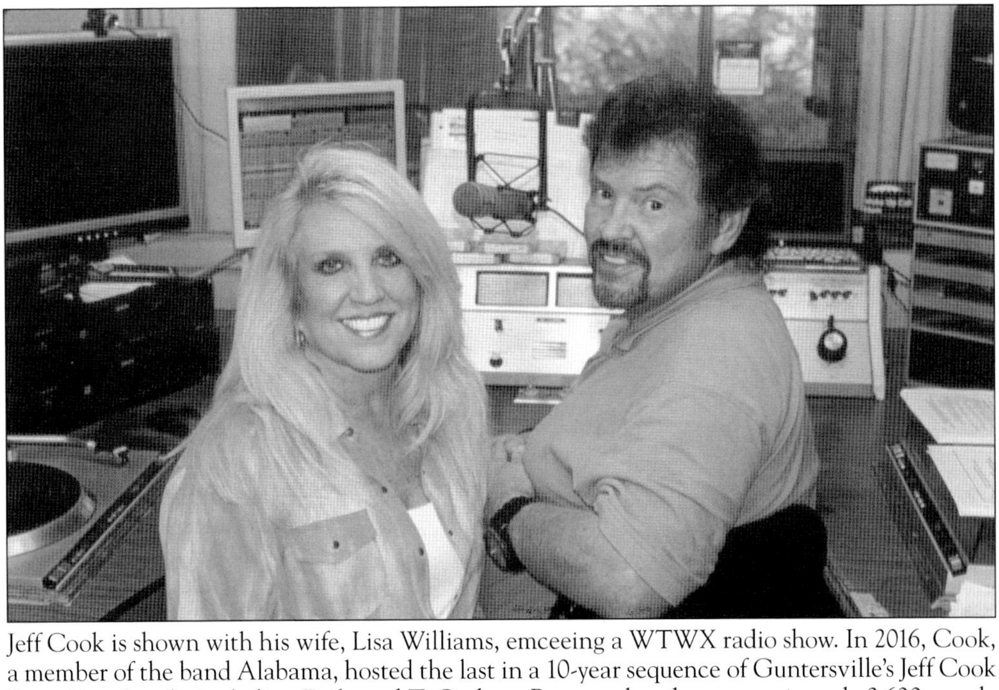

Jeff Cook is shown with his wife, Lisa Williams, emceeing a WTWX radio show. In 2016, Cook, a member of the band Alabama, hosted the last in a 10-year sequence of Guntersville's Jeff Cook Days. Four bands, including Exile and T. Graham Brown, played to approximately 3,600 people at Civitan Park. Rep. Robert Aderholt, Gov. Robert Bentley, Randy Owen, and Teddy Gentry attended to wish Cook a happy birthday. (*Advertiser-Gleam*.)

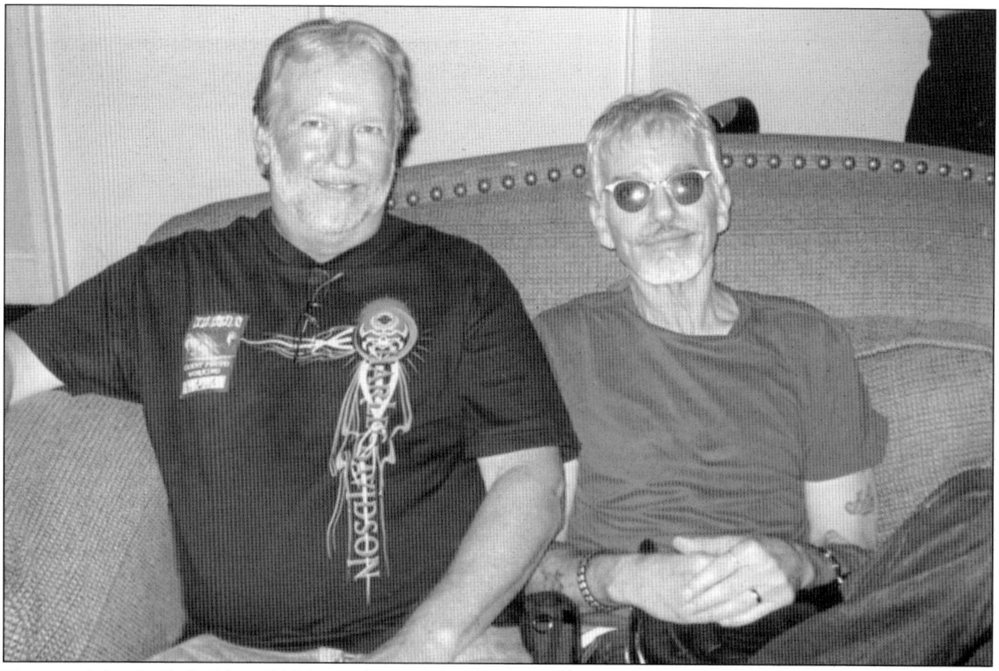

Dennis Mitchell (left), a 1972 graduate of Guntersville High School, is shown with musician and actor Billy Bob Thornton. In August 2018, Mitchell saw Thornton and the Boxmasters play at the Merrimack Hall Performing Arts Center, a theater converted from an old cotton mill, in Huntsville, Alabama. Mitchell, who had backstage passes, met Thornton and the rest of the band after the show. (Dennis Mitchell.)

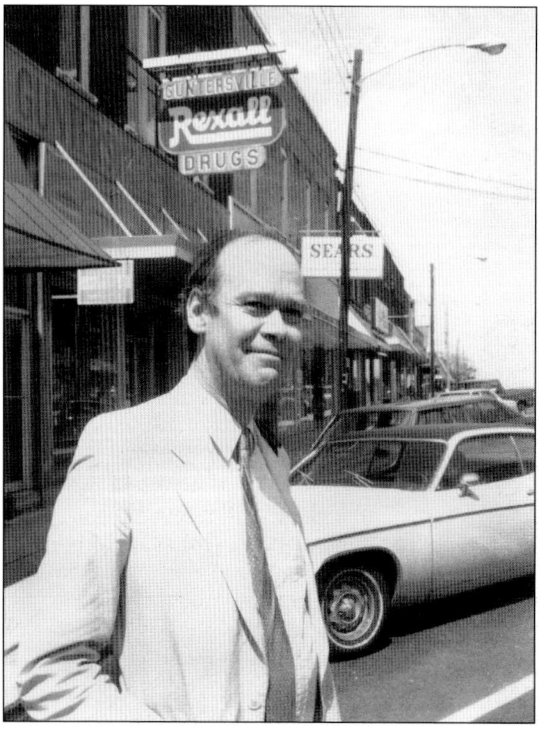

Jonathan Raban, distinguished travel writer, chose Guntersville as one of a handful of US cities to visit for his book *Hunting Mr. Heartbreak: A Discovery of America* (1990). He rented a residence, borrowed a dog named Gypsy, ate in all the restaurants, attended parties, spoke to high school classes, and went to church. After it was published, the book enticed some readers—a few of them international—to visit Guntersville. (*Advertiser-Gleam*.)

While in Guntersville, Jonathan Raban (pictured) often went by the name Rayburn because that was how locals pronounced his surname. Among those quoted in his book are William Bennefield (pharmacist), Ed Neely (realtor), Bob Hembree (mayor), George Kappler (industrialist), Les Click (principal), Katherine Duncan (historian), Al Fant (store owner), Claude Hundley III (lawyer), and Dot Moore (Whole Backstage Theatre). (Karen Ducey.)

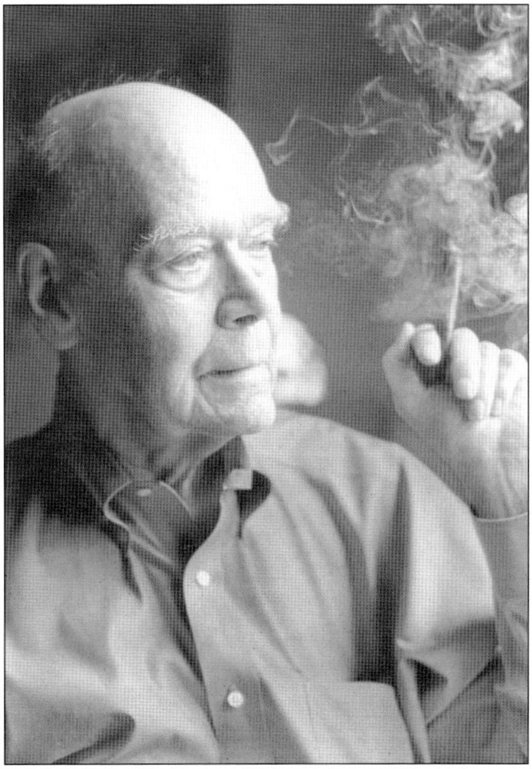

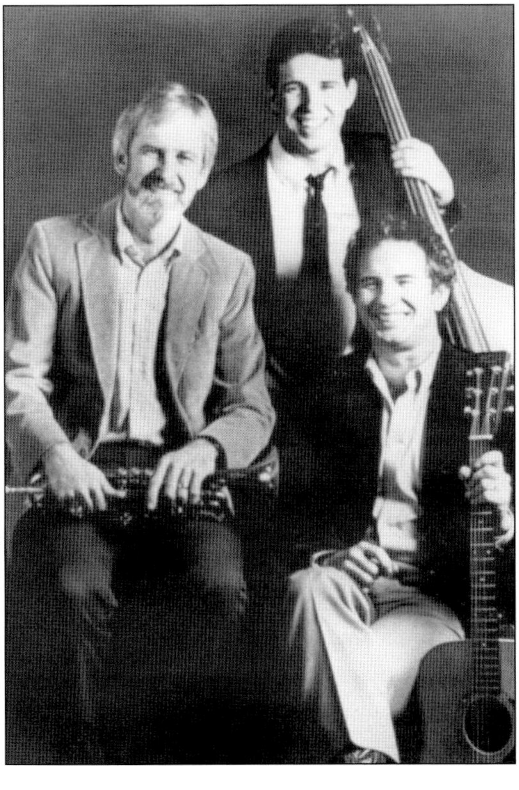

Three on a String, a trio from Birmingham, often performed in Guntersville. Shown are, from left to right, Bobby Horton (guitar, banjo, dobro, trumpet, and bass), Jerry Ryan (guitar and harmonica), and Brad Ryan (bass). They performed folk, country, bluegrass, and classical songs. The group's goal has always been "to provide a show that creates a good feeling with the audience." (*Advertiser-Gleam*.)

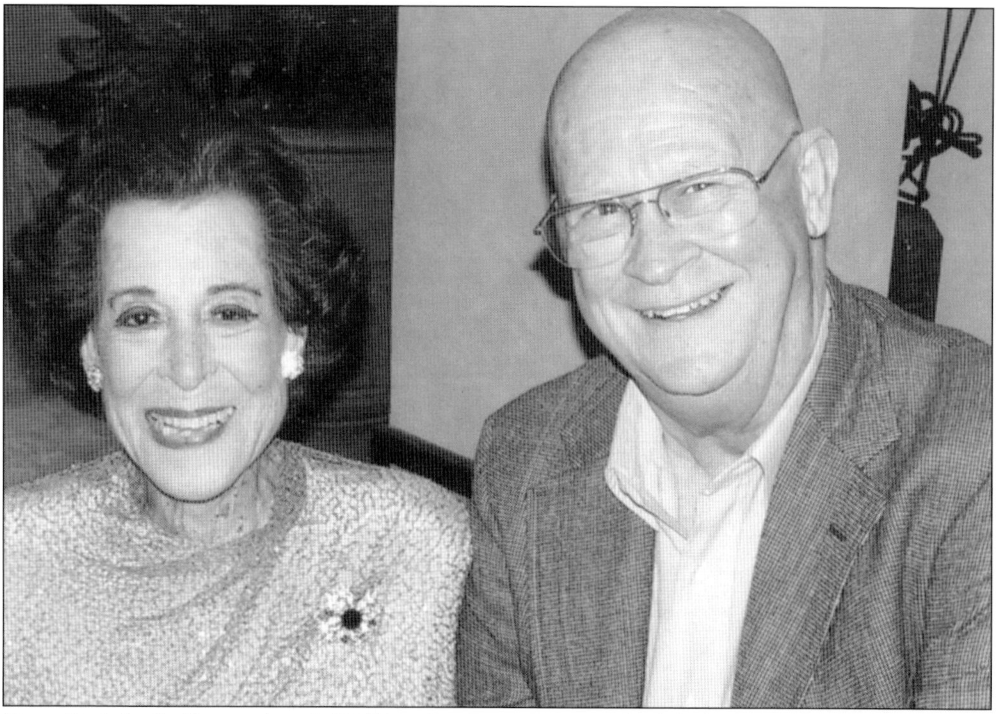

Kitty Carlisle (left) posed with William E. "Sonny" Lewis (right) during a Birmingham event at which she spoke about her life as the wife of playwright Moss Hart. Carlisle was delighted to learn of Lewis's career as a costume designer in Las Vegas and Hollywood. Over the years, Lewis met many celebrities, including Liberace, Jim Nabors, Doris Day, Barbra Streisand, Diana Ross, and Elvis. (Sonny Lewis.)

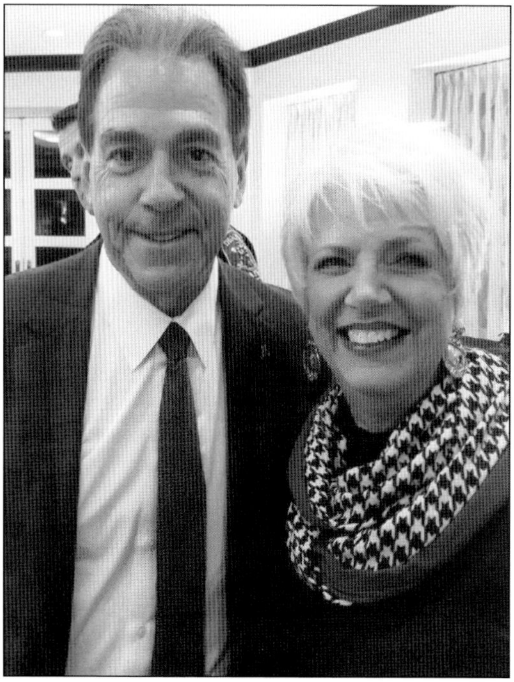

Shown at a pregame event with University of Alabama head football coach Nick Saban in Tuscaloosa is Betty McGowin Jones (right), city clerk for Guntersville, attired in her herringbone scarf. At the event, Saban greeted fans in preparation for the day's competition. A devoted Alabama fan, Betty, the daughter of Virginia and Clifford McGowin, is married to Warren Jones Jr. (Betty McGowin Jones.)

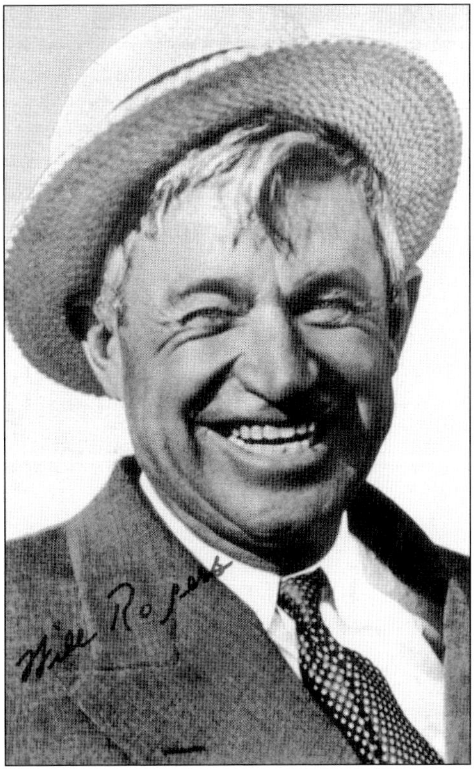

Cowboy, actor, reporter, and humorist Will Rogers grins from this vintage postcard. Periodically, the Whole Backstage Theatre performs *The Will Rogers Follies* to commemorate an association with this great-grandson of John Gunter, the founder of Guntersville. Born in the Cherokee Nation, Rogers never visited Guntersville. At the time of his death in 1935, however, he had scheduled a trip to Guntersville. (*Advertiser-Gleam*.)

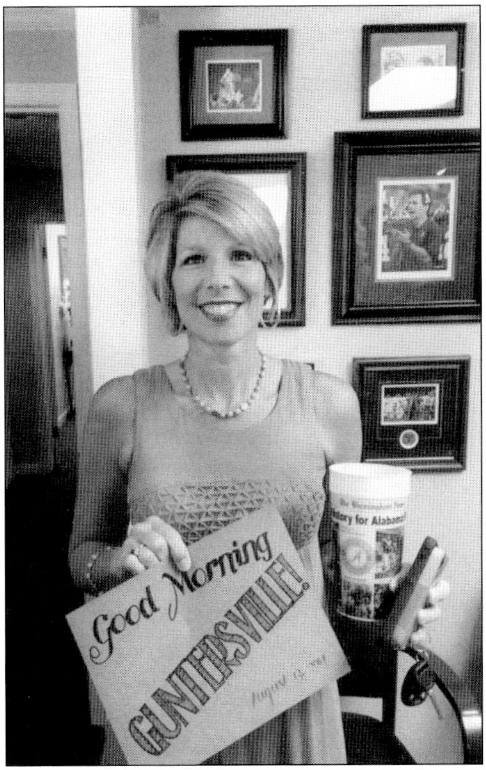

Leigh Barnett Dollar, a certified public accountant and the daughter of George and Dianne Rains Barnett, always wanted to become Guntersville's first woman mayor. Leigh's wish came true, and when this book was published in 2020, she was serving her second term. Her political aspirations were inspired by her father, who served as mayor from 1972 to 1976. As mayor, Dollar has focused on tourism, recreation, and infrastructure. (Morri Yancy.)